VIOLATED

VIOLATED

EXPOSING RAPE AT BAYLOR UNIVERSITY
AMID COLLEGE FOOTBALL'S
SEXUAL ASSAULT CRISIS

PAULA LAVIGNE and MARK SCHLABACH

CENTER
STREET®

NEW YORK   NASHVILLE

Center Street
Hachette Book Group
1290 Avenue of the Americas, New York, NY 10104
centerstreet.com
twitter.com/centerstreet

First Edition: August 2017

Center Street is a division of Hachette Book Group, Inc. The Center Street
name and logo are trademarks of Hachette Book Group, Inc.

The publisher is not responsible for websites (or their content)
that are not owned by the publisher.

The Hachette Speakers Bureau provides a wide range of authors for speaking
events. To find out more, go to www.HachetteSpeakersBureau.com
or call (866) 376-6591.

Print book interior design by Timothy Shaner, nightanddaydesign.biz

Library of Congress Cataloging-in-Publication Data has been applied for.

ISBNs: 978-1-4789-7408-6 (hardcover), 978-1-4789-7407-9 (ebook)

Printed in the United States of America

COR/LSC-C

10 9 8 7 6 5 4 3 2 1

AUTHORS' NOTE

The allegations against Baylor University by former female students—
who say their reports of sexual assault or domestic violence were
ignored—date back more than a decade. As far back as the problems went into the past, by spring 2017 it was clear that they would also
extend into the foreseeable future. In late May 2017, Baylor was under
investigation, review, or monitoring by the Texas Rangers, McLennan
County District Attorney's Office, Big 12 Conference, National Collegiate Athletic Association, U.S. Department of Education, and Southern Association of Colleges and Schools Commission on Colleges, and
was defending six federal Title IX lawsuits. There were five pending
criminal cases against former football players and one against a fraternity president.

Because of the pending litigation, investigations, and certain legal
agreements, several individuals key to Baylor's sexual assault scandal
refused to agree to an interview or answer questions. Others would
only talk to us as long as we did not use their names. We used pseudonyms for any woman who alleged being the victim of sexual assault,
physical assault, or domestic violence unless she specifically consented
to the use of her name or went public with her story and her name.
That would include Jasmin Hernandez and Dolores Lozano. We also
used pseudonyms or granted anonymity for certain other individuals
whose identity could possibly reveal the identity of an alleged victim
or who requested it specifically as a condition of being interviewed.

We did not name student-athletes or students accused of crimes unless their names appeared in police or school investigatory records.

On numerous occasions over several months, we requested interviews with former Baylor president Kenneth Starr, former athletic director Ian McCaw, and former head football coach Art Briles. Starr, McCaw, and Briles were also sent a list of questions addressing specific issues and allegations raised in this book. Starr and McCaw did not respond to the interview requests or the list of questions. Briles did not respond to requests for an interview; his attorney Mark Lanier said Briles, who had reached a financial settlement with the university, could not answer any of the submitted questions unless we secured written permission from Baylor officials for Briles to do so, but the university denied that request. We spoke on the record with three current Baylor regents: Kim Stevens, J. Cary Gray, and David Harper and exchanged written questions with then-chairman Ron Murff. We spoke to dozens of other sources both on and off the record throughout the book, including former assistant football coaches and former university employees. We also requested an interview with former Baylor football player Sam Ukwuachu, but he never responded, outside of sending us emails he'd sent to other media. We submitted a request with the Texas Department of Criminal Justice to interview Tevin Elliott, who is currently incarcerated in a Texas prison, but he declined to meet with us.

Our research is backed up by copious documentation, which we obtained through public records requests, websites, and other sources. We reviewed trial transcripts for the Elliott and Ukwuachu criminal trials, read dozens of police reports from Waco and Baylor police, analyzed criminal incident databases, and pored through legal filings in more than ten federal and state lawsuits. With all the pending litigation and investigations, more details will likely surface, but we have captured, to date, the most comprehensive narrative of what unfolded in Waco, Texas, and later became a nationwide cautionary tale.

CONTENTS

CONTENTS

CONTENTS

The Bible tells a story, in the second book of Samuel, about a young woman named Tamar, who was the daughter of King David. Her half brother Amnon was in love with her. He wanted to have her so badly he pretended to be sick one day, and he tricked their father into ordering Tamar to take care of him. As she was making him bread, he ordered the servants out of the room.

> *And when she had brought them unto him to eat, he took hold of her, and said unto her, "Come lie with me, my sister." And she answered him, "Nay, my brother, do not force me; for no such thing ought to be done in Israel. Do not thou this folly. And I, whither shall I cause my shame to go? And as for thee, thou shalt be as one of the fools in Israel."*

But Amnon didn't listen. He raped her. And then he cast her out. She tore off her long, beautiful robe signifying her as one of the king's virgin daughters. With her face in her hands, she went away crying. She was told to keep quiet. She would live as a desolate woman in her brother Absalom's house.

To make matters worse, their father, King David— no stranger to sexual scandal himself—did not punish Amnon. The king loved him and he was his firstborn son. The king's inaction would breed a hatred and desire for revenge within the family. Soon Amnon was murdered and the entire kingdom of David was in turmoil.

INTRODUCTION

In January 2014, Jasmin Hernandez saw her accused rapist sent to prison. Some would say she received justice. And, truthfully, she did get a lot more than most sexual assault victims. But her life was forever altered. She now lives with her parents in Southern California, attends a nearby college, sees a therapist regularly, and is unsure of her future. It's not the life she planned when she enrolled at Baylor University in the fall of 2011, on an academic scholarship, with plans to become a nurse anesthetist, and full of all the energy and ambition of a college freshman embarking on her own.

There are lots of Jasmins out there. According to national statistics, at least one in five college women experience some type of sexual assault. Many survivors' stories are never told, but their dreams are shattered and their lives are turned upside down nonetheless. Their friends don't know why they dropped out of college. Why they became addicted to painkillers. Why they can't sleep without a bolt on their bedroom door. But those women are out there, and their stories need to be heard.

In this book, you'll read many stories about women like Jasmin. You'll read about Erica, a Baylor volleyball player, who alleged she was gang raped by several football players at an off-campus party in 2012. You'll learn about Jennifer, a Baylor student, who said she and another woman were gang raped by several football players at a party in 2012, and you'll find out what was happening behind the scenes as a university resisted, but eventually had to confront, the realities playing out on its campus.

Many details of the women's stories are difficult to read. Not only were they violated sexually and physically while attending Baylor, but school officials who were supposed to be there to protect and support them also ignored them. That's why so many of the women we interviewed for this book say they were incredibly offended by Baylor officials' indifference to allegations of sexual assault and domestic violence. They are offended because they expected more from the world's largest Baptist university.

Many things stood in their way. They encountered a city police department that was inconsistent in its investigations and withheld police reports involving students and student-athletes. A campus police department operating in a veil of secrecy that was more interested in issuing parking tickets and liquor violations than in helping women who came to them for help after an assault. An honor code that made women afraid to report being raped lest they get in trouble with the university for being at a party and drinking. And administrators, employees, and coaches who received reports of domestic violence or sexual assault and never shared the information, keeping secret the heightened and growing risk to women as they stepped foot on the Waco campus.

Jasmin, a Baylor freshman at the time, was one of five women who reported to police that they were either raped or assaulted by football player Tevin Elliott in incidents from October 2009 to April 2012. In August 2015, a jury convicted Sam Ukwuachu of sexual assault (his conviction was later overturned by an appellate court, which ordered a new criminal trial), and in April 2016, a woman accused Bears defensive end Shawn Oakman of raping her.

Throughout the spring of 2016, details emerged of other cases—some years ago—where women came forth with stories of rape or domestic violence, often naming Baylor football players as their alleged perpetrators. For months, the scandal played out on TV, radio, and online, in message boards and social media: Who knew? What did

they do? Did Bears football coach Art Briles know? Did Baylor president Kenneth Starr know? The victims were cast as villains, jeopardizing the future of a successful and sacrosanct football program. And
Baylor's Christian values were called into question.

Behind closed doors, the thirty-two voting members of Baylor's
board of regents—a who's who of Texas's tony elite and mostly Baylor
Baptist alums—were being briefed on a most important investigation,
one the university itself commissioned shortly after the Ukwuachu
conviction. Philadelphia law firm Pepper Hamilton was tasked with
reviewing the school's response to sexual assault complaints, and after
eight months, it didn't have much good to say about Baylor or its football program.

Finally, in May 2016, the regents broke their silence: The findings were damning and worse than they could have imagined. They
found not just ignorance, but willful intent in trying to silence women
who reported being sexually assaulted by some Baylor football players.
They found university officials retaliated against victims and ignored
survivors' needs for counseling, academic support, and, most of all, justice. And they found a problem that went far beyond their beloved
football program.

Action was swift. Briles, who had guided the Bears to at least a
share of its first two Big 12 championships and was rewarded with
more than $5 million per season, was suspended with the intent to ter-
minate. Starr, a former federal judge and independent counselor, who
investigated U.S. president Bill Clinton's infamous affair with a White
House intern, was removed as president but allowed to stay as chancellor. Athletic Director Ian McCaw was sanctioned and put on probation. Within weeks, they all either resigned or were fired.

For the first time ever, a major Division I university ousted its
president, athletic director, and head coach of one of the most prominent football programs in the country, playing in a brand-new, multi-
million-dollar stadium. It gave the women of Baylor something denied
their peers at other universities—accountability. Finally, there was an
acknowledgment of wrongdoing and penance.

But it wasn't over for Baylor. Within a year, it would end up defending seven federal Title IX lawsuits (with one dismissed in late May 2017), facing two U.S. Department of Education investigations, and an inquiry by the NCAA. The Big 12 Conference voted to withhold a portion of Baylor's share of millions of dollars in revenue until it was convinced actual changes were being made. And there was still the possibility of more criminal charges, after the McLennan County District Attorney's office and Texas Rangers, the state's highest law enforcement agency, launched an investigation into whether student-athletes should be charged for unprosecuted assaults, and if university staff in any way might have hindered a woman from reporting her assault.

It's astonishing and head shaking that there were so many reported sexual assaults at Baylor. But there was power in numbers, a power that a single incident at a school that hits the news here and there doesn't have. That's not to say those other schools don't have the same volume; they might, and the numbers indicate that some indeed do, but the threats, intimidation, deterrence, and hopelessness keep victims from coming forward.

The struggle and the fight of women like Jasmin has been out there before. But never has the struggle, the fight, and the *victory*. And that is a game changer not just for her and the other women at Baylor, but for all the Jasmins at all the schools on all the campuses across America. If they can win at a minefield like Baylor, they can win anywhere.

Jasmin is still in Southern California. It's unknown whether she'll prevail in her lawsuit against Baylor. But she's no longer a face in the shadows. She's the face of a revolution.

CHAPTER ONE

THE PARTY

Waco, Texas
April 14, 2012

Parties were happening all over Waco, Texas, on the night of April 14, 2012, as Jasmin Hernandez and her friends left their South Russell dormitory and headed off the Baylor University campus, singing along to rap music and ready to have a good time. They'd dressed up a bit—Jasmin wearing a camisole top under a loose-fitting shimmery teal sweater that her friend Shannon encouraged her to buy at Forever 21 to brighten up her wardrobe, instead of wearing the same old plaid flannel shirts and grandpa sweaters Shannon thought made Jasmin look too much like a tomboy.

Shannon and her friends lived in the same dorm as Jasmin, who had been invited into their group earlier that spring after running into them at parties. They'd spotted her riding her longboard around campus, and a few of them longboarded too. One of them approached her with a compliment about her funky hunter's cap with fuzzy earflaps, and they started talking. Jasmin, who had left the towering palms and ocean views of Southern California in the fall of 2011 for the landlocked, stubby landscape of central Texas, was in her second semester at Baylor and looking for a new group of friends. She'd had a falling-out with the ones she'd met the previous fall. She'd had a brief fling with another female student in the group, and she felt outed among those friends.

Since high school, Jasmin knew she was different, that she had feelings for other girls, and wasn't as interested in boys as her friends were. But she saw how her classmates at the private Lutheran high school she attended in Yorba Linda, California, mocked the one girl who came out as being gay, and Jasmin kept quiet. She knew her parents also wouldn't approve. The message she heard at home from her parents was that God loves everyone, but being gay was not okay and anyone who is, needs to change. She knew the people in her life cared about her and loved her, but she thought if they knew the truth about who she really was, they would leave her.

Escaping that fear was one of the allures of Baylor; she felt freedom in being 1,200 miles from home, even if it was at a Christian college that, at the time, listed homosexual acts as a violation of its sexual conduct policy. But it was a constant struggle. For Jasmin, religion was a source of security, as it was all she had known. But it was also a source of shame and guilt. As she headed into college, she at first decided she was going to put religion first, and a place like Baylor would help her do that. She figured if she didn't act on her urges, and never told anyone about her sexuality, then it wouldn't matter who she was inside, and God would be happy with her for her restraint. A campus visit to Baylor sealed the deal for her that it was where she wanted to be. "Everyone just seemed so excited to be there," Jasmin said. "It wasn't even like they were talking about Baylor as a school. It's like they were talking about it as a friend."

Attending Baylor also fit her desire to become a nurse anesthetist, because she could get into the nursing program there much easier than she could at any of the California schools she'd considered, and, always a good student in high school, she had qualified for an academic scholarship. At Baylor, Jasmin branched out. She was so invested in the fact that "things would be different." She had been a varsity swimmer for all four years in high school, and although she wasn't on par to become a varsity college athlete at a Division I school like Baylor, she wanted to stay in athletics. She joined an intramural rowing team, getting up well before dawn to glide through the still waters of the Brazos River, counting the seemingly endless yards every morning by familiar land-marks on the bank. And on weekends, she went with her friends to football games and fraternity parties where drinking alcohol was the norm.

Drinking at parties wasn't the tame, restricted Jasmin from high school, but she was having fun and she felt safe among her group. That was until she found herself attracted to another girl—an attraction she had believed was mutual—but the other girl confided in their friends that she was uncomfortable with Jasmin's advances. Jasmin dropped out of their group, afraid of the ridicule she'd witnessed among her high school classmates. Her new friends were less into football, but they still enjoyed parties and going on adventures in and around Waco. Jasmin didn't have a car, so she appreciated the opportunities to get off campus.

Shannon Valverde was one of Jasmin's new friends. So was Catrina Gonzales, or "Cat," as everyone called her. And that night as they headed off to the party, Cat was excited. She'd been hanging out with a Baylor football player, Tevin Elliott, whom she'd met on the way to chapel services awhile back. He'd invited her to a party to cel-ebrate his friend and teammate Glasco Martin's birthday and the end of spring football practices. Cat talked to her friends excitedly about it. She wasn't exactly dating the football player, but they'd been hav-ing sex and to her friends, at least, he was "Cat's guy." The group of friends took two cars, and eventually ended up heading toward Aspen Heights, a complex of townhome-style rental houses southeast of cam-pus. The fact it was gated really didn't matter, because Baylor students knew the security code, and cars soon lined the street along the house Martin shared with two other teammates near the back of the com-plex, not far from a swimming pool and sand volleyball court.

Jasmin and her friends were among the first to arrive, but the crowd grew quickly. The lights were off, hip-hop music was blaring, and people were soon packed shoulder to shoulder to where students had to elbow their way through the crowd to come in or out, jug-gling their red Solo cups filled with alcoholic punch, and spilling out on the front porch and out the back door. The party would grow so big and so loud that someone eventually called Waco police to have it shut down. Jasmin and her friends knew no one at the party outside of their group, and for a brief time some of the girls left to check out another party down the street, but they soon returned. At one point, Cat started introducing Tevin to her friends.

Several were excited to meet Tevin. Jasmin wasn't awestruck like the rest of her friends. She'd never heard his name before, and although she'd gone to football games that year and enjoyed the pageantry and social aspect of cheering on the Bears, she didn't really follow the sport. At the time, the only player she could name was quarterback Robert Griffin III, who would go on to win the school's first Heisman Trophy that fall.

When Jasmin was introduced to Tevin that night, she exchanged a polite, "Nice to meet you," and stepped aside as her friends were vying to get one-on-one photos with him. Tevin asked her, "You don't want a photo with me? Don't you know me?" She told him she didn't. He was surprised and shook his head. "He was like, 'You should want a photo with me,'" Jasmin said. But she didn't. Moments later, all the friends gathered for a group picture, and Jasmin joined in. She didn't stand next to Tevin, but she soon noticed him reach around, put his hand on her waist, and pull her in close. It was a small tug, but one strong enough to give Jasmin a weird vibe. Tevin himself wasn't drinking, but Jasmin and her friends said he was pouring shots of vodka for others.

Jasmin usually loved to dance at parties, mostly out on the dance floor alone or shaking to the beat in a group in a style her friend Caitlin Sears described as "jumpy." That night, she doesn't remember dancing. Her friends don't recall seeing her dance with anyone. Tevin, his brother, Tarnaine Elliott, and a teammate, who were also at the party that night, would say years later under oath that Jasmin was dancing with Tevin.

All the bodies crammed together had turned the dance floor into a sauna, and the football players, including Tevin, had taken their shirts off (he later testified in court that Baylor players liked to call

themselves the "shirt-off boys"). Tevin remembers Jasmin twirling and
dancing to the blaring music. Dancing so close, in fact, that she was
rubbing on his chest and making him think she wanted to go down
on him. But Jasmin denies all of that. Her next memory is of making
her way through the crowd to find the bathroom, and returning to the
party to find her friends gone. Jasmin, only five feet, three inches tall,
strained to see her friends over the crowd, but she spotted Tevin. She
asked him if he knew where her friends were, and he told her they
went outside. She didn't believe him. She didn't understand why they
would dart out of the house while she was in the bathroom. She tried
to search the dark room, and moved into the kitchen with Tevin. She
remembered him saying, "Here, they went outside. They went outside," and then his hand closed around her wrist. As he started to lead
her out, Jasmin thought he was being odd, but she had been drinking
and was having trouble standing her ground. There was that bad vibe
she had gotten from him earlier, but she countered by reasoning that,
as he was dating her friend Cat, she had nothing to fear from him.

As Tevin led her out of the house, Jasmin asked him where they
were going, and he insisted they were looking for her friends. Jasmin
became defiant and demanded he take her back in. She tried to pull
her wrist away, but Tevin wouldn't let go. Instead he picked her up
and started to carry her, cradled like a child and gripping her tight. He
kept walking away from the house, across the parking lot and street
that ran along the back of the complex, and toward a grassy sloped
area by a set of stairs near the clubhouse and volleyball court.

Jasmin was plagued more with confusion, anger, and frustration
than fear, and even though other partygoers were still within earshot,
she did not scream. Years later she would be asked why she didn't
shout out, shriek at the top of her lungs, and she wished she had a better answer. But the truth is, she says she doesn't really know, other than
assuming that she could still reason her way out of his grasp without
making a scene.

She kept her focus on Tevin. She'd said no, shouldn't that be
enough? Then she clawed at him, trying to get him to let her go. She

pleaded with him, thinking if she convinced him this wasn't a good idea, he would take her back: *She wasn't interested in him. He was dating her friend. If he put her down now, they could go back to the party and he could find someone who was interested in him. No. No. No. No.*

And then Jasmin dropped her last bargaining chip. "Hey, look, I am gay. I do not like men. Just take me back, just take me back. I bet there are people who would love to be with you. So how about we both go back and hang out with girls who want to be with us?" But Tevin ignored her.

There was a single yellow bulb on a storage shed casting a dim light on the muddy slope where Tevin put her down. For Jasmin, that's when the reality of what was about to happen hit her, that despite her protests, her belief that "no means no," she was being overpowered by a six-foot-three, 250-pound football player. Instead of becoming frantic or fighting or screaming for help, she shut down. She remembered what a girl she had met at a Baylor orientation camp told her about being raped: *If you stop resisting, it hurts less.*

As Tevin pulled her underwear and jeans down, spread her legs, and entered her, she looked up at the dark sky. She felt like an object, like a thing that was being used. She disassociated herself from her body, a body that was being violated. She felt pain. Her vagina was on fire. She had been shoved into the dirt and someone was on top of her. It hurt, and she waited for it to be over. When he finished, they both got up.

Disoriented, Jasmin let Tevin lead her away, but they ended up walking toward a gated swimming pool. Suddenly, near the swimming pool gate, Tevin grabbed Jasmin and pushed her up against the fence. Pulling down her jeans and underwear a second time, he stuck his penis in her vagina from behind, crushing her against the fence as he thrust into her.

Once Tevin finished, he started to head back to the party. Somewhere, Jasmin doesn't remember when or how, her sweater and top were removed, and she said out loud that she couldn't find them. Tevin found her shirt for her, and then walked off into the night.

Once Jasmin had her clothes on, she got her bearings and started to walk back toward the houses. Mud stained her knees and the back of her jeans near the waistband, pollen strands hung off her sweater, and leaves were in her hair. Still not sure which direction to go, Jasmin approached a group of students and asked if she could walk with them to the party. As soon as she reached the house, she saw some of her friends standing outside. Cat had returned from taking one of their friends back to the dorms. She pushed the lock button on her car, looked up, and saw something that shocked her: Jasmin, walking toward her, crying, shaking, and completely disheveled. Cat grabbed her hand and led her through the crowd to find their other friends.

Jasmin hadn't said a word through her sobs until she saw her friend Kandace Little. Jasmin blurted out, "I think I was just raped."

CHAPTER TWO

MAKING A STATEMENT

Waco, Texas
April 15, 2012

After Jasmin Hernandez frantically exclaimed to her friends that she'd been raped, Kandace Little asked if she was joking, and the question set Jasmin off into an expletive-filled rage: "Of course I'm not joking. Why do you think I would make that up?" She told her friends that "some asshole" had picked her up, carried her to the volleyball court, and raped her. Catrina Gonzalez drilled her: *What color shirt was he wearing? Did he have tattoos? Was he black or white?* Jasmin shook her head. "I don't know. I don't know," she repeated, although something about her made Cat suspect that Jasmin knew more than she was saying.

Jasmin's friends immediately called Shannon Valverde, the mother hen of the group. As Shannon came out the back door, Jasmin was crying so hard it was almost impossible to make out what she was saying. But Shannon did hear the word *rape*. That put her into action, making a decision right then that would cement Jasmin's future. Shannon was the one who'd stay calm under pressure. She was a titan, a real badass who had once, as a lifeguard in high school, saved a man from drowning at a pool and performed CPR on him until medics arrived. And she was the one, that night, who told everyone: "We're going to the hospital. Everyone in the car, right now."

Shannon wasn't thinking about how her actions would affect the future, and certainly not a future almost two years away in a courtroom in Waco, Texas. She was worried about getting help for Jasmin, even if it was only something to calm her nerves in that very moment. On the way to the hospital in Shannon's car, Jasmin sat in the front passenger seat, crying and holding Shannon's hand as the latter gave her the rundown of what was likely going to happen: *They're going to ask you a lot of questions. They'll want to do an exam and take pictures. The police will come to talk to you.*

It was around 2:00 a.m. when Jasmin and her friends pulled into the emergency room at Baylor Scott & White Medical Center–Hillcrest and went into a mostly empty lobby. Jasmin hadn't spoken much on the car ride there about what happened. She'd asked Shannon if she was going to get in trouble for drinking alcohol because she was only eighteen. She cried, and both Shannon and Caitlin assured her it wasn't her fault and that she was going to be okay. The only thing Jasmin really said about the assault was that "it was Cat's man who had done it." She hadn't remembered his name, but Shannon figured it was Tevin.

The triage nurse took Jasmin into a room right away, and Shannon and Caitlin later joined her, turning on the television and trying to joke with her about a nature show featuring a giraffe. Shannon and Caitlin were only trying to keep the mood light, because some serious things were to come. A Waco police sergeant showed up, and the first thing he noted in his report was that Jasmin was "cutting up and joking and she was making light of being sexually assaulted." When he asked her what happened, she said, "He stuck his dick in my pussy and I told him I don't like dick." Jasmin was loud—there's no disputing that—but she was not amused, despite what the officer observed. She was angry. Someone had overpowered her, she had lost control, and she was there—at a hospital, having to write down what happened to her in a statement for the police. She was angry at having to recount every detail, as best she could, about what just happened, and to confront her own struggles with sexuality in such a crass way. "I've been violated as much as I can," she later told an officer.

When Jasmin reached the part in her statement where she was trying to tell Tevin to take her back to the party, she stopped writing. She paused. She had told him she was gay. Should she put that in there? Could she put it in an official record that her mom—maybe her friends, maybe anyone—would be able to see? Yes, she decided, and began to write: *I told him, no, that I'm gay. He said that that's alright. I tried telling him maybe 3 more times before he took off my jeans and underwear and started rubbing his penis on me. I told him please no. He said it was okay and I continued to tell him I only like girls.* She described the second assault: *I said no, I really don't like penis and I didn't want to, but once again he had sex with me (his big black penis was inside me) and I hated it and it hurt and I almost couldn't breathe.*

As Jasmin wrote she reasoned that her friends would either support her, or they would take her back to the dorms and never speak to her again. It was a risk. She turned to Shannon and Caitlin, and while sobbing, said, "I'm gay. I'm gay." Shannon responded, "I know." In fact, Shannon had had a hunch since she first met Jasmin, noting her tomboy attire and her chill demeanor. Instead of being repulsed, both friends told Jasmin they loved her.

Jasmin was taken aback. She thought the best-case scenario would have been for the two friends to say, "That's okay." She certainly didn't expect such an outpouring of acceptance and love. Even in the midst of such chaos and hurt, that moment became one of the most meaningful of Jasmin's young life. "It's a completely different feeling from everything else that night," Jasmin said. "It's a completely separate event for me, that conversation. It went, for me, the fear of the worst next incoming tragedy. A tragedy on top of another one. Now on top of this, I'm going to lose all my friends. That's fine. I don't need anyone. I just braced myself for it, and I received the complete opposite. I received the most supportive, encouraging, the most loving encounter, beyond what I could ever imagine." Shannon described Jasmin as being notably calmer after that, as if a weight had been lifted. It would give Jasmin the strength for what would come next, when a nurse met her in an exam room to conduct the physical exam.

The clothes Jasmin had been wearing that evening—her new sweater, her muddied jeans and shoes—had been bagged for evidence, and she was wearing a hospital gown when she first met with nurse Michele Davis. She was on an exam table waiting for a sexual assault exam (one for which she would later receive a hospital bill in the mail). Davis, too, noted that Jasmin was angry. She asked Jasmin to rate her pain on a scale from one to ten; Jasmin said a seven or eight. After Jasmin lay down on the exam table, Davis pulled out a colposcope—a magnifying device with a light—to examine Jasmin's genitalia. She snapped several photos. A few were of a dime-sized, bluish-purple bruise   like a blood blister—on Jasmin's hymen, a clear sign to Davis that it was likely the result of nonconsensual sex. And there were specks of debris that looked to Davis like dirt. She ran cotton swabs on Jasmin's vagina and anus, and also swabbed her mouth, to send samples in for DNA testing.

It was after 4:00 a.m. by the time Davis finished her exam and Jasmin was able to leave. Shannon drove her back to their South Russell dorm, where Jasmin fell asleep, still in the hospital scrubs she was given at the hospital because they had taken her clothes for evidence. Jasmin had been a virgin before that night. She lost that label and picked up a new one: victim.

* * *

Cat hadn't gone to the hospital with Jasmin and her friends that night. Instead she stayed at the party, but she was upset about what happened. She turned to someone she thought she could trust. She turned to Tevin. Back at the party, Cat found Tevin sitting in his white Cadillac Escalade with the door open. She wanted to go for a drive, to clear her head, and she asked him to go along. She followed him back to his apartment, where he dropped off his friends and then hopped in Cat's red Chevy Cruze.

But they weren't driving long when Cat received a call saying that Jasmin needed her purse—which was still in Cat's car—so they headed to the hospital. Cat told Tevin what little she knew about what happened. She remembered Tevin seeming astonished, and asking whether the hospital would try to do a DNA match, and if it did, then "that's that" and they'd know whoever did it—almost as though he was trying to comfort her, to let her know it would be taken care of. Cat and Tevin stopped by the hospital but didn't go in, and Kandace and another friend met them in the parking lot. If these friends knew about Tevin, they didn't let on. Jasmin had asked some of them at the hospital not to tell Cat, for fear that Tevin would find out before she figured out what she wanted to do. Cat had heard only that the man who attacked Jasmin was someone they all knew, maybe a friend of another football player? It was all they talked about on the way back to the dorms, where Tevin and Cat dropped off her friends, and then back at his house, where she stayed the night.

The start of Cat's relationship with Tevin—unbeknownst to her friends at the time—already showed some potential warning signs as to his behavior. Several weeks earlier, when they'd first met on campus, Cat hadn't been looking for a physical relationship with anyone. Tevin had remarked on her journal—brand-new, with an owl on the cover. She had planned to write in it all the ideas she had for what she wanted to do with her life, and the type of person she wanted to be. She'd had a total of two sexual partners by that point, and she had no interest in becoming someone who slept around. Tevin asked her to lunch, but she had plans so they exchanged phone numbers and soon arranged to meet on a suspension bridge near campus, where they talked about their lives and plans for about fifteen minutes one evening. Tevin talked a lot about himself, and boasted about a tattoo of Jesus he had on his chest. But his ego didn't matter so much, Cat thought. She was a freshman all the way from Corpus Christi, Texas, and if anyone was showing her attention, she was okay with it.

A few weeks later, they were making out at Tevin's apartment when Cat stopped and told him, "I don't want to have sex with you today. This is all that's going to happen." It became heated again, and she told him again to back off. But at one point, as Tevin pushed her further and further, Cat felt she lost control and was in too much of a compromised position to stop what was about to happen. So she gave in and let Tevin have sex with her. As he drove her home, she figured she deserved what happened by putting herself in that situation. She decided to make the best of it with Tevin, because she really didn't want to simply jump to another guy. They hung out after that, but Cat didn't really enjoy it. Tevin got on her nerves. They didn't like the same things. They argued. She pushed the night's events of her first time with Tevin to the back of her thoughts. So much so, that the significance of it wouldn't cross her mind until years later, when she said she received a surprising phone call from Tevin's father about the upcoming trial. But on the night of the party in Waco, the memories of her first encounters with Tevin would take a backseat to the bombshell she was about to get from Jasmin in fewer than twenty-four hours.

* * *

When Jasmin woke up hours later, for a split second she thought the night's events had been a crazy dream. That was, until she looked down and saw that she was wearing hospital scrubs. And it hit her again: *I was raped.* The rage returned and she became resolute. The previous night at the hospital, she told a Waco police detective that she didn't want to press criminal charges against Tevin. She didn't want to ruin his life. Looking back on that night, she reasoned she had probably still been in shock. But that next morning, awake and aware and still very angry, her mind was made up. She had suffered. She would seek justice. *No one does this to me and gets away with it.* Tevin wronged her, had violated her. She steeled herself for what would come next, but she knew she couldn't do it alone. It started with a shower—and an extremely difficult phone call.

* * *

Twelve hundred miles and two time zones away, in Yorba Linda, California, Candice Hernandez was cleaning her closet on a Sunday evening. Candice and her husband, Ostes, worked in the boom-or-bust real estate market, and although they'd moved Jasmin and her three younger brothers into different houses as they grew up, they'd always remained in Yorba Linda, an affluent Southern California suburb coincidentally associated with one of the nation's biggest cover-ups. It's the hometown of the late U.S. president Richard Nixon, whose presidential library there was once accused of glossing over Nixon's role in the Watergate scandal, in which the former Republican president tried to cover up certain aspects of the infamous break-in of the Democratic National Committee headquarters, and which led to his resignation in 1974.

The Hernandezes enrolled their children in private, religious schools and became entwined with the community. Candice and Ostes raised their family in a Christian home, and Baylor's Baptist affiliation was a huge plus for sending their oldest child off to college. It was a long way from their "Yorba Linda bubble," but it was a safe, small, Bible-based school, and Jasmin's parents had done their research. They spoke to Jasmin's high school counselors who'd sent students to Baylor before. They twice visited the campus in Waco and went on all the parent tours. Candice and Ostes and another couple specifically asked one of the tour leaders about campus sexual assaults, and the woman responded, "Oh, no, sexual assault is so low here," Candice recalled, and said the woman proceeded to boast about the school's low rate of drinking and drug use, and rattled off statistics about how safe Baylor's campus was.

But Candice wasn't naïve. Although she didn't want Jasmin to drink, she knew it was likely inevitable. She warned Jasmin about being aware of her surroundings, checking in with her roommate, and staying on campus as much as possible. Her daughter seemed to be making a good transition to college. She had a good group of friends, was taking part in activities, and was getting decent grades. So when Jasmin called, and Candice picked up the phone and heard, "Mom, I was raped," her first knee-jerk response was, "Are you kidding me?"

Candice was in complete shock as Jasmin relayed the details of what happened, and the distance between them never seemed greater. "You never prepare for something like that all your life," Candice said. Then she had to break the news to Jasmin's father. "I was dumbfounded," Ostes said. "It's like when someone close to you passes away, you can't believe it because you just talked to them or you just saw them or something like that. That was kind of what went through my mind. Is this really happening? Is this really going on?"

As soon as Candice hung up the phone, she went online and pulled up airline websites. The earliest flight she could get was the next morning into Austin, putting her into Waco the next afternoon. She left Ostes home to take care of the boys. She prayed all the way.

CHAPTER THREE

WAKE-UP CALLS

Waco, Texas
April 16, 2012

Candice Hernandez checked into a nearby hotel and had Jasmin stay with her for a few days while they figured out what to do. Waco police interviewed Jasmin at the hospital and would be investigating her alleged assault by Baylor football player Tevin Elliott because it happened off campus. Candice decided they needed to also alert campus police, thinking they could offer Jasmin some form of protection from the fellow student who attacked her.

The officers' response stunned Candice when they visited the police station on campus. "They said, 'There's nothing we can do.'" She was offered a business card, but that was it. Candice pressed on, explaining that this involved a football player and her daughter standing right next to her. The officers simply told her she'd have to talk to Waco police. "I would have thought they would have written his name down, at least on a sticky note," she said, but no one took down any notes, even if only as a means of giving someone a heads-up in case anything else happened down the road. "No report. Nothing, nothing, nothing in writing. It shocked me."

They drove down the road to the Waco Police Department, where they met with Officer John Rozyskie, from whom Candice received great reassurance. He said all the right things to Jasmin: It wasn't her fault. It was okay if she was drinking. But he needed Jasmin to come back several times to answer questions, review photos, and talk to other officers. Candice knew it was necessary, but she was worried about Jasmin having to think about her case in the midst of final exams and endure the emotional burden of constantly being asked to revisit the night's events.

Candice wanted to take her back to Yorba Linda, California, but Jasmin insisted she wanted to finish the semester, even if she woke up every morning worrying about her grades in the midst of everything else. So Candice went online and started searching Baylor's website for possible resources. She couldn't find anything specific to sexual assault. She looked for contact information under "Academics" on the site. After a few calls, and a few transfers, she ended up speaking to a woman—whose name she did not write down. "I made sure I used the word *rape* and not sexual assault. I told her, 'My daughter was raped. She's missing a lot of class time because she has to go to Waco PD. Is there anything you can do to help her with either making up finals or making up class time?'" The response Candice heard is one that is burned forever in her memory. The woman told her, "Mrs. Hernandez, I'm sorry that happened. But even if a plane fell on your daughter, there's nothing we can do to help her."

Candice lost it. It was a sad message: No one at Baylor was going to help her daughter. Jasmin did build up the nerve to tell a couple of her professors, and she received a more sympathetic ear. Her religion teacher sympathized with the reason for her absences and relayed a story about a friend who was sexually assaulted as well. When a trip to the police department posed a conflict with a psychology test, she told her professor and was allowed to take the test at a different time.

Candice knew, and so did Jasmin, that right then she was operating on autopilot, but that at some point soon, the gravity of what happened and what was to come was going to hit her. A Waco police officer suggested she get counseling, and gave her information about therapists in town, but Jasmin didn't have a car. She didn't want to take the bus, and she turned down the police department's offer of arranging for someone to pick her up and take her to appointments. It was a nice offer, but she felt it was too much to deal with and involved yet another person knowing what happened. Her mom kept her on task, having Jasmin focus on meetings and phone calls with detectives. But she could tell it was already wearing on Jasmin, whose normally bubbly demeanor had been replaced by a somewhat distant and detached personality.

Candice went back online and discovered what she thought was a solution: At that time, Baylor students were entitled to seven free on-campus counseling sessions each semester. Jasmin agreed. Baylor was still her home, a place where she felt comfortable, and this was a way for her to get the help she needed, without feeling as though it was yet another burden. When Jasmin called to make an appointment, she was told they were booked until the end of the semester. She explained she was having a crisis, but they still said there was no one who could help. She could sign up right then for appointments next fall—close to four months away—but even that wasn't guaranteed. Candice tried, but was told the same thing. They were too busy. They told her to seek a counselor off campus, citing that Jasmin had "too many problems" for their counselors to handle. Jasmin understood the message. She was a dysfunctional rape victim, and she had no answers. Then, not knowing what Baylor was supposed to be doing for her, she simply felt like she was just out of luck, and that trying anything else at that point would be useless. But she was still functioning, going through the day-to-day. The worst wouldn't hit her until months later. Her mom suspected as much even then, which is why she at least wanted Jasmin to start on counseling, to get the free sessions to which she was entitled.

"This is not where I dropped her off," Candice would say publicly years later. "When we dropped her off, there was love and compassion and unity and safety, and there was nothing like that from this university." During Candice's conversations with people at Baylor, she felt as though they couldn't get her off the phone fast enough. The high expectations she'd had of this Christian caring community came crashing down when she realized that everyone was turning a blind eye to her daughter, all the while she kept hearing about the new football stadium and how great the Bears were going to be that coming season. She realized how important football was to the university, where images of the team were inescapable and the stadium glowed like a beacon along the Brazos River.

Candice had to get back to her husband, Ostes, and their three boys. It had been about five days, and she hated to leave. She left Jasmin, knowing she'd be back in a few weeks to pack her up and bring her home for the summer. Those weeks were brutal for Jasmin. "A lot happens when you don't study for finals and are having a mental breakdown," she said. Religion class was one of the worst. "I grew up completely religious and I was like I can't even touch this subject right now," she said. She had hoped to raise her GPA to the required 3.0 to keep her academic scholarship. Instead, she failed one class, scored two Cs and a D, and took an incomplete, leaving her with a 2.66 GPA. No one at Baylor ever reached out to her regarding her reported rape, she said. The only acknowledgment from the university came at the end of the semester, when she received a letter informing her that her scholarship was in jeopardy.

Throughout the semester she occasionally noticed a large, white SUV with tinted windows driving past her dorm, almost as if it were circling, with music blaring so loud the bass notes made the building rumble. She learned it was Tevin's white Cadillac Escalade, distinct because of a pair of novelty testicles hanging from near the trailer hitch. She felt Tevin's presence behind her, in front of her, to the sides of her, always circling her.

* * *

Candice made one other phone call during the time she was in Waco. She called the office of Baylor football coach Art Briles. She thought that if he didn't know already, he should be aware of what one of his players did. The Hernandez family had great respect for coaches. Jasmin had been on the varsity swim team in high school, and she ran cross-country. Her brothers Matt and Elijah played football, and their teammates were always hanging out at the Hernandez house, swimming in the pool, playing in the backyard. The coaches they knew kept a close eye on their players. So they thought surely Briles would take action on something so serious yet they never got to speak to him.

Briles had come to Tevin's defense before, when the player was caught plagiarizing, which was a violation of Baylor's academic honor code. It was his second violation, and after he failed to respond with an appeal, the provost's office suspended him for the fall 2011 semester, which meant he'd miss football season. More than two months after the appeal deadline, Briles personally intervened on his behalf, emailing then-president Ken Starr and asking for a late appeal. Starr accepted Tevin's appeal letter—which appeared to have been written by an athletics department academic advisor—and overturned the provost's decision to suspend him. Starr also allowed the athletics department, and not the standardly appointed judicial affairs department, to oversee Tevin's probation. Judicial affairs staff complained, and with good reason, because when Tevin failed to show up for class, was in danger of failing, and was caught cheating—all violations of his probation— athletics department officials did nothing. In emails that would be released years later in a legal case, one athletics department employee informed then athletic director Ian McCaw of Tevin's lapses, "Wow, what is this kid thinking?" McCaw simply responded, "Unbelievable!"

Briles knew about Tevin's alleged rape of Jasmin the very next day after she had reported him to police, according to text messages he exchanged with an assistant coach that were released in the legal case. The assistant coach wrote, "Tevin just called and told me Waco PD took him down to swab his mouth. He also went to see a lawyer who took his case. I would think he will be charged pretty quick," to which Briles responded, "Dang it."

* * *

Nurse Michele Davis made a phone call too. One of a nature she'd never made before in her career, even after conducting hundreds of sexual assault exams. Davis had examined Jasmin that night, and she was also director of the Sexual Assault Nurse Examiner Program in McLennan County and four surrounding counties. Even if she didn't conduct all of the exams herself, she oversaw the nurses who did. Davis and her colleagues were the front line. A woman might not press charges. She might not call the police. She might not alert anyone at school. But, at the very least, she might want to see a nurse, if only to get emergency contraception or be tested for a sexually transmitted disease.

Davis and her colleagues weren't divided among jurisdictions, like law enforcement agencies, either. Women shared details with Davis and her nurses that they would tell no one else, and they promised to protect their privacy. Yet Davis kept notes, filed reports in her office, and compiled her own statistics based on the women who came to see her or her nurses. So when it came to sexual assault in and around Waco, few people were as positioned, educated, and experienced to see the big picture as Davis.

And on the night when she examined Jasmin, what she saw and what she heard made the hairs stand up on the back of her neck. She had seen this profile, this pattern, before, and recently. She'd worked on cases involving serial rapists, and right then she thought she had another. "You get that sense, 'Oh, gosh, this is not good.' I knew that I had to intervene. I felt like, as a nurse, our duty is to protect the public as well as to take care of our patients."

When Waco police arrived later that day to pick up Jasmin's rape kit, Davis told them that she thought they were dealing with a repeat offender and they should look into prior reports. "He fit the profile of some other victims that we'd had—at least two or three. That's what I told the police. There's a connection here you need to look at," she said. Then she picked up the phone and called an official in Baylor Judicial Affairs, one she'd met while serving on the school's sexual assault advisory board, which mainly worked to provide educational information for freshman orientation sessions at Baylor. She didn't want to violate her patients' privacy, so, avoiding revealing Jasmin's identity, she gave him the case numbers of criminal cases with Waco police. She told him that she believed the perpetrator was a potential threat to the public—and to Baylor students—and that the Baylor official should confer with Waco police.

"It's the only time I've ever made a call like that," she said, wondering years later what would—or would not—have happened if she hadn't picked up the phone.

CHAPTER FOUR

ONE IN FIVE

By the time of Jasmin Hernandez's assault in the spring of 2012, almost five years had passed since the U.S. Department of Justice released its oft-cited statistic that one in five women would experience some type of sexual assault while in college. It was a figure that would be debated, dismissed, and doubted but later backed up by further research that proved the same. By the spring of 2012, sexual assault had become a serious concern on American campuses, mostly because mainstream media was finally beginning to take notice of the epidemic. And the Barack Obama administration was promising sweeping changes. What is perhaps most surprising about Baylor University's indifference to Jasmin and other female students who said they were sexually assaulted there is that administrators didn't recognize what was happening at other colleges and universities around the country.

At schools large and small, college presidents were realizing the risk associated with minimizing allegations of rape and interpersonal violence. Already, victims who claimed administrators didn't do enough to investigate their allegations or accommodate them after assaults were suing schools in federal court under the provisions of Title IX, the federal law that provides equal access to educational opportunities regardless of gender. Indeed, the public acceptance of slapping assailants on the wrist and simply saying, "Boys will be boys," was finally coming to an end.

On March 26, 2012, about three weeks before Tevin Elliott raped Jasmin on a muddy slope behind the Aspen Heights clubhouse, *Washington Post* political writer Melinda Henneberger authored a tragic story about a woman who committed suicide only ten days after she said she was sexually assaulted by a Notre Dame football player. Henneberger, a Notre Dame graduate, wrote the story for the *National Catholic Reporter,* and media outlets around the world picked up her report.

Henneberger documented the death of nineteen-year-old Lizzy Seeberg, a student at St. Mary's College, which is across the street from Notre Dame in South Bend, Indiana. On August 31, 2010, Lizzy and a friend were dancing and listening to music with two Fighting Irish football players in one of the men's rooms. After one of the players and Lizzy's friend left, the other player, who was later identified as line backer Prince Shembo, allegedly kissed Lizzy's neck, pulled down her tank top, and sucked and licked her right breast. Seeberg said she was crying and froze as the alleged assault began. On the way back to St. Mary's, she texted her therapist, who was treating her for anxiety and depression. "Something bad happened," Lizzy texted the therapist.

That night, Lizzy wrote a handwritten statement about the incident, and she and a friend signed and dated it. The next day, Lizzy went to a hospital, where a nurse swabbed her lips, neck, and breasts for DNA. The hospital called a police officer, and Lizzy gave him her statement, along with the top and bra she was wearing the previous night. After Lizzy met with the police again a few days later, one of Shembo's teammates texted her with a warning: "Don't do anything you would regret. Messing with notre dame football is a bad idea."

On September 9, Lizzy had a panic attack while sitting through a mandatory freshman seminar on sexual assault. She failed to show up for a therapy session the next day, and a counselor found her unresponsive in her dorm room. Paramedics and emergency room doctors tried to resuscitate her for nearly ninety minutes but failed. She was buried on September 17 with a cowboy hat she wore to country music concerts and a foul ball she'd caught during a Chicago Cubs game at Wrigley Field.

Lizzy's parents met with Notre Dame campus police six days after they buried their daughter. According to Henneberger's reporting, police officers told them they weren't sure when they'd continue to investigate the case because it was football season "and there's a lot of underage drinking." Notre Dame president John Jenkins declined to meet with her parents. Five years after Lizzy's death, her father, Tom Seeberg, said he still hadn't received an incident report from campus police.

Following a disciplinary hearing in February 2011, Notre Dame officials found Shembo "not responsible" for sexually assaulting Lizzy. Police never charged him with a crime. The U.S. Department of Education's Office for Civil Rights still opened a Title IX investigation into how Notre Dame handled allegations of sexual assault by students. For the first time in at least thirty years, the OCR launched its inquiry without first receiving a formal complaint. After a seven-month investigation, the OCR reached a settlement with Notre Dame, which promised, among other things, to speed up its investigations and do more for victims who reported assaults.

The Notre Dame story wasn't the only sexual assault scandal that might have served as a warning for Baylor officials. Only three days after Henneberger's story about Lizzy's death was published, the University of Montana in Missoula announced that it had fired football coach Robin Pflugrad and athletics director Jim O'Day. Montana president Royce Engstrom made the decision during the middle of spring practice. On the day the dismissals were announced, associate athletics director Dave Guffey told the *Missoulian* newspaper: "Shocked is a good way to describe it. Disbelief. . . . It could have major negative ramifications on Grizzly athletics and Grizzly football for a long time to come. Speaking from my perspective, it's pretty scary."

But a sexual assault scandal that rocked Missoula and the Montana football program had already had a devastating effect on several women who said they were raped or assaulted by Grizzly football players. An independent investigation by retired Montana Supreme Court justice Diane Barz found that nine sexual assaults involving students were investigated, including a December 2010 incident in which two women accused several players of gang-raping them. In January 2013, Montana running back Beau Donaldson was sentenced to thirty years in prison, with twenty suspended, after pleading guilty to raping a childhood friend. He was released on parole in June 2016. Grizzlies quarterback Jordan Johnson was also accused of raping a woman on February 4, 2012, but he was later found not guilty of sexual intercourse without consent.

In an unprecedented development, the U.S. Department of Justice and U.S. Department of Education simultaneously conducted their own investigations into how alleged assaults were handled by the university and local law enforcement. In a scathing twenty-page report, the Justice Department said the county prosecutor's office ignored sexual assaults so frequently that it was placing "women in Missoula at increased risk of harm." The Justice Department found that county prosecutors pursued charges in 14 of the 85 sexual assault cases referred to them by police. The Justice Department reached resolution agreements with the Missoula Police Department and University of Montana, which promised to improve the way it investigated sexual assaults.

But perhaps the most headline-grabbing case—and one involving a high-profile football program and a star player—would unfold on a national stage at the same time accusations against Tevin Elliott were picking up steam. On December 7, 2012, Florida State University student Erica Kinsman told police in Tallahassee, Florida, that a man sexually assaulted her at his off-campus apartment. Kinsman had a sexual assault examination at the hospital the next day, and Tallahassee police and FSU officials were notified of the incident. Then, about five weeks later, Kinsman identified Seminoles quarterback Jameis Winston as her attacker after recognizing him in class. A Tallahassee police detective contacted Winston and told him he'd been identified as a suspect in a sexual assault, but Winston declined to meet with police. The next day, his attorney, Tim Jansen, showed up at police headquarters and turned over two affidavits from Winston's teammates, Chris

Casher and Ronald Darby, who said they saw the woman having consensual sex with Winston. Police put the case in "open/inactive" status in February 2013 because they said Kinsman refused to cooperate. Police never interviewed Winston and didn't process DNA evidence from her rape kit. (Kinsman was originally identified as Jane Doe in police and court records, but she publicly identified herself in the 2015 documentary *The Hunting Ground* and in civil lawsuits against Florida State and Winston.)

In November 2013, after Winston guided the Seminoles to an undefeated record and emerged as the leading Heisman Trophy candidate as college football's best player, Tallahassee Police reopened the investigation after receiving media requests for incident reports related to the alleged rape. State Attorney Willie Meggs, whose office wasn't informed of the incident eleven months earlier, opened his own investigation and interviewed Kinsman. After DNA analysis completed by the Florida Department of Law Enforcement confirmed that Winston's DNA matched a sample taken from Kinsman's underwear, Winston's attorney said his client had consensual sex with her. On December 5, 2013, following a three-week investigation, Meggs announced his office wasn't charging Winston with sexual assault. "We have a duty as prosecutors to determine if each case has a reasonable likelihood of conviction," Meggs said at the time. "After reviewing the facts in this case, we do not feel that we can reach those burdens."

More than a year later, Winston was also cleared of violating FSU's student conduct code during a disciplinary hearing adjudicated by retired Florida State Supreme Court justice Major Harding. In a letter to Winston, Harding wrote: "This was a complex case, and I worked hard to make sure both parties had a full and fair opportunity to present information. In sum, the preponderance of the evidence has not shown that you are responsible for any of the charge violations of the Code. Namely, I find that the evidence before me is insufficient to satisfy the burden of proof." Harding also wrote that he did not find "the credibility of one story substantially stronger than that of the other. Both have their own strengths and weaknesses."

If nothing else, the Winston case put FSU and other schools investigating allegations of sexual assault under a microscope. "It caught the nation's attention," said John Clune, one of Kinsman's attorneys. "That was the biggest thing. When I first started doing Title IX cases, nobody had any idea it had anything to do with sexual assault. Winston was the first time people made the connection and understood that Title IX and sexual assault went hand in hand."

In January 2016, FSU officials agreed to pay Kinsman $950,000 to settle a federal lawsuit she filed against the school for its handling of her Title IX complaint. As part of the agreement, FSU agreed to commit to five years of sexual assault awareness programs and to publish annual reports of those programs. FSU did not admit liability as part of its settlement. In fact, FSU president John Thrasher said the school decided to settle the case because avoiding trial and millions of dollars in legal fees was financially responsible, "even though we are convinced we would have prevailed." Winston, who led the Seminoles to a national championship in 2013 and won the Heisman Trophy the same season, was the No. 1 pick by the Tampa Bay Buccaneers in the 2015 NFL Draft. He signed a four-year, $23.35 million contract with the team. In December 2016, Winston reached an undisclosed settlement with Kinsman to end the federal lawsuit she filed against him, as well as a countersuit he filed against her.

Clune said media attention surrounding the Winston case prompted more women to come forward with their allegations of sexual assault. "Everything feels like it was, in a good way, gasoline on the fire once Florida State hit," he said. "Everything seemed to accelerate."

The fact that Winston was the star player on college football's best team in 2013 made it a bigger story, but Clune also sensed that media changed their tone in reporting sexual assaults. "They understood. They weren't victim blaming. They were giving intelligent analysis and getting good views on their pieces and articles and that snowballed as the media became more and more attentive to these issues," he said.

With each case, there would be public outrage. But with each case, as history has shown, there were always more cases. In 2004, a female student at Arizona State University accused running back Darnel Henderson of raping her in her dorm room. In the summer before his first year at ASU, Henderson had already been accused of improper behavior toward women, including exposing his genitalia to female staff members, but football coach Dirk Koetter persuaded administrators to let him enroll. Police investigated the woman's rape allegations, but the county attorney's office declined to pursue charges against him. The woman and her family filed a federal Title IX lawsuit against the coach and university, during which it was discovered university officials destroyed emails related to Henderson's behavior toward women. The woman received $850,000 in a settlement, and the board of regents agreed to establish a women's safety czar at all three of its campuses—Arizona State, the University of Arizona, and Northern Arizona University.

At the time of that settlement, in January 2009, Joanne Belknap, a professor of sociology at the University of Colorado, told ESPN's Lester Munson: "This is a new day. Universities always protect the male athlete. It has happened forever. But this settlement will make things significantly better."

Diane Rosenfeld, another expert in women's violence issues and a lecturer at Harvard Law School, told Munson: "This could be our turning point. Instead of privileging athletes, we will now approach the goal of a culture of sexual respect."

Two years later—prompted by the still-increasing number of reports of sexual assault on college campuses and heightened public awareness—the U.S. Department of Education pushed the issue further into the forefront with the issuance of sexual violence guidelines in what has become known as the "Dear Colleague letter." Surely, if any university, including Baylor, hadn't realized that rape and sexual violence on campus weren't a problem by then, a mandate by the highest education office in the nation certainly should have made that clear.

CHAPTER FIVE

THE CRUX OF TITLE IX

Women shouldn't be getting sexually assaulted in college. That's obvious. But to fully understand Baylor University's failures, and those of U.S. colleges in general, it is vital to know what was expected of the institutions that take in hundreds of thousands of our sons and daughters every year.

If a student would have gone to Baylor's website in the spring of 2013 and tried to find information about how to report a sexual assault, he or she likely would have struggled. Let's say the student managed to make his or her way to the Web page for Baylor's Judicial Affairs Office, which at that time was overseeing sexual assault investigations. There would be a lot of information about Baylor's drug and alcohol policies and what to do if one is caught drinking or smoking marijuana. There would be an in-depth description of Baylor's policies on plagiarism and what would happen to someone who violated the school Honor Code for academic integrity. There would be testimonials from students who'd suffered the consequences of being caught drinking, cheating, hazing, using pornography, and even "inappropriate blogging," but there would be absolutely no mention of sexual assault on the main page. A student searching the site would see that Baylor logged 152 violations of its alcohol policy in 2011-2012, but only two for what was termed "sexual misconduct." Only if you clicked several links into the student code of conduct would you find Baylor's brief "sexual misconduct" policy, which mentioned sexual assault in the context of incest, fornication, adultery, homosexual acts, and sex outside of marriage. It said students, faculty, or staff could be sanctioned for sexual misconduct, and the person sanctioned would receive counseling and assistance "so the sanction imposed may be a catalyst for redemption in his or her life." Something that came closer to a list of resources for sexual assault victims and ways to make a report came a few links deep into the "students" section.

For Jasmin Hernandez and many of the other women who reported being sexually assaulted at Baylor, the actual reported rape, attempted rape, or other act of violence or violation was only the beginning. The fear of running into their alleged assailants on campus kept some of them from going to class or participating in activities. Friends shunned them. Friends of the accused student harassed them. Grades dropped. Scholarships were lost. Some didn't get therapy, and the crushing effects of anxiety, depression, and posttraumatic stress disorder took its toll. Even for those who received regular counseling, their college experiences were marred forever.

When Jasmin, for example, would sit down to study in the months following her rape and leading up to the trial, she said she couldn't keep the material in her head. "I felt very spaced out. Kind of detached, not focused. I would kind of say with my 'head in the clouds,' but not with the dreamy connotation. Just very dissociative." She saw herself transition from a super-friendly girl who was eager to branch out and meet new people into someone who sought security with a core group of friends and had become somewhat socially withdrawn. A former honors student, she lost her scholarship and was told that no one could help her academically after having been raped by a football player. She stuck it out at Baylor for another year after her assault, during which she said the emotional turmoil took its greatest toll. Her mom noticed the change when Jasmin came home for Thanksgiving and seemed very isolated and often overreacted to even innocuous events. Her friends noticed her being more withdrawn. She ended up dropping out after her sophomore year and moving back to Yorba Linda.

She eventually enrolled in a community college. But even there she faced assumptions, by people who didn't know what had happened, that she'd simply partied too hard at Baylor or couldn't handle the rigors of a more prestigious school. It had caused incredible strain on her family, particularly with her dad, with whom Jasmin did not want to discuss the rape. Once, while riding in the car with him, Jasmin became upset when he wouldn't stop trying to talk about her case. She opened the door while Ostes was still slowly driving up a big hill near their home, and she jumped out and ran down the hill. "You just don't realize the ripple effect," her mother said.

In April 2011, a year before Tevin Elliott sexually assaulted Jasmin, university officials received a nineteen-page letter from the U.S. Department of Education's Office for Civil Rights laying out specific details about how colleges and universities should respond to reports of rape and other forms of sexual violence and how institutions were supposed to make students, faculty, and staff aware of such incidents. That letter also outlined actions that Baylor or any college should take to protect and assist students who report sexual violence.

The directive, which became popularly known as the Dear Colleague letter, specifically stated that every school should have someone dedicated to overseeing its response to sexual violence complaints — someone whose other job responsibilities didn't create a conflict of interest. Additionally, it stated that information on how to contact that person, and what those complaints covered, must be prominently displayed on the institution's website. Baylor didn't.

The letter repeatedly mentioned how schools should widely publicize their grievance procedures regarding sexual violence. There was no such publicity at Baylor. It stated that school law enforcement employees should notify alleged victims of their right to file a complaint with the school. According to many women, Baylor police officers didn't. It laid out recommendations that all students, faculty, coaches, and administrators be trained on how to respond when they heard of an allegation of sexual violence. At Baylor, they by their own admission were not. It stated that "a school that knows, or reasonably should know, about possible harassment must promptly investigate to determine what occurred and then take appropriate steps to resolve the situation," regardless of whether there was, or wasn't, a criminal investigation. That had not been the practice at Baylor. The words *prompt* or *promptly* appear eighteen times in the letter. It is dated April 4, 2011. Yet, even years later, those appropriate steps—and several other provisions in the letter—were still not in place at Baylor.

The Dear Colleague letter outlined schools' obligations to respond to complaints of sexual harassment and sexual violence. Its guidelines apply to all schools that receive federal funds, which is almost every college and university in the United States, about seven thousand total, according to the U.S. Department of Education. Private institutions, including Baylor, qualify because they accept students who pay for their tuition with federal grant money.

The purpose of the letter was to provide clarification to a federal civil rights law that had been around since 1972 known as Title IX. Although its impact on gender equality has been broad, the law itself is brief: "No person in the United States shall, on the basis of sex, be excluded from participation in, be denied the benefits of, or be subjected to discrimination under any education program or activity receiving federal financial assistance." Although Title IX doesn't even mention athletics—and the law applies to all aspects of education such as admissions, financial aid, treatment of pregnant students, and discipline—it has mostly been associated with college sports. And in that sense, it has always generated controversy and demanded clarification.

Title IX was widely promoted as the genesis behind giving female students equal athletic opportunities, as they were woefully underrepresented in collegiate sports at that time.

That part of Title IX people knew, but how it applied to rape was still a point of confusion. The general concept is this: Title IX was designed to ensure equal opportunity in education for both sexes. When a woman or man is harassed or assaulted on the basis of her or his sex, the conduct creates a "hostile environment" to where it "interferes with or limits" the student's ability to continue her or his education. Thus, having to attend school in that type of environment is discriminatory and denies a student the equal opportunity promised in Title IX.

At the start of former U.S. president Ronald Reagan's administration in 1981, the U.S. Department of Education's Office for Civil Rights issued a policy memorandum stating that Title IX prohibits sexual harassment, using a definition that is still in place today. The department's first investigation into a Title IX complaint as a form of sexual violence was in 1988, after a female high school student in Gwinnett County, Georgia, alleged that her coach and teacher had harassed her and had coerced her into having sex. The district was found to be in violation. That case also made its way to the U.S. Supreme Court, which in 1992 ruled for the first time that plaintiffs could sue for monetary damages under Title IX. For many alleged victims that became a more effective way to go after an institution that wasn't complying with Title IX than filing a complaint with the U.S. Department of Education. The department has the ability to withdraw federal funding from schools that don't comply with Title IX, although it hasn't done so at least within the past ten years. It generally strikes resolution agreements with schools that outline what actions they'll take to remedy the situation.

In 1995, former University of Nebraska student Katherine Redmond filed a Title IX lawsuit against the university alleging that the school didn't investigate her report, made in 1993, that football player Christian Peter had twice sexually assaulted her on campus two years earlier. The suit made national headlines as the Huskers had recently won a national championship and would go on to win again at the end of the 1995 season. Redmond settled her suit for $50,000 in the spring of 1997, only months before Nebraska would win yet another national title.

Then, in 2002, University of Colorado student Lisa Simpson filed a lawsuit against the university alleging that officials within the football program knew of, and tolerated, a pattern of illicit behavior that included sexual assaults during school-sponsored visits by football recruits. Simpson claimed she was gang raped by several football players during one such visit in 2001 and that the university, which investigated her allegations, declined to take appropriate action. After a federal appeals court overturned a lower court's ruling to dismiss the lawsuit in 2007, the two sides reached an agreement that gave Simpson $2.5 million and instituted several changes in how the university addressed Title IX sexual violence complaints.

In 2008, the Obama White House would begin to raise the profile of campus sexual assaults, later creating a special task force, putting the onus on college and university administrators to help prevent assaults and proactively address them when they happen.

Catherine Lhamon, who served as assistant secretary for civil rights at the U.S. Department of Education from 2013 to 2017, said a pattern of noncompliance with Title IX in terms of addressing sexual violence prompted the 2011 Dear Colleague letter. The Dear Colleague letter was quickly followed by increased media attention to the issue, including a segment by the CBS newsmagazine *60 Minutes* on a University of the Pacific women's basketball player who said she was raped by three members of the school's male basketball team.

In the ensuing years, Title IX lawsuits against universities relating to sexual assaults increased, as did complaints coming into federal education officials about how institutions responded to sexual violence. Complaints went from nine in 2009, to 108 in 2014, when the department issued yet another set of clarifying guidelines on sexual violence, and then up to 318 by April 2017. "I do not think that's because there's a higher incidence of sexual violence in schools," Lhamon said. "I think it reflects greater national awareness and expectations that the Office for Civil Rights will be responsive."

There was pushback against the department's enforcement of Title IX when it came to sexual violence, especially in the area of investigating allegations and punishing those the school found responsible. In recent years, male students started filing Title IX lawsuits accusing the schools of expelling, suspending, or otherwise punishing them as a result of a poorly conducted investigation and denying them due process. Title IX investigations rely on the "preponderance of evidence" standard used for civil legal proceedings. That means an accused student can be found responsible if the adjudicator determines there's a 51 percent chance the allegations against the accused are true. It's a much lower requirement than the "beyond a reasonable doubt" standard for criminal convictions. And what complicates many university-led Title IX investigations is that there is often a criminal inquiry or trial occurring at the same time. Although that can make it difficult for university investigators, the U.S. Department of Education has stated clearly that a school can't wait for a criminal case to conclude, nor does a criminal inquiry relieve the school of its separate responsibility to investigate.

That standard has been attacked from all sides. Critics routinely argue that schools shouldn't be in the business of adjudicating crimes and should stay out of sexual assaults and related criminal incidents altogether. Those who want schools out of the sexual violence adjudicating business argue that employees aren't trained to properly handle such cases and lack the resources and subpoena power to get needed evidence.

In defending why schools have a role in addressing sexual assault complaints, Lhamon cites a case from Southern Methodist University in Dallas involving a male student who alleged another male student raped him. The school directed him to the police, and the accused student ended up being indicted for sexual assault. But back on campus, the accused student's friends harassed the student who complained— catcalling him in the cafeteria, knocking on his door late at night, prank-calling his room. "He felt increasingly unsafe," Lhamon said. "He went to the school. He talked about the kind of harassment that was taking place for him, and the school said, 'There's nothing for us to do. This is now a criminal matter.' Well, it's not a criminal matter. The criminal justice system doesn't touch that kind of harassment that's at school." In that case, the student dropped out and, as Lhamon points out, was denied the equal opportunity to his education. The criminal justice system can, although not always, punish the alleged perpetrator, but its job is not to take care of the victim back at school, which is also where Title IX and university administrators come in.

In the debate over how Baylor and other universities adhered to Title IX, the guidelines for supporting complainants and ensuring their safety would get less attention than how schools conduct investigations. But the guidelines have been seen as vital in helping sexual assault complainants feel safe on campus and continue their education and participation in activities, whether that's a sports team or campus choral group.

According to guidelines, help can include:

- providing an escort to ensure that the complainant can move safely on campus
- ensuring that the complainant and alleged perpetrator do not attend the same classes
- moving the complainant or alleged perpetrator to a different residence hall
- providing counseling services
- providing medical services
- providing academic support services, such as tutoring
- arranging for the complainant to retake a course or withdraw from a class without penalty
- ensuring that any changes do not adversely affect the complainant's academic record.

According to Title IX, schools are directed to take those steps to protect the complainant as soon as they become aware of an incident, regardless of the status of an investigation. In one of the Title IX lawsuits filed against Baylor, ten women alleged the university failed them. Their alleged perpetrators included a football player, fraternity member, campus coworker, even an assistant in president Ken Starr's office. Although the incidents happened in different years and different circumstances, they share a similar spiraling effect: Assault leads to emotional trauma, emotional trauma leads to poor performance in school, bad grades lead to lost scholarships and, in some cases, when victims are unable to pay for school or cope with stress and anxiety, they drop out. All along the way, victims state school officials ignored, discouraged, or prevented them from seeking help. "Professors refused to provide her with accommodations," read one allegation in the lawsuit.

One woman, upon reporting her rape to campus medical staff, "received only an external stomach evaluation. She was not provided a rape kit, much less a proper examination." Another woman reported ducking into an assistant dean's office to avoid running into her alleged perpetrator on campus. After the dean found out about her assault, she wasn't offered help, but was instead encouraged to withdraw from classes because her grades had plummeted. Another woman said her alleged perpetrator's friends harassed her. Several women reported being turned away from the counseling center. One tried to commit suicide by slitting her wrists. Others described prescription drug abuse and panic attacks. One woman, not in the lawsuit, would report being terrified in the aftermath of a domestic violence incident: "I haven't seen a student as scared and upset as she was in a long time. She mentioned that she lives in constant fear, 24 hours a day she is scared that [her alleged assailant] or his friends will come beat her up," according to a statement from an academic services employee, which was included in a 2017 legal filing in a defamation case against Baylor.

Much of the focus on how Baylor failed to address sexual violence has been on what happened after 2011, but the lawsuit with the ten women describes dismissive behavior toward sexual assault complaints that goes back, in some cases, more than a decade. There were specific incidents happening with football players as well, including a March 23, 2010, arrest of cornerback Antareis Bryan for physically assaulting his girlfriend. She told police he became violent with her after she told him she wanted to break up with him and they struggled over some items in her apartment; officers observed she had a bloody lip and red marks on her upper arms. A record from the McLennan County District Attorney's Office noted that Bryan completed a pretrial diversion program and the case was essentially dropped in July 2011. The Waco police report notes that, upon finding out that Bryan was a football player, officers notified Baylor police, who asked Baylor football coaches to bring Bryan into the police station when he showed up for practice, and the report indicated that one of the coach's staff members brought Bryan in. Through his attorney, Briles said he didn't recall that incident. Baylor records show that Bryan played in eight games, starting twice, during the following fall 2010 season. Bryan did not respond to multiple requests to talk to us for this book. The woman would end up again reporting Bryan for assault almost a year later, but in that case police determined there wasn't enough evidence to pursue charges. Neither case ever made it into the media. Briles, through his attorney, and a former assistant coach said they recalled police coming to Baylor's NFL pro day in March 2011 and taking Bryan into custody. But Briles didn't know why and didn't follow up because police were handling it and Bryan was no longer a Baylor player at that point, his attorney wrote. It ended up being in connection with the report of attempted ATM thefts in 2009 and 2010, including one from the school library which apparently failed because the tires on the dolly went flat.

In a March 2017 ruling in the case of the ten anonymous women whose alleged assaults spanned from 2004 to 2016, U.S. district judge Robert Pitman wrote that if, as the women claimed, there was a pattern of misinforming students as to their rights under Title IX, failing to investigate assaults and discouraging women from coming forward, the university had put them and their peers at a "heightened risk" of sexual assault. Critics and media also noted that despite being informed of multiple sexual assaults between 2008 and 2011, Baylor, in its annual report to the U.S. Department of Education, reported no such assaults on its campus during that time period.

Baylor was not alone in failing various provisions of Title IX, even after the new guidelines were issued in 2011. In spring 2017, the U.S. Department of Education Office for Civil Rights had 236 schools under investigation, for more than 300 alleged violations. But Baylor's case was unique—in scope and effect—and illustrative of the widespread impact of failing to address sexual violence. The question is: How did it get so bad at a place that prided itself on being a caring Christian community that was different from everywhere else?

CHAPTER SIX

RISE OF BAYLOR

I n the fall of 2001, Baylor University's leadership laid out an ambitious ten-year plan to transform the school from a regional denominational college to a national research institution that would be on par with the likes of Harvard, Princeton, Yale, and other "Tier One" schools in *U.S. News & World Report*'s rankings of the top universities in the country.

What would set Baylor apart from the aforementioned institutions, according to its leaders, was that it would continue to embrace its unwavering Christian identity. For nearly 175 years, Baylor has held firm to its conviction that the world needs a university that is "unambiguously Christian." On its website, Baylor boasts: "In a world where faith is often the casualty of a serious pursuit of academic achievement, Baylor is a special place."

"Some people think Baylor's mission sounds very idealistic and it does," regent J. Cary Gray told us. "We are going to integrate academic excellence in a Christian setting. We are going to be unapologetically Christian and integrate academic excellence and do it in a caring community. That sounds very idealistic and it's hard because most people in American culture today think that's not even possible."

Indeed, few other American universities have fought to maintain their Christian heritage as much as Baylor, the world's largest Baptist university, with more than 16,000 students. Chartered in 1845, at the suggestion of Rev. William Milton Tryon and district judge R. E. B. Baylor, it is the oldest continually operating university in Texas, having first opened its doors in Independence in 1846 (it consolidated with Waco University in 1886 to form Baylor University in Waco).

Ever since, Baylor has been a place that put as much emphasis on teaching students about Jesus Christ and faith as on biology and economics. In its Student Code of Conduct, Baylor makes it clear what it anticipates of its students: "We expect that each Baylor student will conduct himself or herself in accordance with Christian principles as commonly perceived by Texas Baptists. Personal misconduct either on or off the campus by anyone connected with Baylor detracts from the Christian witness Baylor strives to present to the world and hinders full accomplishment of the mission of the University." Among other things, Baylor students are prohibited from consuming alcohol, using illicit drugs, cohabiting, and having premarital sex. In fact, dancing wasn't even allowed on campus until 1996, more than 150 years after the school opened.

In the fall of 2001, then president Robert B. Sloan and other Baylor leaders asked tens of thousands of alumni to fall in line with another bold plan that would dramatically alter the course of the university for decades to come. Instead of remaining a smaller, regional university that catered to Baptist families from Texas and other parts of the country, Sloan and other leaders wanted to transform Baylor into a nationally recognized research institution, which would attract scientists, professors, and students from all over the world, and, of course, millions of dollars in federal research grants that might potentially come with them.

The "Baylor 2012" strategic plan was more ambitious than anything Baylor had done in its past. Over ten years, the university, among other priorities, wanted to build a $2 billion endowment; increase its doctoral program offerings from 14 to 20; increase the percentage of students living on campus from 29 percent to 50 percent; and dramatically raise the average SAT score of its incoming freshmen.

"The underlying premise was Baylor was going to be a national research university and one of the only unapologetically Christian national research universities," Gray said.

Of course, the price of trying to become a nationally recognized research institution wasn't cheap. Baylor spent $400 million on the construction of facilities, including a $103 million science building and $45 million industrial research facility. Baylor issued $247 million in bonds for campus construction and amassed sizable debt for the first time in its history. From 2001 to 2004, the university hired 184 new tenure-tracked faculty members. As a result, tuition and fees for students more than doubled from $18,233 in 2002 to $40,396 in 2012, according to the *Waco Tribune-Herald*. Baylor also accepted more students to help cover rising faculty salaries and infrastructure costs, and its bottom line ballooned. In 2002, the university reported about $329 million in revenue. By 2012, revenue had more than doubled to $749 million. Even after expenses that year, it had $87 million in net income. But that was for 2012 alone, as over time, the university amassed more than $2.7 billion in assets.

Some critics of Baylor's new vision argued that the university was becoming too expensive for middle-class families and that, more important, its renewed focus on science, research, and technology was another step toward becoming a more secular institution. But others saw the new vision—and particularly Sloan's implementation of it—as a move toward making Baylor too staunchly religious.

As Baylor's campus footprint rapidly expanded and its enrollment swelled, lines were being drawn in the central Texas dust. On one side were Baptist fundamentalists (or conservatives), who generally believe that God inspired the authors of the Bible and thus its text is to be interpreted literally because it was "written without error." On the other side were the Baptist moderates, who believe in the Bible but leave some wiggle room in its interpretation. In other words, as *Texas Monthly* writer Michael Hall eloquently wrote in a 2003 story about Baylor's spiritual war, moderates and liberals are the "Baptists who don't go to church every Sunday" and "who like Baylor just as it has always been, a place where you could get a good, strong undergraduate education while the bells in the McLane Carillon played 'Amazing Grace.'" The conservatives, Hall wrote, clamored for change, "for progress, new programs, new buildings, and deeply religious professors who will bring back the faith they say has been diminished at Baylor." As he summed it up, "It's the difference between being a good school in a Christian environment and a good Christian school."

The tug-of-war between Baptist fundamentalists and moderates had been fought on Baylor's campus for decades. In 1990, when fundamentalists tried to seize control of the Baptist General Convention of Texas, which elected every member of Baylor's board of trustees, then university president Herbert Reynolds, a moderate, amended the university charter to allow the general convention to elect only nine of the thirty-six members of the board.

One of the harshest critics of Sloan would be the nonprofit Baylor Alumni Association (now known as the Baylor Line Foundation), which was separate from the university and published a magazine called the *Baylor Line,* which Sloan—and some of the regents—took issue with when it editorialized against his policies or printed stories about controversial topics, including drug and alcohol abuse on campus. According to many alumni, the residual effects of Sloan and his supporters on the board of regents in some ways laid the groundwork for why Baylor was so far behind the curve in addressing sexual assault.

"It's a culture of, 'We don't talk about our problems,'" said former Baylor Alumni Association president Tom Nesbitt. "It's a toxic, horrible part of our culture that we don't talk about our problems. It's viewed as disloyalty. These are disloyal people. These are rabble-rousers."

"With the alumni divide, you could almost calculate the split by when someone had graduated or been most engaged with the university," said Karla Leeper, a former chief of staff to two Baylor presidents. "There were people who thought the [status quo]—a smaller, very teaching-focused institution that was low priced for a private institution—was the way it should be. Then there was a different vision, which was more of a research institution with a greater national profile, higher price tag, and a very different philosophy."

Unfortunately for Sloan, the timing of Baylor's grand plan couldn't have been worse. The announcement of Baylor 2012 came a year before the university endured one of its darkest periods. In the summer of 2003, Baylor basketball players Carlton Dotson and Patrick Dennehy told their coaches that someone had stolen $300 from their apartment and that their teammates had threatened them. The coaches didn't take the threats seriously, so Dotson and Dennehy purchased handguns. Dennehy, a transfer from the University of New Mexico, shared an apartment with Dotson, a transfer from Paris Junior College in East Texas.

On June 19, 2003, Dennehy's family reported him missing. A few days later Dotson showed up in his native Maryland and Dennehy's abandoned SUV was found in Virginia. In late July, Dotson was arrested after he called police and said he was hearing voices and needed help. He told FBI agents that people were trying to kill him because "he is Jesus, the son of God."

National media descended on Waco, which, only ten years earlier, had been the site of a fifty-one-day standoff between members of the Branch Davidian religious sect and law enforcement at the Mount Carmel Center outside town. An April 19, 1993, raid ended with David Koresh and seventy-five of his followers dying in a fire. Waco was in the spotlight again for all the wrong reasons. After a six-week search, police found Dennehy's decomposed body in a field near Baylor's campus. Dotson told the FBI that he and Dennehy went to gravel pits for target practice on June 13. Dotson claimed Dennehy pointed a gun at him. When it jammed, Dotson said, "Father, please forgive me," and shot his friend. An autopsy report showed Dennehy, twenty-one, was shot above the right ear and once toward the back of his head.

An ensuing Baylor investigation uncovered that basketball coach Dave Bliss had improperly paid up to $40,000 for tuition and other expenses for Dennehy and another player, a violation of NCAA rules. The inquiry also revealed that the coaching staff covered up positive drug tests for several players. But the most stunning revelation was that Bliss had instructed two players and assistant coach Abar Rouse to tell law enforcement officials that Dennehy was a drug dealer and used money from drug deals to pay his tuition. Bliss told the players that Dennehy couldn't refute their stories because he was dead. "It doesn't have to be the same story," he told them. "It just has to have the same ending." Unwilling to participate, Rouse made secret recordings of Bliss and turned them over to a newspaper reporter, who published their contents the next day.

Bliss and athletics director Tom Stanton resigned, and the school self-imposed sanctions, including a postseason ban in 2003–04. In June 2005, Dotson pleaded guilty to murdering Dennehy and was sentenced to thirty-five years in prison. At the time, Sloan told reporters: "We ask ourselves, 'How did it happen?' But it did happen here."

Leeper was a communications studies professor at Baylor at the time of Denney's murder.

"We were very aware, always, of that history," Leeper said. "It was hard not to be because almost every time one of your teams was doing something well, almost every story would start out, 'You might remember . . .'"

In September 2003, the Baylor Faculty Senate passed a no-confidence vote against Sloan; it reaffirmed the vote in May the next year. In December 2004, when Baylor's faculty was asked if they wanted Sloan to remain president, 85 percent voted no. At the time, Sloan believed his unpopularity was the sign of a much deeper issue. In a February 2005 article in *Baylor Magazine* titled "Identity Crisis," he was quoted as saying, "The central question for Baylor, whether we're talking about academic freedom or the controversy right now over 2012 and me, is what is the character and shape of Baylor? Who are we? Are we a Christian institution or not? That is the central question that Baylor faces, and particularly faces today—and it's in some sense the elephant in the room that people sometimes don't want to talk about."

Sloan stepped down as Baylor's president in June 2005 and worked the next two years as chancellor. Bill Underwood was named interim president, and John M. Lilley became Baylor's new president on January 1, 2006. The son of a Louisiana Baptist minister, Lilley earned three academic degrees from Baylor in the 1960s, and had previously worked as president at Penn State University–Erie and the University of Nevada–Reno. Lilley was considered to be someone who understood Baylor's Christian mission, as well as its aspirations of becoming a nationally renowned research institution. Most important, he was thought to be someone who could unite Baylor's divided constituencies.

After less than three years on the job, however, the board of regents fired Lilley on July 24, 2008, saying he was unable to unite the school's students, faculty, and administrators. During Lilley's tenure, the university was criticized for offering freshmen a $300 bookstore credit to retake the SAT after they had already enrolled, and a $1,000 merit scholarship if they raised their scores by at least 50 points. Critics said it was a manipulation of standardized tests to increase Baylor's ranking by *U.S. News & World Report.* David E. Garland, a professor of Christian Scriptures and dean of the Truett Theological Seminary, was named interim president.

"I think unfortunately, Baylor has a lot of people who love the university and are very connected to it," Leeper said. "So when you have an argument over the institution and have that level of connection, passions are going to run pretty high."

Six years into its ambitious ten-year plan, Baylor was again searching for a new university president—its third in four years. Its two-year search would end with a man who was very familiar to Baptists and people around the world.

CHAPTER SEVEN

JUDGE STARR

Only two weeks after Judge Kenneth Starr—yes, that Ken Starr—officially took office as Baylor University's fourteenth president, he already was facing a massive crisis. Two Big 12 Conference schools, Colorado and Nebraska, announced they were leaving for the Pac-10 Conference and Big Ten Conference, respectively. On June 11, 2010, ESPN reported that Texas, Texas Tech, Oklahoma, and Oklahoma State were also preparing to leave the Big 12 for the Pac–10, and Missouri and Texas A&M were deciding whether to depart for the Pac-10–or the Southeastern Conference. If those schools left and the Big 12 dissolved, Baylor would be left without a place at college sports' main table, potentially costing it tens of millions of dollars in broadcast rights and other revenue every year.

Just three days earlier, Starr had written a guest column that was published in the *Waco Tribune-Herald* and the *Dallas Morning News*, in which he tried to assure alumni, faculty, students, and fans that he and his executive council were doing everything possible to protect Baylor's interests. "Let me make our perspective clear: Baylor emphatically supports the Big 12. We are proud of our role in the conference and we want to see it prosper. . . . What we do know is this: the Lone Star state schools of the Big 12 should stick together. That's what's in the best interests of Baylor, of Texas, and of our own community, here in Waco."

In the end, cooler heads prevailed. Only Missouri and Texas A&M departed for the SEC and those defections didn't happen until a year later. In many respects, it was an early victory for Baylor's new president. The Big 12 was still in business, and the Bears and their in-state rivals were still a part of the league.

"He understood the importance of the front porch," said Karla Leeper, Starr's chief of staff from 2010 to 2014, of athletics being a university's most visible arm. "I think quite frankly during all the conversations about the Big 12 and about whether Baylor belonged, there was some pretty stinging criticism. To keep our front porch in that neighborhood was important to the university in a number of respects."

Many Baylor alumni and faculty members probably remembered their new president from his earlier time as President Bill Clinton's nemesis during the Whitewater and Monica Lewinsky investigations. Being in the middle of big, important issues was Starr's calling card throughout his successful legal career, and it would largely become his management style as Baylor's president. More than anything, he loved being in the public eye, whether it was while he argued thirty-six cases in front of the U.S. Supreme Court or enthusiastically ran onto the field in a green and gold Baylor Line jersey with freshmen before football games.

Starr wasn't an obvious choice to replace John M. Lilley. Although Starr was a fifth-generation Texan and devout Christian, he had very limited experience in academic administration. He was the dean of Pepperdine University's School of Law when Baylor hired him. He had previously taught law at New York University and was a visiting professor at George Mason University and Chapman Law School in Orange, California. He'd spent much of his life practicing law, as a partner at Kirkland & Ellis LLP in Chicago; solicitor general of the United States under President George H. W. Bush; federal appellate judge for the District of Columbia under President Ronald Reagan; and, perhaps most famously, as an independent counsel for five investigations, including the infamous Whitewater case.

From 1994 to 1998, Starr investigated the Clintons' controversial Whitewater land deal and the suicide of White House counsel Vincent Foster. He expanded the inquiry to include Bill Clinton's alleged romantic relationships with Paula Jones and Lewinsky, a White House intern, which eventually led to Clinton's impeachment, only the second of a president in U.S. history. Clinton was acquitted in a subsequent trial before the U.S. Senate. Starr later said he regretted the investigation took so long and "brought great pain to a lot of people."

Despite his being widely regarded as someone who divided the country as an aggressive prosecutor during the highly charged Whitewater investigation, the Baylor regents believed Starr would do what former presidents Robert Sloan and Lilley didn't—unite the school's divided alumni and faculty. He was a legal scholar and staunch advocate of Christian values, which were the foundation of Baylor's mission. And the regents were banking on Starr's notoriety and familiar name helping the school reach its goal of a $2 billion endowment.

"He was a very effective public presence for the university," Leeper said. "He clearly loved the students. You've seen the pictures of him running with the Line. He was just as excited to be with student government or the model UN team. He was very interested in working with things related to students."

Starr was a big sports fan, and Baylor's athletics teams enjoyed unprecedented success under his watch, and, as a result, historic increases in alumni giving. The 2011–12 academic year is often referred to as the "Year of the Bear" by Baylor alumni and fans. In addition to quarterback Robert Griffin III winning the Heisman Trophy, the women's basketball team became the first NCAA squad—men's or women's—to finish 40-0 and win a national championship. Lady Bears star Brittney Griner was named national player of the year. The men's basketball team, coming off NCAA sanctions from the Dave Bliss scandal, started 17-0 and reached the Elite Eight of the NCAA tournament. That spring, the Baylor baseball team won forty-nine games and came just shy of making it to the College World Series.

The first time Starr met football coach Art Briles at a reception on June 1, 2010, Starr asked the coach what he needed. "We need an on-campus stadium," Briles told him. "It is a need, not a want." The Bears had played at Floyd Casey Stadium across town since 1950. After sixty years, the stadium was crumbling and had fallen woefully behind the facilities at other Big 12 schools. If Baylor was going to stay in the conference—and recruit better players to be more competitive—it needed a new on-campus stadium, Briles told him.

In 2014, Baylor opened McLane Stadium, a $266 million venue named in honor of alumnus Drayton McLane Jr., a billionaire and former owner of Major League Baseball's Houston Astros, who made the largest donation in school history for its construction. Privately, Starr told people close to him that he had aspirations of Baylor becoming the Baptist version of Notre Dame, the Catholic university in South Bend, Indiana, which is known as much for its football tradition as its sterling academic reputation. The sparkling new stadium on the banks of the Brazos River was the first step toward reaching that goal.

By all accounts, at least publicly, Starr seemed to be very happy working as Baylor's president, and the regents and faculty seemed satisfied with the job he was doing. Baylor's student enrollment was growing rapidly, its academic standing was rising, and its athletics teams were winning like never before. In November 2013, the regents extended Starr's contract and appointed him to the additional post of chancellor, which would give him greater responsibilities in promoting the Baylor brand and mission. His salary increased from about $586,000 to $721,000, and would exceed $1.3 million by 2015. In January 2014, the Baylor Faculty Senate, which twice gave Sloan votes of no confidence, took a rare step in endorsing Starr's contract extension. "The Baylor Faculty Senate congratulates Judge Ken Starr on his appointment as chancellor and commends his service and leadership as Baylor's president, especially his spirit of cooperation and shared governance," the resolution read.

Jim H. Patton, a professor of neuroscience, psychology, and biomedical studies and faculty senate chairman at the time, said Starr won over his early doubters with his humble and congenial personality.

"He clearly values debate, lively debate that doesn't put him off or change his character," Patton told insidehighered.com on January 31, 2014. "He values loyal and respectful opposition. He never misses an opportunity to thank folks for their service and even when it is necessary to be critical. I have always detected a positive, redemptive note in what he has to say. People who have principled differences in worldview from his still like him because he is unflaggingly polite and considerate."

Behind the scenes, though, Baylor's regents and administrators had growing concerns about Starr's management style. He came to Baylor having no experience in upper management of a university. While he seemed more than engaged in big decisions and issues related to students, they said he was largely disinterested in the day-to-day operations of the university. He delegated much of those duties to vice presidents and other senior officials, and, as a result, there was massive turnover in his cabinet. During Starr's tenure as Baylor's president, for instance, there were five different provosts (chief academic officers), including interims.

"There were a lot of instances where the president was not engaged in the day-to-day management of things," Leeper said. "There were some areas, if he was interested in that area, where he would be more engaged. . . . He did not have much of a desire to dig down into the operations of the institution."

Members of the board of regents suggested the massive turnover in senior staff members led to poor communication and lack of coordination at the highest level of the administration. "The level of turnover was a problem," one regent said. Senior administrators who remained ended up having to take over much of the day-to-day work, including managing the university's interactions with the board of regents, which was typically a president's job, but one they said Starr was reluctant to do. "It just became a strange administration to serve in when that nexus of communication is broken," said one senior administrator.

The lack of communication and coordinator impacted not only the senior level of Baylor's administration, but athletics as well.

CHAPTER EIGHT

COACH BRILES

In the fall of 2011, Jasmin Hernandez was one of thousands of fresh-men on the Baylor University campus. And while she couldn't name the starting running backs or comment with authority on coaching strategy, she did love the pageantry of football. She loved the games. She loved the excitement. And it was an exciting year. After decades of mediocrity or worse, Baylor football was on the rise and, that winter, quarterback Robert Griffin III would win the Heisman Trophy. And while Jasmin knew who Art Briles was, and that he was an important figure on campus, she didn't know how their paths would soon cross and he would factor into her very personal future.

Briles's ascension from a dusty, West Texas town to the upper ech-elon of college football started with tragedy. When he was a player at the University of Houston, his parents, Wanda and Dennis Briles, and his aunt, Elsie "Tottie" Kittley, were killed while driving to one of his games at the Cotton Bowl in Dallas on October 16, 1976. His father had coached him in high school, when Briles led Rule High School to the Class B state championship game as a senior in 1973.

"It was kind of a hopeless time, to say the least," Briles told ESPN in 2013. "It kind of jolts the soul and spirit, you know? All of the sud-den, you look down and there's not a net anymore. When you're falling, you're falling. One day everything is good and then the next day you're wondering where you're going for Thanksgiving and Christmas."

After burying his parents and aunt, Briles returned to Houston, but only to pack his bags and turn in his football equipment. No matter what others told him, Briles believed he was largely responsible for his loved ones' death. If they weren't driving to Dallas to watch him play, he told himself, they wouldn't have been in the car that fateful morning. For the next forty years, Briles would rarely talk about the accident, even with his wife and children. He felt too much guilt about what happened. "I do," Briles said. "I really do. If I hadn't been playing, it would have never happened. They were coming to see me."

After leaving Houston, Briles went back to Rule, where he moved in with his girlfriend Jan and her parents. Briles knew he was lucky to have Jan; she had planned to attend the game with his parents but stayed behind for a friend's bridal shower instead. Briles joined Jan at Texas Tech University in Lubbock the next fall, and then on Christmas Day 1977 he asked her to marry him. "If there's a shining light out of all of it, that's it," Briles told ESPN. "Jan could have been in the car, too."

Upon graduating from Texas Tech, Briles took an assistant coaching job at Sundown High School, outside Lubbock, which was the start of what would become a twenty-one-year career coaching at Texas high schools. He moved to Sweetwater High School, near Abilene, the next year. In 1988, he was named head coach at Stephenville High School, a Class 4A school located about seventy miles southwest of Fort Worth, which can't be missed due to the giant fiberglass Holstein cow in the town square noting it as the No. 1 dairy county in Texas. Under Briles, the Stephenville Yellow Jackets, who hadn't reached the state playoffs since 1952, won Class 4A state championships in 1993 and '94 and 1998 and '99. Briles's teams were known for their fast-paced, high-scoring offenses, and six of his quarterbacks, including future NFL player Kevin Kolb, played at Division I colleges.

In 2000, Briles joined Texas Tech coach Mike Leach's staff as a running backs coach. He spent three seasons in Lubbock, working with many of college football's brightest young talents: former

University of California, Berkeley coach Sonny Dykes, West Virginia coach Dana Holgorsen, and future Texas Tech coach Kliff Kingsbury.

After the 2002 season, Briles became the first former Houston player hired to coach his alma mater. He inherited a program that was only two years removed from a 0-11 finish and had only two winning seasons in the previous twelve years. But Briles guided the Cougars to a 7-6 record and the Hawaii Bowl in his first season in 2003. After going 3-8 in 2004, Houston played in three consecutive bowl games from 2005 to 2007.

After rebuilding Houston, Briles was eager to try to do the same thing on a bigger stage. When the Baylor job opened at the end of the 2007 season, he was interested, even though the Bears had been one of the worst teams in the country for years. His agent, Jeff Nalley, called a well-known Texas sportswriter with ties to Baylor for help. So when the sportswriter called Baylor booster J. Cary Gray, a Houston attorney (he wasn't yet a member of Baylor's board of regents), and told him that Briles was willing to leave Houston, Gray listened.

"[He] told me that Briles thought he would be a good fit," Gray recalled. "He thought Baylor was a sleeping giant and a real opportunity. He thought he could stay at Houston and win seven, eight, or nine games and no one would care. He could win seven, eight, or nine games at Baylor, stay there for the rest of his career, and they'd build a statue of him."

Athletics director Ian McCaw, not the board of regents, would select Baylor's new coach and he had to get the decision right. He had fired former coach Guy Morriss after the Bears lost their final eight games to finish 3-9 in 2007, their twelfth consecutive losing season. With the university trying to build a $2 billion endowment and reach the rest of its goals in the "Baylor 2012" strategic plan, choosing the right coach was paramount.

Baylor had been searching for coaching stability for nearly two decades. After legendary coach Grant Teaff retired following a twenty-one-year tenure from 1972 to 1992, the Bears fired four coaches in the next fifteen seasons, and only one of them, Chuck Reedy, had a winning record when he was terminated (he went 23-22 in four seasons). In fact, after Baylor joined the Big 12 Conference in 1996, it finished last in the South Division in eleven of twelve seasons.

"It wasn't just the significance of having a football program," said former Baylor chief of staff Karla Leeper. "The ultimate collapse of the Baylor football program had become a metaphor for sort of a really negative period in Baylor's history."

Despite what others told him about Baylor, Briles left the winning program he'd built at Houston for one of the worst programs in the country.

"I didn't view it maybe the way many other people did," Briles told ESPN in 2013. "To me, it was a chance for accomplishment. You can have opportunity anywhere. It was a chance for people to accomplish something."

Baylor's turnaround didn't happen quickly. There was too much work to do. Briles surrounded himself with coaches who knew him best. His son Kendal coached the team's wide receivers, and his son-in-law, Jeff Lebby, coached running backs. Two of his longtime assistant coaches at Stephenville High School and the University of Houston—offensive coordinator Philip Montgomery and offensive line coach Randy Clements—also joined him. They installed a system in which the Bears played very fast on offense, often scoring in under two minutes and running more than ninety offensive plays per game.

The Bears went 4-8 in each of Briles's first two seasons, before finally turning the corner with a 7-6 record in 2010. They upset Texas, 30–22, in Austin, their first win over the Longhorns since 1997, and lost to Illinois, 38–14, in the Texas Bowl, their first postseason appearance in sixteen years. Finally, there was reason for optimism. The Bears were winning and had the country's most exciting player in Griffin. Baylor went 10-3 during Griffin's Heisman Trophy–winning season in 2011, tying a school record for victories in a season, and defeated Washington 67–56 in the Alamo Bowl, its first bowl win since 1992.

After the big breakthrough in 2011, Baylor was becoming a destination for top high school recruits, instead of only an afterthought. But there was also reason for concern. Before the 2012 season, Briles recruited a handful of players who had been dismissed at their previous schools because of off-field problems. One of them was receiver Darryl Stonum, a native of Stafford, Texas, who was kicked off the University of Michigan's team following two drunken driving arrests and another for driving with a revoked license, a violation of his probation. Briles also recruited former Penn State defensive lineman Shawn Oakman, who was dismissed by the Nittany Lions after he was arrested on charges of disorderly conduct, harassment, and retail theft during a dispute with a female store clerk.

Briles and his assistants also recruited former Colorado State linebacker Mike Orakpo, who was dismissed by the Rams following a fight that injured four people, two seriously, and led to a drug investigation that uncovered evidence of marijuana and anabolic steroids in his apartment. Orakpo was listed on Baylor's roster shortly before the 2012 season started, but then his name was removed. He transferred to Texas State University and played there instead.

During Big 12 news conferences in Dallas in July 2012, Briles told reporters that he believed in giving players second chances. "When I went through some tough times, people were there to help me and pick me up, and give me an opportunity," he said. "I feel a duty, a need, and a desire to help other people maybe when things aren't always going their way."

Baylor president Ken Starr later defended Briles's willingness to help troubled players and give them second chances, in an interview with ESPN's Joe Schad in June 2016.

"That's what Art Briles was doing, working on those young men's lives to shape their character, to make sure they get an education, that they become good, young men," Starr said. "Yes, in retrospect it would have been a lot safer to say to these young men, 'No, we're not going to give you a second chance.' But that's not America."

Starr also suggested it was Baylor's responsibility, as a Christian university, to help troubled players find their way.

"I can't disagree with that kind of policy that you decided to give second chances to young men with a very tough past," Starr said. "Shawn Oakman grew up without a father. He grew up with a cocaine-addicted mother. He was homeless. He lived in a car as a young man in Philadelphia. Do we want to take someone like Shawn Oakman in? From our worldview, from our Christian perspective, we say yes. We don't say, 'We will never, ever take any chances.'"

With Oakman and others leading Baylor's dramatic turnaround, the Bears became one of the best teams in college football. They finished 8-5 in their first season without Griffin in 2012, but then won at least ten games in each of the next three seasons. In 2013 and 2014, Baylor won eleven games and at least a share of Big 12 regular season titles for the first time in school history. In 2014, the Bears finished the regular season with an 11-1 record, but were left out of the inaugural four-team College Football Playoff in a very controversial decision. Big Ten champion Ohio State was the final team selected for the playoff, ahead of Baylor, and won a national championship.

Despite the Texas-sized disappointment, the Bears were suddenly among college football's elite programs.

"We were in the valley for a long time, but we'd been to the mountaintops before," Starr told ESPN in 2013. "We knew we had mountains to climb, but we'd climbed them before. Art Briles has taken us to the mountaintop again. That's where people want to be, looking out."

CHAPTER NINE

"HOW DID ANYBODY FIND OUT ABOUT ME?"

Waco, Texas
March 27, 2012

On Friday, April 27, 2012, Baylor football coach Art Briles announced that Tevin Elliott had been suspended for an "unspecified viola-tion" of team rules. (He would end up being expelled from Baylor about a month later.) On Monday, April 30, the *Waco Tribune-Herald* published a story with the headline BAYLOR DEFENSIVE END ARRESTED ON SEXUAL ASSAULT CHARGE, followed, in the ensuing days, with more stories about Jasmin Hernandez's assault, even though her name was redacted from the police report and wasn't in the newspaper articles. Samantha* was standing in her kitchen when her mom handed her the newspaper. As she started to read the story about Elliott's arrest, her first thought was, *Holy crap! How did anybody find out about me?*

Samantha had good reason to be confused. Only a few weeks ear-lier, she too had gone to Waco police and told them Tevin raped her. Samantha was also a Baylor student-athlete—and to this day doesn't want to say which sport, for fear she'll be identified. But it was through her sports association that she became Facebook friends with Tevin and the two occasionally texted. Her story is a compilation of what was doc-umented in an April 2012 Waco police report, her testimony in court in January 2014, and a story two years later by ESPN's *Outside the Lines*.

---

* Pseudonym

On March 27, 2012, Samantha was a few months away from graduating, and she needed a heavy desk moved upstairs into a bedroom she planned to convert into an office. It was a Tuesday night, around 7:00 p.m., and Tevin agreed to help. Samantha didn't think anything of it. She knew other Baylor football players and they seemed like good guys, and she had no reason to have her guard up. She thought she could trust Tevin, and, after moving the desk, the two started to watch a movie.

At first, Tevin casually flirted with her, saying he watched her in the workout room and such, and then he started touching her. It was playful wrestling at first, but then he moved to kiss her. Samantha pushed him away, saying she wasn't interested in a sexual relationship. He kissed her again, and again Samantha told him to stop and behave. But Tevin didn't stop. He kept kissing her, and started touching and grabbing her more forcefully. Samantha felt capable of self-defense as she had been taking classes in American Kenpo, a type of martial art, but right then, she was very aware of her size, only five feet, two inches and 110 pounds, compared to Tevin's towering football build. She became afraid, very afraid, of what was happening. With a mix of fear and confusion—*Wait, this guy's a friend? Is he still just playing? What's going on?*—Samantha froze.

Tevin picked her up, threw her over his shoulder, and carried her upstairs. Samantha's yellow Labrador retriever followed them, and Samantha saw Tevin use his foot to push the dog back. "I knew that when he kicked my dog down the stairs, I was like, 'This is going to get violent.'" Samantha yelled at Tevin to put her down and told him no several times. She beat on him with her fists. He carried her into her bedroom and put her facedown on her bed, at first telling her that he only wanted to give a back massage. Samantha's thoughts were racing. He clearly didn't understand "no." "You don't know if you should, like, play nice and try to veer it back to normalcy and kind of be like, 'Hey, stop. Like, okay, don't do that,'" Samantha would say, while trying to explain her actions to a jury months later. "Or if you should be, like, a jerk about it and raise your tone of voice. But then, what if he matches that? You know?"

But Tevin wasn't interested in a massage. He pulled Samantha's pants down and forced himself in her. Samantha was paralyzed. *What's going on? How did I get here? Wait, I'm a good girl. This doesn't happen to girls like me.* It could have been five minutes. It could have been an hour. She turned over and made eye contact with Tevin. "No. Seriously, stop. Like, really, stop," she recalled saying. "You're scaring me." Tevin stood up, put his pants on, and left.

Samantha sat on the stairs, confused. She couldn't process what happened. She called her friend and went over the details of the evening, and her friend told her to take a bath and get some sleep and she'd come over in the morning to talk about it. Samantha kept going over what she could remember. Did she do something to encourage him? Should she have fought harder? Was this rape or maybe just a misunderstanding?

What came next was a decision that Samantha, to this day, knows most people won't understand, and it's one she herself has tried to block. On Thursday, two days after she'd invited Tevin to her condo, she invited him back and had consensual sex with him. At first, she figured maybe somehow that could make it right. That if she had sex with him again it would mean they were somehow in a relationship and it would make her feel better about what happened. But it had the opposite effect. It made her realize, with absolute certainty, that what had happened two days earlier was rape. Samantha withdrew. She stayed home. Skipped class.

Samantha's decision to have sex with Tevin after her alleged rape has been a studied phenomenon. Researchers at Ohio University questioned sixty female college students—who had described some sort of unwanted sexual intercourse after the use of force, threat of force, or administration of drugs or alcohol to lower their resistance, which was the legal definition of rape in Ohio—to determine, in part, whether the women considered the incident as rape or not, and how they responded. Among other findings, the researchers reported that "sexual assault does not invariably dissuade a woman from maintaining a relationship with a perpetrator. Indeed, nearly a third of the victims maintained a

relationship with their assailant and a quarter of the victims continued to have sex with the man after the event. It is not known, however,
whether the sex was forced or voluntary," according to their study published in the February 1996 issue of the *Journal of Abnormal Psychology*.

After that, Samantha struggled with what she should do. "When
something like that happens to you, the last thing you want to do is
pick up the phone and talk about it with a police officer and be like,
'Hey, guess what just happened to me?' I wanted my mom. I wanted
my dog. And I wanted to be home."

Samantha didn't leave her condo until Sunday, when she decided
to go to church. She invited Phoebe*, a friend she'd met a couple of
weeks earlier. Phoebe wasn't a Baylor student, nor was she from Waco.
She went to a local community college. But the two hit it off, and
Phoebe agreed to join Samantha and some friends that Sunday for
church. During the lunch afterward, the talk turned to Baylor football. Phoebe expressed disgust, and launched into a story about when
a Baylor football player who was visiting her roommate poked Phoebe
with a broomstick, cornered her in her kitchen, and tried locking her
in her room, so she called the police. Samantha's face went white—
and Phoebe noticed. When they were in the car to leave, Phoebe asked
Samantha if she was okay. Samantha asked Phoebe, "You said that
guy's name was Tevin Elliott?" And Phoebe replied, "Yeah." Samantha responded, "You know, that guy raped me."

Phoebe got goose bumps at the mere mention of the name. She
peppered Samantha with questions and asked if she filed a police
report. Samantha hadn't and she was reluctant. Phoebe pressed her
again. "You need to file a report. If you don't, he's just going to get away
with it again." Part of Samantha wanted to forgive Tevin, because it
was in her nature to do so, but another part knew Phoebe was right
and she needed to be concerned for who might be next.

Samantha avoided Tevin's text messages and phone calls that day.
That night, when she pulled into the parking lot near her condo, Tevin

---

* Pseudonym

pulled in behind her, blocking her in. Samantha got out of her car, terrified of what might happen, but Tevin simply asked her a question: "We're cool, right? Like the other night, it's cool?" Samantha responded, "Yeah, it's fine," and hurried into her condo.

Phoebe was there, as the two were going to stay in, make dinner, and have a girl's night. She remembered seeing Samantha rush in, slam the door, and lock it. She looked like a ghost. "Tevin's downstairs," she said to Phoebe, who panicked, peeking out the blinds to see if he was still there. Phoebe had one directive to Samantha, "Call. The. Police. You need to get them over here." Samantha did, and at least four Waco police officers came to her condo. Samantha told one of the officers she was afraid that Tevin would retaliate against her.

Samantha wrote five pages of a statement before she had to stop, unable to finish. Phoebe chimed in. She told one of the officers about her incident with Tevin from last fall and that she'd made an incident report. The officer left for a bit and came back to where Phoebe, Samantha, and Phoebe's boyfriend—who had also come over—were sitting on the couch. Phoebe recalled the officer saying that he had run Tevin's name through the system. The officer said, "We don't want to alarm you," and told them that there had been other reports like this involving Tevin. Phoebe said she looked at him in shock. She was astounded at it all, and still amazed at the sheer coincidence of having even met Samantha—she told her mother it was a "divine intervention"—and then supporting her in pursuing her case.

According to the police report, Samantha told the responding officer on April 1, 2012, that she wanted to pursue criminal charges, and she filled out and signed a form indicating she wanted to prosecute. But two days later, Samantha called Waco police again and told them she was afraid of Tevin retaliating against her once he found out she'd reported him. On April 4, 2012, Waco police detective Charlotte Mathews called Samantha to set up an appointment for her to come in. But Samantha wanted a different detective—a male—someone who would be a more fatherly figure, someone she felt capable of standing up to a football player. Samantha's mother, who had driven three

hours from south-central Texas, called Waco police as well, request-
ing the same. Mathews noted in the police report that it was "odd"
that Samantha had requested a male detective, and there was no indication that any effort was made to accommodate her. Samantha and
her mom persisted, but Mathews stayed on the case. When Samantha
didn't show up for her appointment, the detective began to doubt her,
writing that, "any reasonable person that wanted the police to pursue a
case . . . would at the bare minimum meet with the detective to express
her feelings, fears, expectations, etc."

In the police report, Mathews noted that she tried to call Samantha, but got a recording that the number was no longer a working
one. She decided to close the case out as unfounded. She also indicated
that Samantha's stated "fear of retaliation" didn't make sense, writing, "When [Samantha] cried and told Tevin to leave during the initial sexual encounter, he stopped having intercourse with her and left
as she asked." And, finally, she wrote that the report could be closed
out based "solely on the fact that [Samantha] believed there could have
been a misunderstanding" during the sexual encounter on March
27. The detective then filled out a form to have the evidence officers
obtained at Samantha's condo destroyed.

Samantha and her mother decided to see if someone at Baylor
could help, and they ended up scheduling a meeting with the school's
chief judicial officer, Bethany McCraw. McCraw came from a small
town north of Corpus Christi, Texas. She earned two degrees from
Baylor and had been an employee for the university since 1982. At that
time, McCraw oversaw all areas of student conduct in and out of the
classroom, from plagiarism and other violations of academic integrity,
to drinking or smoking marijuana on campus, and all the way up to
sexual assault.

On April 10, 2012, Samantha and her mom went into McCraw's
office on campus. Samantha recalled their initial exchange.

"Why are you here?" McCraw asked her.

"Well, Tevin Elliott," Samantha said. "I don't know if you know
Tevin Elliott."

"Yeah," McCraw responded.

"He raped me," Samantha told her.

"Yeah, you're the sixth girl to come in and tell me this," McCraw said.

"Oh my gosh, six?" Samantha asked incredulously. "Well, why are there six? Does the football team know about this? Does Art Briles know about this?"

"Yes, they know about it," McCraw replied, according to Samantha. "But it turns into a he said, she said, so there's got to be actually a court decision in order to act on it in any sort of way." (Briles would deny having known about any such reports, in a response to a lawsuit filed years later.)

Samantha said she also asked about a restraining order from Baylor, and McCraw told her that it would simply be the university sending Tevin a letter telling him to stay away from her, "and then you kind of hope for the best," because the university really had no way to monitor him. Samantha declined to request one. She said it seemed as though McCraw was dissuading her from taking any criminal action. But McCraw did offer to help Samantha out with finals, seeing as she'd missed several classes already.

"I'm like, *Okay. Well, I guess my only option is to graduate and get the heck out of here,*" Samantha recalled thinking of her exchange with McCraw. "And she was like, 'Okay, well, we'll make that happen.' Like 'Shoo, shoo, run along. Okay, got it. Let's just get her graduated,' you know?"

When contacted, McCraw said it was not her recollection of the conversation but refused to comment further, according to an ESPN "Outside the Lines" story from January 2016. Baylor officials would not allow us to interview her for this book.

The next few weeks were difficult on Samantha, and her mother had already noticed a change in her usually outgoing and confident daughter. She was withdrawn and quiet. She couldn't focus. Samantha, whose fierce independence had propelled her through five years of college on her own, and to invest in a condo in Waco, now couldn't sleep without her mom in the house. Her mother moved in, and planned to stay until graduation, when Samantha could move back home.

Several days later, she saw the newspaper. It was a story about Tevin—and the sexual assault involving Jasmin. She panicked. She thought no one was going to find out about her. But then she kept reading. "I find out it's about someone else. I was just, like, 'Oh my God.'"

CHAPTER TEN

PRIOR KNOWLEDGE

Waco, Texas
September 28, 2011

A t that point, Samantha knew only one other woman who had reported Tevin Elliott, and that was Phoebe. As it turned out, Baylor University, and its athletic department, had been aware of her, too.

On March 29, 2012, only two days after Samantha said Tevin raped her, Baylor officials sanctioned him and put him on disciplinary probation as a result of the incident involving Phoebe. Baylor officials had known about Phoebe's reported assault as far back as November 18, 2011. That's when Baylor's judicial affairs coordinator, David Murdock, sent Tevin a letter notifying him that he was in violation of student disciplinary procedures and had engaged in misconduct by having "unwanted physical contact with a female student." The letter, which was copied to chief judicial officer Bethany McCraw and senior associate athletic director Paul Bradshaw, asked Tevin to call their office to schedule a meeting to discuss the charges. On the same day, a records technician with the Baylor Judicial Affairs office sent an email to Bradshaw that contained a copy of Tevin's police report. At the same time this information came to athletic department officials, Tevin was also under academic probation.

The incident occurred on September 28, 2011, at Phoebe's apartment at The Grove, a popular apartment complex for Baylor students.

Though Phoebe didn't go to Baylor, she'd wanted to. She had been accepted into Baylor, granted financial aid, chosen her classes—even auditioned for the dance team—and was ready to pick her dorm when her father fell ill in July 2011. The family, not knowing what sort of financial situation they were facing, decided to hold off on sending her to Baylor. Phoebe enrolled at nearby McLennan Community College for her first semester, with the hope she would start at Baylor in the spring. She chose an apartment complex that featured a roommate-pairing service and she ended up with two Baylor students. But within a couple of weeks she realized it wasn't a good match.

On that late September day, when Phoebe stepped out of her room, she saw her roommate with a guy she'd brought over before—a Baylor football player named Tevin Elliott. Phoebe had prior run-ins with Tevin. Once, he asked to borrow her laptop to check Facebook and instead pulled up a bunch of porn sites, which he tried to persuade Phoebe and her roommate to look at. He'd squeezed Phoebe's butt and fondled her breast—all advances that Phoebe, who had a boy-friend at the time, rejected. Tevin also talked a lot about football and how good he was, which didn't interest Phoebe at all. She remembered one exchange in which he boasted about "how hard he could hit peo-ple and how they wouldn't get off the ground" and he was "so good and that nobody could beat him."

She recalled Tevin's reaction when he saw a T-shirt from Texas Christian University, a big football rival of Baylor. Tevin became angry and started drilling them, "Do you like TCU? You know we beat TCU?" He grabbed the T-shirt off a table and threw it in the trash. Phoebe and her roommate were shocked, and when they protested, saying it was, "only a T-shirt," Tevin first picked Phoebe's roommate up and held her against the wall. Then he did the same to Phoebe, all the while asking if they liked TCU. Phoebe demanded he put her down. She wasn't sure if he was joking or not, but it didn't matter.

When Tevin came back the second time, it was late morning and Phoebe was still in her pajamas, just about to get ready for classes. She was lying on the side of her roommate's bed talking with her about plans for the evening. Tevin walked into the bedroom holding a broom and started poking Phoebe with it, shoving the handle toward her vagina from behind. "I jumped up and was like—I don't usually have a bad mouth—but I was like, 'What the hell are you doing?' and he just kind of looked at me with this really creepy look. And I was like, 'Don't ever touch me,'" Phoebe told us.

Phoebe walked out of the room and into the kitchen, where she tried to make a sandwich for lunch. But Tevin came up behind her, pinned her into a corner with his body, and began pushing into her with his pelvis. He pressed his face right up to hers and whispered in her ear. He said the two of them were "going to get to know each other a lot better." She threw her elbows back to hit him and was finally able to duck out under his arm. She punched him on his back, "I told you not to touch me," she said, and he flashed that look again, as if he wanted her to challenge him.

Phoebe said she had planned to finish getting ready at her boyfriend's apartment. She had to step back into her bedroom to get her cell phone. As she was unlocking her door, Tevin came up next to her, staring down, and said, "Are you mad at me? Do you want to hit me?" Phoebe said no, fearing that anything else might provoke him.

Phoebe unlocked her door, walked five steps to her nightstand to grab her phone, and turned around to see that Tevin had come into the room and shut and locked the door behind him. She ran to the door and tried to unlock it, but Tevin leaned against the door and kept his hand on the handle. Phoebe banged on the door and screamed for her roommate. Tevin laughed. She tried to push past Tevin but he picked her up under her arms—touching her breasts as he did so—and put her back.

Phoebe was terrified. She didn't know what to do next. Could she lock herself in her bathroom? If Tevin tried anything further with her, would she be able to fight him off? She even debated whether she could jump out her second-story window. Phoebe kept screaming for her roommate, who came to the door and knocked, asking what was going on. As soon as Tevin heard her, Phoebe said he let out an exasperated sigh and moved away. Phoebe unlocked the door, pushed past her roommate, and ran out of the apartment. She went to her boyfriend's place and told him what happened. She called her mother. "It's the phone call you never want to imagine receiving," Phoebe's mother, Judy*, said. "She was crying, and I said, 'What happened? What happened?'" Phoebe was too upset to talk, so her boyfriend got on the phone. Judy told her daughter to immediately call the police and she did.

Waco police detective Fabian Klecka came to meet Phoebe and her boyfriend at The Grove's clubhouse around 2:00 p.m. Phoebe relayed the entire story. She also told Klecka that she believed Tevin was "very sexually charged in nature" and "that she knew what he was after." Klecka then made a point of detailing the efforts he made to make sure Baylor police were aware of Phoebe's incident. Klecka wrote at the top of the report's narrative in all-capital letters, "ATTENTION BAYLOR PD-DETECTIVE BRENT HOWELL." Klecka noted in his report that he drove to the Baylor University Police Department to meet with Howell. Howell told him that Tevin had been a suspect in a sexual assault at a Baylor nightclub—a case that Waco police investigated in March 2011. Howell also told him that Tevin "had been a suspect (in) several other offenses at the Baylor PD."

On October 7, another Waco police officer asked Tevin to come to the police department for questioning. Tevin denied ever picking up a broom to threaten Phoebe, and he said he never tried to trap her in her room. He even agreed to take a polygraph test to prove it, but there's no indication that the officer ever actually administered one.

Klecka initially suspected Tevin of unlawful restraint and assault. In the officers' final review of the case, they decided there wasn't enough evidence to charge Tevin with unlawful restraint, but there was for misdemeanor assault. Under Texas law, someone who "intentionally or knowingly causes physical contact with another when the person knows or should reasonably believe that the other will regard the contact as offensive or provocative" can be cited with what's known as a Class C ticket, which can carry up to a $500 fine but no jail time.

---

* Pseudonym

Tevin was issued a Class C ticket on November 4, 2011. He paid the fine, and in municipal court that's technically considered a conviction. Klecka made a point to note in the report that while Phoebe's incident didn't merit an investigation for sexual assault or attempted sexual assault, he wrote, "it was apparent that Tevin's conduct and mannerisms were in fact leading to the fact that Tevin was not getting the point that he was being told 'no.'"

Phoebe never spent another night in the apartment. Her mother and father, who was still in a wheelchair at the time, immediately made the three-hour drive from their home west of Austin and stayed in a hotel room with her that night. They described Phoebe as shaking and scared. "Just the look of fear in her face," her father said, recalling that day. The very next day, with her parents' help, she moved out and transferred to another apartment within the same complex. Her roommates—including the one who was seeing Tevin—whispered to each other as Phoebe packed her belongings. She never talked to them again.

Either that day or the next, Phoebe's mother called the Baylor Police Department and spoke with an officer she believed was Lieutenant Kevin Helpert. She told him she wanted to talk to someone in the athletics department and meet with Bears football coach Art Briles and make him aware of the situation. Judy and her husband had concerns if someone like Tevin was representing the football team. "There is an acknowledgment that comes when you look somebody in the eye," Judy said. "I wanted that young man to know what he had done was wrong. We did not raise our daughter that way, and his actions were wrong and not accepted." But she said the officer told her that it would not be the best thing to do at that time.

The only response Phoebe said she ever received from Waco police was a phone call about the time they issued Tevin's citation on November 4, 2011. She and her parents were disappointed the police didn't do more, and that officers told them Phoebe wouldn't qualify for a protection order. She was worried that Tevin would come after her. A few days later, Phoebe said she saw Tevin's white Cadillac Escalade, distinguishable by its rumble and the pair of silver novelty testicles hanging from the back bumper, drive by her apartment. The next morning, Phoebe climbed into her car—a white, 1998 Nissan Maxima—and felt like it was sinking on one side. She got out and froze at what she saw: both passenger-side tires were slashed, key marks covered her hood, and the word *bitch* was spray painted in gold on her rear fender. Phoebe pointed out that gold happened to be one of Baylor's colors.

She called Waco police and an officer came out. "Do you have any idea who would want to do that?" she recalled the officer asking. "I do absolutely have an idea," she responded. Even though Phoebe told the officer about what had recently happened with Tevin, she said the officer didn't dust for prints, didn't take pictures, and never followed up with her after she made the report—even though the officer noted in the report that Phoebe believed it was a retaliatory act. Phoebe remembered driving to the body shop, slumped down in her seat, sunglasses on, and crying all the way, embarrassed and knowing what was written on her car.

"After that, I was super-paranoid to go out anywhere. He knows what I drive. He knows where I live," Phoebe told us. "This total paranoia that I had gotten over a couple months before was back in an instant. I didn't want to go anywhere alone."

On November 9, 2011, Phoebe's mom called Lieutenant Helpert at Baylor police and told him what happened with her daughter's car. She followed up with an email the next day, which she shared with us. She forwarded photos of the vandalism to Helpert and asked him to keep her informed of whatever action Baylor was taking. Helpert acknowledged her email five minutes later. But that was the last time Judy or Phoebe said they ever heard from Baylor officials, and it was a double blow after their letdown with Waco police. "I don't think the whole justice system is a failure, but I think what is going on in Waco is," Phoebe said.

Phoebe never did enroll at Baylor. After her experience with Tevin, she wanted nothing to do with the school. Football was everything then, and she knew that he was still playing.

CHAPTER ELEVEN

IMPLIED CONSENT

Waco, Texas
March 19, 2011

Although the Waco police report indicated that Baylor police knew that Tevin had been investigated for sexual assault at a Waco nightclub— one that was reported on March 19, 2011—there's no indication that university officials attempted to look into that allegation that fall, although Baylor's police chief, Jim Doak, knew about it within days of it being reported.

The alleged rape at the nightclub didn't result in any charges. According to the police report, it started with a chance meeting between Tevin and Leslie*, a Texas Christian University student. Leslie was on her way back to Fort Worth, Texas, from a spring break trip with her friends, one of whom had a friend in Waco. The group decided to stop there for the night.

Leslie and her friends went to a fraternity party around 9:30 p.m. A couple of hours and a few drinks later, they went to Club Energy, a Waco nightclub that featured hip-hop and rap music. Tevin and Leslie were introduced and started dancing. He talked to her about football and asked her to spend the night. She said she didn't think that would happen, but that she might come back and visit him.

At one point, they separated: Tevin went to talk to his teammates and Leslie went to check on a friend who wasn't feeling well. Tevin

---

* Pseudonym

75

found her again later and they started dancing, then kissing, and then Tevin suggested they find somewhere "out of the way." It was almost 1:00 a.m. when Tevin led Leslie off the dance floor, past the bar, and up the stairs into a unisex bathroom, where he lifted her on a counter and they began to make out. Tevin ran his hands up her thigh twice and she twice told him to stop. He asked her if she was on her period, and she said yes. He asked when she'd be finished, and she said, "Today or tomorrow."

The report continues, noting that Tevin kept kissing her and trying to slide his hand between her legs. At one point, he grabbed her underwear. She told him no, and spread her legs farther apart to try to keep him from taking her underwear off. Her underwear were down to her knees and then with his right hand near her vagina, Tevin ripped out her tampon and threw it in the toilet. He shoved one of his fingers in her vagina, and although she told him no, she didn't do anything physically to stop him.

Leslie told police that Tevin then lifted up her dress, took it off, and threw it to the side and continued to kiss her. He then pulled down his pants. As Tevin continued to finger her vagina, she grabbed his penis. But when Tevin tried to put his penis inside Leslie, she told him to stop and put her hands out to block him. She said Tevin told her, "Don't worry, I'm as clean as shit," and continued to have sex with her. She asked if he had a condom and he told her he'd pull out before he ejaculated. She again said no. Tevin stopped briefly, but started again, and Leslie decided right then to give up and let him finish.

About five minutes later, Tevin pulled out and ejaculated—Leslie wasn't sure where—and pulled up his pants and said, "I better leave first so people don't think we did anything," and he left. Leslie jumped off the counter, put her clothes back on, and left the bathroom. As Leslie came down the stairs and passed her friend, she told her that she "needed to leave right now and that she just wanted to go home." After they had left the club, Leslie told her friends what happened, and one of them convinced her to go to the hospital.

After giving her statement to police, a victim services advocate met Leslie and transported her from the Baylor Scott & White Medical Center–Hillcrest to Providence Health Center, where a nurse—Michele Davis—was ready to conduct a sexual assault exam. It would be one of the exams Michele remembered years later, even though Leslie never gave her the name of the person she said assaulted her that night.

Two days later, while reviewing the case, Waco police detective Kristina Woodruff was beginning to have doubts. She noted that Leslie let Tevin keep his finger inside her vagina while she masturbated his penis. She noted that after Leslie said no to sex, and Tevin kept going, she asked him if he had a condom. "By asking him if he at least had a condom, she is again consenting," the detective wrote. She continued, noting that once Leslie admitted to giving in to Tevin's actions, "She doesn't attempt to fight, pull away, push him away or tell him no."

Detective Woodruff decided to call Leslie to discuss her concerns. Later that afternoon, Leslie called back and told her that she didn't want police to take any action against Tevin, she didn't want to press charges, and she didn't want her sexual assault exam kit processed. Leslie told the detective it was a "he said, she said" situation, and that even she realized that what she did and said might be considered "implied consent." It struck Woodruff that Leslie would use such a technical legal term, to the point she even noted it in her report.

Woodruff agreed not to pursue the case further or contact Tevin, but she noted in her report that officials at Baylor were already aware. Doak, Baylor's police chief, contacted her supervisor asking about the case, and she wasn't sure how he would have heard about it. Woodruff guessed word made it back to Baylor from a former football player.

The report states, "She said [name redacted] was a former football player and that he probably did tell coach what Tevin had done, but that she didn't want to pursue this and she doesn't want him to get in trouble with his football either." The name is redacted in the police report narrative but listed among witnesses that night was the name of a player on Baylor's practice squad in 2007.

Woodruff ended the report by writing, "There is not a SEXUAL

ASSAULT because she does not try to get him to stop and goes along with it. In her statement, she even states that she spreads her legs. She gives the reason of trying to keep her underwear on, but he is in the process of putting his penis in, so that to me is another implied consent. CASE UNFOUNDED."

Tevin played in all twelve regular season games in 2011, starting five of them, including the game against the Oklahoma Sooners on November 19, 2011—the day *after* Baylor's Judicial Affairs Office sent him the email notifying him he was being investigated. It was also the day *after* the athletics department received the police report about Phoebe's assault. But Briles would state in an April 2017 response filed in a lawsuit that he was unaware in November 2011 of Tevin's misdemeanor assault conviction; McCaw would state in a separate filing that he was "without knowledge or information sufficient to form a belief" as to whether he knew.

Tevin would also tell a reporter in December 2015 that none of his coaches ever spoke to him about the incident. "I don't even know if they knew. I just kept playing ball, kept going to school," he said.

During the 2011 season, Tevin was tied for second on the team with eight tackles for losses, and he recorded three sacks. In the October 8 game against Iowa State, he returned a fumble 86 yards for a touchdown. On Christmas morning, it was announced that Tevin had a knee injury and would not play in the Alamo Bowl matchup against the Washington Huskies.

The Bears ended their season with a 10-3 record and were ranked No. 12 in the final ESPN/*USA Today* coaches' poll, and 13th in the Associated Press Top 25—the highest final ranking Baylor had achieved since 1986. Months later, after the team finished four weeks of spring drills, Tevin would suit up one last time for Baylor. It was for the Bears' spring scrimmage on Saturday afternoon, April 14, 2012, only hours before he would meet Jasmin Hernandez at his teammate's birthday party.

CHAPTER TWELVE

THE PROSECUTOR

A few days before Baylor football coach Art Briles suspended Tevin Elliott from the team, Tevin called his mother, Sureka Holmes, in Mount Pleasant, Texas, and informed her of the serious accusations that Jasmin Hernandez made against him. "Momma, this girl is trying to say that I raped her," Tevin told her.

"What are you talking about?" Holmes asked her youngest son. "Tevin, what's going on? Who is this girl?"

Tevin told her that he'd met Jasmin through another female friend at a party. Holmes asked if he'd had sexual intercourse with her. Tevin admitted he had but was adamant it was consensual. "I told him not to let anyone question him," Holmes said. "Where we're from, you can't trust the police. I told him to let me figure out what was going on."

On Monday, April 30, 2012, Waco police arrested Tevin at his apartment for sexually assaulting Jasmin during the party at Aspen Heights. Waco police detective John Rozyskie had obtained DNA samples from Tevin a week earlier by taking swabs from the inside of his cheeks. When Tevin's DNA matched the samples taken from Jasmin's body and underwear during a rape exam at the hospital, police believed they had sufficient evidence to charge him with second-degree felony sexual assault, which carries a maximum sentence of twenty years in prison in Texas. Tevin's mother and uncle, Rodrick Elliott, made the three-hour drive from Mount Pleasant to Waco to bail him out of jail. During Tevin's arraignment, Judge Matt Johnson of the 54th State District Court agreed to release him on $10,000 bond.

McLennan County assistant district attorney Hilary LaBorde would ultimately have to decide whether Jasmin was telling the truth. LaBorde had spent the previous twelve years prosecuting hundreds of cases involving murderers, pedophiles, human traffickers, and child abusers. Incredibly, she had never tried a sexual assault case involving an adult victim and adult suspect. When Jasmin's case reached the district attorney's office, another prosecutor asked LaBorde if she was interested in helping. LaBorde had never heard of Tevin Elliott; she initially believed the suspect was Tevin Reese, a Baylor wide receiver. She agreed to help and was eager to learn more details about the alleged incident.

LaBorde earned a bachelor's degree in history and political science from California State University, Bakersfield in 1998 and then attended Baylor Law School from 1999 to 2002. The same year LaBorde graduated from law school, she was hired by the McLennan County District Attorney's Office to work as a Child Protective Services attorney and handle cases involving children in state custody due to neglect and abuse. In 2011, she was promoted to chief prosecutor of the Crimes Against Children Unit and prosecuted cases ranging from endangerment, to sexual and physical abuse, to human trafficking and murder.

Jasmin's case was new ground for LaBorde. Tragically, every one of the sexual assault cases she had previously tried in court involved child victims. For whatever reason, there weren't many adult sexual assault cases reaching the district attorney's office. "I don't think many of them make it to the police," LaBorde told us. "I think then even fewer make it out of the police department to the district attorney's office."

In fact, LaBorde is unaware of a single sexual assault case reported by the Baylor Police Department during her tenure at the district attorney's office. Each of the sexual assault cases involving Baylor students was investigated by Waco police, and then a small number of them were turned over to the district attorney to decide whether there was sufficient evidence to charge the suspect with a crime. In many cases, the female victims decided they didn't want to pursue criminal charges, or police decided there wasn't enough evidence to secure a conviction.

While Baylor police are responsible for investigating any crimes reported inside campus boundaries, including sexual assaults that might have occurred at dormitories, Waco police handle any crimes reported outside the campus footprint, including those that might have occurred at off-campus houses and apartments where students typically live. The Baylor Police Department had a staff of 49 people during the 2016–17 academic year, according to the school's website, including 37 officers, 10 dispatchers, an office manager, and a Clery Act specialist. The Jeanne Clery Act, a consumer protection law passed in 1990, requires universities that receive federal funding to share information about campus crime and their efforts to improve campus safety.

LaBorde believes Baylor police's small jurisdiction is one of the reasons it didn't refer a single sexual assault case to her office since she started working there. But she believes there's another reason as well.

"I also think it's that those girls don't want to make a report," LaBorde said. "I think it's both things. My understanding of the statistics is that it's the least reported crime we have. We have too many barriers, in my opinion, for women to come forward. If they're having to deal with a university that's a barrier, if they're having to deal with the police that's a barrier, and then they have to deal with us."

National statistics support LaBorde's beliefs about college women being reluctant to report sexual assaults. In a 2015 survey commissioned by the Association of American Universities, nearly one-fourth of undergraduate women at twenty-seven colleges and universities reported being sexually assaulted by force or when they were incapacitated, usually due to alcohol or drugs. According to the survey, 27.2 percent of female college seniors reported they experienced some kind of unwanted sexual contact, from touching to rape, since enrolling in college.

The survey of 150,000 students was conducted at many of the nation's most respected campuses, including every Ivy League institution except Princeton. It showed that only 5 percent to 28 percent, depending on the type of specific behavior, were reported to police or a school's judicial affairs or Title IX office. The most common reason for not reporting incidents of sexual assault or sexual misconduct, according to the survey, was that it was "not considered serious enough." Other reasons included victims saying they were "embarrassed, ashamed or that it would be too emotionally difficult," and also that they "did not think anything would be done about it."

"They want to keep it to themselves," LaBorde said. "They don't want to tell their parents. They don't want to tell anyone. They take on blame they shouldn't. I also think we aren't training our police to investigate them appropriately, so they're not making it from the police to the DA's office. I'm seeing a very small percentage of women, who have decided that no matter what—no matter the roadblock they're going to face—they're going to pursue their case."

Through LaBorde's courtroom experience, training, and education, she also developed another theory about rapists: They rarely act on their abhorrent desires only once. Many of the sexual predators she prosecuted for targeting children involved multiple victims. She also believes rapists rarely attack only one woman.

"It's not something that happens one time," LaBorde said. "It's something they do many times. I think that's why we have such a high percentage of college freshmen that are going to have some kind of sexual assault experience, and yet we have so few offenders. They do it more than once."

CHAPTER THIRTEEN

ON TRIAL

McLennan County Courthouse, Waco, Texas
January 21, 2014

When a new McLennan County Courthouse was constructed on Washington Avenue in downtown Waco at the start of the twentieth century, few expenses were spared during what was a cotton boom in central Texas. More than anything, Waco's leaders wanted the courthouse to be the city's most imposing civic building and an undeniable symbol of criminal justice.

The neoclassical courthouse, which was designed by renowned architect James Riely Gordon, features three statues, pilasters, and ornate columns. When the courthouse opened in 1901, Themis, the Greek goddess of divine order, stood at the top of the central dome, holding a double-edged sword in her left hand and a pair of scales in her right. Right below the dome, Justia, the Roman goddess of justice, and Lady Liberty, the American symbol of freedom, stood on the upper roof in case anyone still has doubts about Texans taking crime and punishment seriously.

McLennan County Courthouse has been the site of many memorable trials, including the country's first televised murder trial—four decades before millions of people watched gavel-to-gavel proceedings of former football star O. J. Simpson's murder trial. Harry Leonard Washburn was accused of planting a car bomb that killed his former mother-in-law in San Angelo, Texas, and the trial was moved to Waco, where KWTX-TV broadcast the proceedings.

Tevin Elliott's criminal trial in January 2014 didn't receive nearly as much publicity, but 54th State District Court judge Matt Johnson knew it was different from most trials on his docket. More than twenty months after Tevin was arrested for raping Jasmin Hernandez, he faced two second-degree felony charges of sexual assault. He would be sentenced from two to twenty years in state prison and a maximum $10,000 fine if convicted. Tevin had pleaded not guilty and rejected a plea agreement that would have sent him to state prison for seven years.

Because of Tevin's notoriety and pretrial publicity surrounding the case, the court clerk summoned 48 potential jurors to the courthouse for jury selection on January 21, 2014. They included 32 women and 16 men, and among them were a social worker, radiology nurse, middle school teacher, bank vice president, and a restaurant general manager.

The jurors would not only decide whether or not Tevin was guilty; it was also their responsibility to determine an appropriate punishment if he was found guilty, within the sentencing guidelines established by the state legislature.

Of course, Tevin and his family were hoping his attorney, Jason Darling, would get him acquitted. Darling wasn't Tevin's first choice to defend him. According to his family, a Baylor coach recommended another Waco-based attorney, but they couldn't afford his $50,000 retainer, which included $25,000 in advance. Tevin's father, James Rockwell, located Darling on the Internet, according to Tevin's mother and uncle. And the family would later argue that Darling failed to adequately prepare and represent Tevin at trial.

In Assistant District Attorney Hilary LaBorde's opening statement, she told the jury that Jasmin felt uneasy about Tevin, especially when he grabbed her waist and tightly pulled her closer to him.

Then LaBorde recounted the events that occurred before Tevin picked Jasmin up and carried her behind the Aspen Heights clubhouse, where he allegedly raped her on the muddy slope and then against a fence around the swimming pool. LaBorde told jurors that Jasmin was intoxicated after consuming a couple of shots of vodka and three cups of alcoholic punch. "She was just thinking, *Oh, I guess he's going to help me look outside for our missing friend*," LaBorde told jurors.

During the previous several months, as LaBorde and Assistant District Attorney Robert Moody investigated the case against Tevin, she struggled to detect a link among his victims. What were the similarities between Phoebe, the McLennan County Community College student whom Tevin trapped in her bedroom, and Leslie, the Texas Christian University student who had unwanted sex with him in a nightclub bathroom? There also weren't any obvious links between Jasmin and another former Baylor female student athlete, who told police that Tevin raped her after he helped her move furniture. "I didn't get it," LaBorde told us, more than two years after the trial. "They weren't the same. They seemed so different to me."

As LaBorde struggled to establish a commonality among the women, an intern in the McLennan County District Attorney's office, who was a student at Baylor Law School, developed a theory about Tevin's affinity for each of them: None were romantically interested in him. In fact, at some point each of the women had rejected his advances.

"He doesn't have a lot of empathy," LaBorde told us. "All of them would have communicated with their faces, with their bodies, and with their words that they weren't interested. I think maybe that was exciting, that he felt like he was going to do them a favor."

LaBorde believed Tevin had a personality trait that is prevalent in many rapists: narcissism. When she examined Tevin's Facebook page and other social media accounts, she discovered dozens of shirtless photographs of him, in which he proudly exposed his bulging biceps and ripped abdominal muscles. There were shirtless photographs of Tevin working out in the gym, lying with his infant sons in bed, hiking in the hills outside Los Angeles, and even standing at the site of actor James Dean's fatal car crash. "He had a picture of himself horseback riding with his shirt off," LaBorde said. "I was like, 'What in the world? This is crazy.' I thought he was a narcissist and that's the hallmark feature of sex offenders. It's all about them."

According to LaBorde, Tevin's narcissism is why he targeted Jasmin at the party and sexually assaulted her. He realized she wasn't interested in him—and she had told him as much through her body language and disinterest in taking a photograph with him. But to fulfill his own self-absorbed desires, he had to control and dominate her through fear, according to LaBorde. "I think what you're going to find out is that in this moment, this defendant believed he had an opportunity," LaBorde told the jury. "He had a drunk girl. He got her away from her friends. She had communicated to him in some way that she wasn't interested, and he was going to show her she was wrong."

The prosecution's first witness was Bradley Skaggs, a sergeant with the Waco Police Department. Skaggs was an eleven-year veteran in law enforcement and had previously worked as a detective at the McLennan County Sheriff's Department. He had spent much of his career working as a patrol officer, patrol sergeant, and as an investigator in the Street Crimes Unit. He had only recently been promoted to the Crimes Against Children Unit. Skaggs testified that he'd worked more than one hundred sexual assault cases during his career.

In the early morning of April 15, 2012, Skaggs was patrolling south Waco when he noticed that a sexual assault victim had been waiting quite a while to talk to police at Baylor Scott & White Medical Center–Hillcrest. He decided to take the call. When Skaggs located Jasmin in one of the emergency rooms, he immediately recognized that she was muddy and upset. "I obviously questioned her about why I was there and what happened," Skaggs testified. "And she was able to give me pretty good details, so I don't believe she was intoxicated, but I didn't do any tests to see that."

Once Skaggs finished his initial questioning and provided Jasmin with paperwork to write a formal statement, Waco police officer William Roy arrived and took over the interview. Skaggs drove to Aspen Heights, where he located the pool house that matched Jasmin's description. He observed mudslides on the slope behind the back porch. He discovered an iPod with a zebra-print case lying on the ground. He didn't yet know it belonged to Jasmin. He also spotted a stud diamond earring near the iPod, which would later match the description of an earring Tevin wore that night. Skaggs contacted crime scene technicians to secure the area around the pool house and collect evidence.

During cross-examination, Darling asked Skaggs if Jasmin was joking about the alleged sexual assault when he questioned her. "I didn't take it as a joke," Skaggs said. "To me, she was trying to deal with what happened and trying to make sense of it. That's how she come across to me."

Michele Davis, the nurse who examined Jasmin at the hospital that morning, was the next witness to take the stand. She described to the jury the injuries she observed on Jasmin's genitalia. There was a dime-sized, bluish-purple bruise, almost like a blood blister, on Jasmin's hymen, just beyond her vaginal opening. It was a clear sign to Davis that it was likely the result of nonconsensual sex. Davis testified that in 75 to 80 percent of the women she examines, there are no visible signs of vaginal injuries.

"Would you expect to see this kind of injury from consensual sexual activity?" LaBorde asked her.

"I wouldn't expect it. No, ma'am," Davis replied.

During cross-examination, Darling pushed Davis to elicit testimony from her that Jasmin's vaginal injuries might have been caused by consensual sex. First, Darling asked Davis if she believed Jasmin was intoxicated. When Davis answered that she didn't, he asked if she smelled alcohol on Jasmin's breath. "Not to my recollection, sir," she answered.

Darling then attempted to raise issues about Jasmin's credibility. He pointed out that on the questionnaire Jasmin completed during her sexual assault exam, she indicated she hadn't consumed alcohol in the previous twenty-four hours, which LaBorde had already told the jury wasn't true in her opening statement. Davis didn't request a blood-alcohol content test at the time of the exam.

Darling also pressed Davis to explain to the jury that there weren't any visible injuries to Jasmin's face or neck. Davis testified that there weren't any noticeable injuries to Jasmin's wrists, arms, or legs, which might have indicated that she'd been forcibly held down against her will. In fact, the only wounds Davis notated in her report were the injuries to Jasmin's vagina, which Darling referenced, asking whether they could be consistent with someone who had consensual sex. She said it was possible, but unlikely. "Most patients that I've seen don't have swollen hymens when they have sexual activity," she said.

At one point, Darling even asked if the hematoma on Jasmin's hymen was an injury similar to one a child might suffer when she falls awkwardly on a bicycle seat.

"That's not a normal fall," Davis said. "I mean, this is some type of serious physical injury to cause a hematoma to the hymen."

One person who didn't testify at Tevin's trial—or even appear— was Baylor football coach Art Briles. It's unclear why that didn't happen, but Tevin certainly tried. According to information released in a legal case years later, Tevin texted the coach and asked him if he would testify on his behalf, to which Briles responded, "We need to get your name cleared. . . . Always all in with my players."

CHAPTER FOURTEEN

STRENGTH IN NUMBERS

McLennan County Courthouse, Waco, Texas
January 22, 2014

On the second day of Tevin Elliott's trial, three of the women who came to testify against him held hands with their mothers in a side room of McLennan County Courthouse. They felt power and strength in numbers, but also shock. Shock and anger that it took five victims to get to this point. Disappointment and frustration that it took so long to finally bring him to justice.

When Jasmin Hernandez walked into the waiting room that morning, she was surprised to see so many other women there. It was the first time Jasmin, Phoebe, and their mothers had been together. Jasmin was also meeting Samantha in person for the first time, and she'd never spoken to Olivia*, another one of Tevin's victims. Candice Hernandez, Jasmin's mother, was stunned to learn that Tevin had so many victims.

"I didn't understand until we actually met in the hallway at the trial," Candice told us. "We were all in tears. We were all going back and forth to the bathroom to get tissues. Just looking at each other, we'd fall apart and start bawling in the hallway. It was extremely emotional. When you hear the other stories it tugs at your heart because you've been going through it. It was shocking."

---

* Pseudonym

Jasmin knew she would be taking the stand to testify against him.
But the other women in the room weren't certain they would have
opportunities to share the stories of their assaults with the jury.

Until that point, jurors only knew Jasmin as "Jane Doe," a faceless
pseudonym to protect her identity and privacy. On the stand, though,
she revealed many details of her life at Baylor, including the names of
her roommates and closest friends, academic history, and social habits, including the fact she was gay. "When we were in the courtroom,
it was hard. It was very hard," Jasmin told us.

After LaBorde walked Jasmin through the events that preceded
Tevin scooping her up and carrying her behind the Aspen Heights
clubhouse, LaBorde asked Jasmin if she screamed once he put her on
the ground and pulled her pants down.

"It was shouts," Jasmin testified. "But it was more toward him. I
wasn't asking for external help. I was just pretty much, like, demanding or asking or begging, trying to get his attention, saying, 'No.'"

"Do you have any idea why when you're getting picked up you
don't scream to the people at the party at that point? Did you know at
that point what was coming?" LaBorde asked.

"I'm more of a rational person," Jasmin replied. "So I thought that
expressing the fact that no means no would go into someone's head."

Jasmin told jurors that she said no several times. "In fact, I told
him I was gay. And I was like, 'I'm gay. I'm gay. Take me back.' You
know, 'I'm not interested in you. Find someone who would rather be
for you and would be willing to enjoy.' No interest at all, no possible
interest."

LaBorde asked Jasmin to describe what happened when Elliott
climbed on top of her.

"He is having sex with me, I guess," Jasmin said.

"Had you ever had sex before?"

"No, I was a virgin," Jasmin answered.

"And how did that feel?"

"Uh, not good," Jasmin testified. "It hurt a lot and it was just
unwanted, unplanned for, and I just felt like a thing."

"You felt like a thing?"

"Yeah, not a person," Jasmin said.

After Jasmin identified Tevin as the man who sexually assaulted her, LaBorde asked her why she told Michele Davis that she hadn't consumed alcohol that night, and Jasmin said she thought she had mentioned that to the nurse, noting that she did tell the Waco police officer. If she indeed hadn't, she surmised, "Maybe because I hadn't been drinking for the last few hours that I was in the hospital."

"Is there any doubt in your mind that this defendant knew that he did not have your consent to violate you?" LaBorde asked.

"He knew that he did not have my consent," Jasmin insisted.

"You said, 'No'?"

"I said, 'No.'"

Darling, for the most part, treaded lightly during his cross-examination of Jasmin. He too inquired why Jasmin didn't scream while Tevin was carrying her through the parking lot outside Baylor football player Glasco Martin's townhome. Jasmin had testified that there were people pouring out the door and congregating in the parking lot.

"And at no time did you yell for help, say, 'Please stop, I don't want to go with you,' or anything like that?" Darling asked.

"It was once we had begun passing the people and it was clear we were not searching for my friends and that we were being led away that I was not even questioning," Jasmin testified. "I was sure that something was not right. And at which point I vocalized that to Tevin."

Darling would ask again, "And even then, when you felt kind of weird about the situation, you never yelled for help from the people that were standing outside?"

"I didn't yell for help," Jasmin answered.

Darling continued to push Jasmin to elicit testimony that she didn't resist being carried away. Was she hitting Tevin? Kicking him? Slapping him? "I was pushing back," Jasmin testified. "I didn't kick or claw, or at least successfully do that, but I did try to create a barrier and push—and not lightly. It was an attempted forceful push. It wasn't anything graceful, just for the record."

While other people—even family members and friends—have often questioned rape survivors about why they didn't do more to resist or fight back, freezing and withdrawing is also a natural reaction in high-stress or threatening situations, according to myriad studies on the subject. In a June 2015 op-ed in the *Washington Post*, Dr. James W. Hopper, an instructor in the Department of Psychiatry at Harvard Medical School, explained that in the midst of sexual assault, the brain's fear circuitry dominates and people might not always respond to an attack the way others might expect. According to Hopper, who didn't testify in Tevin's trial, the prefrontal cortex of the brain can be severely impaired, and all that's left may be reflexes and habits:

> Freezing occurs when the amygdala—a crucial structure in the brain's fear circuitry—detects an attack and signals the brainstem to inhibit movement. It happens in a flash, automatically and beyond conscious control.
>
> It's a brain response that rapidly shifts the organism into a state of vigilance for incoming attacks and avenues of escape. Eyes widen, pupils dilate. Hearing becomes more acute. The body is primed for fight or flight. But as we shall see, neither fight nor flight necessarily follows.
>
> Simultaneously with the freeze response, the fear circuitry unleashes a surge of "stress chemicals" into the prefrontal cortex, the brain region that allows us to think *rationally*— to recall the bedroom door is open, or that people are in the dorm room next door, for example, and to *make use* of that information. But the surge of chemicals rapidly impairs the prefrontal cortex. That's because, despite our dominant role on the planet now, we evolved as *prey,* and when a lion or tiger is upon us, stopping to think is fatal.

After Jasmin's friend Shannon Valverde testified about Jasmin's state of mind prior to the sexual assault exam, the prosecution rested. Jasmin returned to the side room in the courthouse, where the other girls and their mothers were waiting. She'd fought back tears on the stand, but couldn't do it any longer.

"Once the door closed, [Olivia] hugged me and so did the other girls," Jasmin said. "And I cried."

Olivia knew Jasmin's pain all too well. She'd met Tevin when he was a high school senior being recruited to Baylor in the fall of 2008. She was a student-athlete in her third year at Baylor and met him at a recruiting party. They developed a long-distance relationship, and when he was preparing to move to Waco the next summer, he told her that his girlfriend from high school was pregnant. Olivia was about to start her senior year at Baylor and wasn't interested in dating a guy who was about to become a father, especially someone who was three years younger than her. So Olivia broke off their relationship, and she told Tevin they could still be friends. She bumped into Tevin in the weight room and on campus that fall, and one day he invited her to see his new apartment. When he tried to make a pass at her, she stopped him and reminded him she wasn't interested in dating anyone. A couple of weeks before Halloween, Tevin asked her to take him to a costume store off campus because he didn't have a car. She agreed and everything was fine.

On Halloween night, Olivia and her friends decided to attend a party that was being hosted by baseball players. Olivia said she had too much to drink that night and was feeling sick by the time she and her friends went to Scruffy Murphy's, a popular bar for students. Around two o'clock in the morning, Olivia's friends took her back to her apartment, and she climbed into bed still wearing her costume. But she woke up naked the next morning and didn't recall much about what had happened the previous night. She checked her cell phone and saw a text message she'd sent to Tevin, in which she told him she wasn't going to make it to a party to see him. She called Tevin that morning, apologizing again and asking him how the party went. After talking to Tevin, Olivia went into her living room, where her roommate was sitting on the couch and watching TV. Olivia asked her roommate how late she'd stayed out the previous night, and she responded: "Not

that late after you. Just a little before Tevin got here." Olivia was confused because she didn't remember him being there, and when she
talked to him only a few minutes earlier, he hadn't said anything about
coming over. Her roommate said when Tevin arrived at their apartment last night, she told him that Olivia was in the bathroom puk-
ing and wasn't feeling well, and that Tevin mumbled something and
pushed past her. At that point, Olivia remembered she was having her
period. She went to the bathroom to check her tampon and it was
shoved really high up inside of her.

"I think that's when I realized it couldn't have been consensual
because you would have to feel that, right?" she told us. "As a man,
you would have to know that there was something blocking him. Like
how could I have been coherent and not said something or done something? That's when I realized that something happened that shouldn't
have happened." Olivia texted Tevin again, asking him if he'd come
over the previous night. When he responded that he had, she asked
him if they'd had sex. He said they did.

Olivia told her roommate that she'd been sexually assaulted and
talked to three of her closest friends about what to do. She couldn't
decide if she wanted to call the police. She knew Tevin had a young
son and she didn't want to ruin his life. She said she'd been taught that
as a girl she was supposed to please people and always look for the best
in others. That night, she went to dinner with Tevin and confronted
him about what happened. He denied raping her and was adamant
she'd wanted to have sex with him. "I remember when I brought it up,
he was almost aggressively denying it to the point that it scared me a
little bit," she said. "So I dropped it."

Olivia never reported the assault to anyone at Baylor. She never
called the police, and never informed the school's Judicial Affairs
Office. She decided she would avoid Tevin for the next six months
until she graduated, and then she'd leave Waco and her secret behind.

"I just said, 'Maybe he made a mistake,'" Olivia said. "'I can focus
on getting out. I can leave Baylor and not think about it again.' So that

was the decision I made, to leave and focus on graduating and not look back."

Five years later, however, Olivia would have to retell the story about what Tevin did to her on that Halloween night. It was a story she now wished she'd told the police back then, wondering if it might have prevented him from assaulting Jasmin and other women.

CHAPTER FIFTEEN

"HE'S NOT COMING HOME"

McLennan County Courthouse
January 22, 2014

The night before Tevin Elliott testified in his defense, he posted the following message on his Facebook page: "Wishing all prayers for me and my family 2mar is a big day for us."

Tevin wasn't the only one concerned about what transpired on the first day of his trial at McLennan County Courthouse. His mother, Sureka Holmes, called her husband, Kevin Holmes, who couldn't attend the trial because of work. "They're going to railroad Tevin," she told Tevin's stepfather. "He's not coming home."

"I knew that first night," Tevin's mother told us.

For more than two years, Tevin's mother had been haunted by allegations that her youngest son raped Jasmin behind the Aspen Heights clubhouse. Tevin's indictment forced him to leave Baylor and transfer to Central Arkansas University, where he'd hoped to finish his college football career. A former Baylor assistant coach recounted a conversation one of his fellow coaches had with an assistant at Central Arkansas before Tevin enrolled there. "We think this guy is guilty. You take him on your own accord. If you want to talk about football, we'll talk about it. But you take him with the thought of us believing that he is guilty," the former assistant recalled. Central Arkansas indeed took Tevin, but intense media pressure and public criticism forced him to leave there as well, and he ended up graduating from Bacone College, a small liberal arts school in Muskogee, Oklahoma.

Even though Tevin hadn't played football since the 2011 season at Baylor, he still harbored hopes of playing in the National Football League. In fact, in the weeks leading up to his trial, he was training for his "pro day"—when he would audition for NFL scouts. But he'd have to prove his innocence and clear his sullied name before he'd ever step on a playing field again.

"I know my child," Tevin's mother said. "I know what I've instilled in him about being respectful toward women. I never had no doubt that he was innocent. I knew he was innocent because I knew Tevin and knew what kind of person Tevin is."

McLennan County assistant district attorney Hilary LaBorde also believed she knew what kind of person Tevin was: a violent serial rapist, who preyed on multiple young women during his three years as a Baylor football player. And she was finally going to have her chance to confront him in front of a jury.

Tevin testified that he met several of his teammates at Bears wide receiver Kendall Wright's house on the night of Saturday, April 14, 2012. Then they left for running back Glasco Martin's birthday party. Elliott said he'd invited Catrina Gonzalez to the party, but didn't know she was bringing her friends, including Jasmin. Tevin told jurors he danced with Jasmin for twenty or thirty minutes after Cat left, which Jasmin vehemently denies.

"We danced not just one song, we danced probably about four or five songs," Tevin testified. "We was starting to draw a lot of attention because, uh, you know, everybody, the football boys, I guess, we call ourselves, like, the 'shirt-off boys.' Everybody takes their shirts off like that. It was real hot in there, too."

Tevin said Jasmin was rubbing his chest as they danced. "She was all on me," he testified. "She was dancing and twirling and stuff. . . . I thought she was gonna go down on me. I was like, 'Oh, what you doing?'" Tevin testified that Jasmin grabbed his hand and wanted him to help her find her friends. He said she led him outside in search of the other women.

As they walked down the street in search of her friends, Tevin said he grabbed Jasmin's waist. "She kind of jumped on my waist and she put her legs around my waist, and she was kissing me all on my neck and ear and stuff like that," he said. "So I kissed her."

After they walked through a crowd of people in the parking lot, Tevin said, he and Jasmin stopped on the other side of the basketball court near the clubhouse. He said they were making out there, and she started taking her clothes off. He said he undressed and they had sexual intercourse. They put their clothes back on and moved to a muddy slope behind the clubhouse. Tevin said he and Jasmin continued to have sex for ten or fifteen minutes. They were kissing and she gave him oral sex.

"And during this time frame did she tell you to stop?" Darling asked him.

"No, sir," Tevin said.

After they had sex on the slope, Tevin said, Jasmin grabbed his hand and led him to a bench area by the swimming pool. He testified that she lay down on a pool chair and they had sex again. Eventually, she stood up, grabbed the fence, and he entered her from behind and they had intercourse for another five or ten minutes. Once they were finished, Tevin said he helped Jasmin find her teal sweater and they walked back to the party together.

"At any time from the time that y'all were in the house to the first spot you went to the last spot, did she ever tell you that she didn't want to be there with you?" Darling asked.

"Never," Tevin insisted.

Near the end of Tevin's testimony, his defense team introduced what his family believed was a "game changer"—a key piece of evidence that they believed would prove his innocence. As Tevin and Jasmin walked to the clubhouse, according to Tevin, his red BlackBerry cell phone recorded a video of their sexual encounter. Apparently, he had inadvertently hit the record button. The video lasted one minute and three seconds, and, according to Tevin, it revealed that Jasmin was moaning while they had sexual intercourse, which, according to Tevin, proved that she was aroused and had consented. Tevin claimed he texted the video to his uncle, Rodrick Elliott, the day after the party to preserve it. Darling played a DVD of the video for the jury.

LaBorde told us she didn't receive a copy of the video from Tevin's cell phone until about a week before his trial. Darling, who had previously worked in the district attorney's office, had hinted to LaBorde that he was in possession of a video that proved Jasmin consented. "His attorney told me at pretrial hearings that he had a video that showed she was really into it," LaBorde told us. "I was like, 'How can that be?' It really stressed me out."

LaBorde told Darling that she wanted to see the video before the trial because she didn't want to prosecute Tevin if he was really innocent. "He gave it to me thinking I didn't want to lose and didn't want to put all of these girls through this if there was no purpose," LaBorde said. "I didn't think it was possible."

When LaBorde watched the video for the first time, she immediately suspected it wasn't recorded on the night Tevin raped Jasmin. The video showed a man and a woman walking, but she couldn't see the woman's face. LaBorde could hear a woman moaning at the end of the video, but she was pretty sure it wasn't Jasmin—and it wasn't even clear if the couple was having sex.

"Once I got it, it was ridiculous," LaBorde said. "It was so obvious he'd made it after the fact, and it was like no sex I'd ever imagined. It was so fake it was stupid. It happened at a party, but there were no people in the background. Everybody admitted that he carried her. But he was swinging his hand and you could see that he wasn't carrying anyone. I was really upset that I'd spent so much time worried about this ace in the hole and it was just stupid."

During LaBorde's cross-examination of Tevin, she asked him why he didn't provide the video to Baylor administrators when they were considering whether to expel him. Why hadn't he given the video to Waco police when he was arrested for raping Jasmin? Why hadn't he provided it to the district attorney's office before he was indicted by a grand jury? Why didn't he show it to officials at Central Arkansas to prove his innocence before they kicked him out?

"You got expelled," LaBorde told him. "You got indicted. You got kicked out of your second school. And you haven't played football since. But you decided to wait until today to play the audio for the first time?" She drilled him about why he never turned the phone over to be analyzed by a professional.

"Because the truth is, you didn't make this on that day, did you?"

"I did," he insisted. "Yes, ma'am."

Tevin told LaBorde that he no longer had the BlackBerry that recorded the video. He insisted he'd texted the video to his uncle, who then texted it to Darling. LaBorde asked Tevin why the phone only recorded for one minute and three seconds and then "magically turned off." He said he believed the phone had a timer. As LaBorde played the DVD for the jury again, she asked him why he couldn't be heard talking in the video.

"Because she's busy kissing on me right now," Tevin answered.

"Okay," LaBorde said. "Where was the kissing part?"

"She was kissing on me," he explained. "My phone's in this hand. She was kissing on my neck right there. We was walking. I was walking."

"So we can't hear that. We just have to trust you, correct?"

"Yes, ma'am," Tevin said. "Just like you have to trust her."

"I'm sorry?" LaBorde asked.

"I said, just like you have to trust her word you have to trust mine, too," Tevin repeated.

It was the opening in Tevin's testimony that LaBorde had been waiting and hoping for. He had testified that he was trustworthy, and LaBorde hoped that it would be enough for her to introduce the other women who alleged Tevin raped them. After LaBorde and Darling met with Judge Matt Johnson in his chambers, LaBorde asked Tevin in front of the jurors, "Mr. Elliott, this isn't the first girl that trusted you, is it?"

Darling immediately objected, claiming LaBorde's question was a violation of Texas Rules of Evidence 404 (b), which prohibits evidence of a defendant's prior bad acts from being introduced at a trial. Darling argued that LaBorde's line of questioning would be highly prejudicial for the jury and wasn't relevant, but Johnson overruled his objection. Johnson's decision allowed the testimony of Samantha, Olivia, and Phoebe.

LaBorde repeated her question: "This isn't the first girl that trusted you," she said. "Is that correct?"

"Excuse me?" Tevin asked.

"This isn't the first girl that trusted you when you took her from one place to another, is it?" LaBorde asked again.

Tevin struggled for words. "I don't understand what you're—on that." LaBorde pounced on him.

"This isn't the first girl that said no over and over and over," LaBorde said.

"I haven't anyone just ever said it, just no," Tevin insisted. "We have consensual."

LaBorde asked Tevin if he knew that Samantha was in the courtroom. She'd accused Tevin of raping her in her apartment, after she'd invited him there to help her move a desk into a spare bedroom. She said Tevin threw her over his shoulder and carried her upstairs, then violently raped her as she repeatedly told him no. "She told you she didn't want to have sex until she was married," LaBorde told him. "You didn't care."

"She never said that toward me," Tevin testified.

"Okay," LaBorde continued. "She was kissing you, and then you carried her, just like you carried Jasmin, from one location up to her bedroom, and you forced yourself on her, didn't you?"

"No. Never," Tevin said, and continued to deny each detail of the assault LaBorde presented.

"Okay," LaBorde continued. "So that's another person that you're claiming consented to have sex with you and then lied about it later."

"Probably after all of this stuff came out in the media, of course," Tevin answered.

"Are you aware that [Samantha] went to the police a month before Jasmin ever met you?" LaBorde asked.

"I wasn't aware of that," he admitted.

Then LaBorde asked Tevin about Phoebe, the McLennan County Community College student who accused him of inappropriately touching her and poking her vagina with a broomstick. Tevin testified that he and Phoebe's roommate were having sex.

"So you have someone you can have sex with whenever you want to, but that isn't enough," LaBorde said. "You want to have sex with all these other people that don't want to have sex with you, too. Is that right?"

"No, ma'am," he answered.

Tevin acknowledged he'd received a Class C ticket from Waco police following the incident in Phoebe's bedroom, in which he closed the door and wouldn't let her leave. "And she didn't know [Samantha] and she didn't know Jasmin, correct?" LaBorde asked.

"Yes, ma'am," Tevin said.

"So these are just three girls that don't know each other that are all saying when they tell you no, you think it means yes?" LaBorde asked.

"I never forced myself on anyone," Tevin insisted.

Then LaBorde asked Tevin about Olivia, who alleged he raped her while she was passed out drunk at her apartment on Halloween night in 2009.

"I never had sex with her when she was passed out," he testified. In fact, he insisted that he didn't even have sex with Olivia on the night in question. "No, ma'am. That's false," he said.

"Are you aware she had a tampon in?" LaBorde asked.

"No, ma'am," he said.

"And it got shoved all the way up to her cervix because you didn't bother to take it out. That would be a pretty strong sign that a woman didn't consent, wouldn't it? That she didn't take her tampon out?" LaBorde said.

"No, ma'am," Tevin answered. "That's false."

"That's not the first time you've ever had an issue with a tampon, either, is it?" LaBorde continued. "Let's talk about what happened at the club with the TCU student. . . . Do you remember having sex at a club upstairs?"

"We never had sex at no club," Tevin said.

"So some random girl just totally made up that you raped her at a club?"

"Wasn't a random girl," he testified. "We met at the club. We never had sex at the club. She actually came to Dallas. She goes to TCU, right?"

"I don't know. How many girls are there? Can you not remember? Because I don't think [Leslie] ever wanted to see you after you raped her at the club."

Tevin testified that he and Leslie had sex at his cousin's apartment in Lewisville, Texas, but they didn't have sex at the nightclub.

"She told you no, too?"

"No, ma'am, she never did," Tevin answered.

"Because she was on her period."

"Never, no, ma'am."

"And you didn't care," LaBorde said. "She shoved you out of herself three times and you just kept shoving it right back in."

CHAPTER SIXTEEN

"GIRL AFTER GIRL AFTER GIRL"

McLennan County Courthouse, Waco, Texas
January 23, 2014

Before the closing arguments in Tevin Elliott's trial, three of the women who accused him of raping or assaulting them—Samantha, Olivia, and Phoebe—took the witness stand and told jurors how the horrific events changed their lives.

"If that doesn't turn you into a Christian or make you believe in God, I don't know what does," Samantha testified. "I forgave Tevin because I'm supposed to forgive. But it is really sad that I read a newspaper article and thought it was about me when it was about someone else. And the only reason why I didn't press charges or anything like that was because I didn't want to make him upset."

Samantha was volunteering as an advocate for sexual assault victims at the time of the trial. "I talk to other girls that have gone through it, and I'm like, 'It's hard to understand that a rape doesn't necessarily mean punching and kicking and screaming and biting and scratching.' It doesn't necessarily mean that that's what no is. No is like, 'Don't put your junk in me.' That's what no means, like no means we're not connected, and clearly he didn't get that."

Olivia told jurors that she felt like Tevin "owned" her after he raped her. She graduated from Baylor in 2010, but encountered Tevin more than a year later when she returned to Waco, Texas, to participate in a career panel for Baylor Athletics. Olivia saw Tevin while she was lounging at a pool with a girlfriend.

"Did he seem remorseful at the pool or that he was sorry or did he talk to you?" McLennan County assistant district attorney Hilary LaBorde asked her.

"No, he just seemed very sure of himself," Olivia answered.

Olivia testified that she'd struggled to maintain relationships with men and referred to herself as "damaged goods" for two or three years. She became convinced that no man could look past the sexual assault and care about her.

"I went through a really difficult time and made some reckless decisions to put myself in kind of dangerous situations, where I would just go places by myself that I probably shouldn't have," she said. "I must have an angel on my shoulder watching out for me after that. My excuse was that I had already been raped so what was the worst that could happen?"

Phoebe testified that her experience with Tevin caused her to constantly look over her shoulder, no matter where she went. "I was very self-conscious about everywhere I went and what time of day it was when I went. . . . It just rattles you," she said. "It changes how you live your life and how you go about it daily."

The last witness to take the stand before closing arguments was Waco Police Department detective Charlotte Mathews. She'd been a police officer since 2002 and had worked as a detective in the Special Crimes Unit since 2008. In April 2012, Mathews was assigned Samantha's case.

During Mathews's testimony, LaBorde showed jurors the Waco police incident reports from Leslie's case on March 19, 2011, when the TCU student accused Tevin of raping her at a nightclub, and Phoebe's case from September 28, 2011. Detective Kristina Woodruff briefly investigated the nightclub incident until Leslie decided she didn't want to pursue criminal charges; Detective Manuel Chavez worked Phoebe's case after she reported Tevin trapped her in her bedroom.

"The records I've just showed you, those would have been offense reports that you would have had access to when you were doing your own investigation, is that right?" LaBorde asked Mathews.

"Yes," Mathews replied.

"And did you review those when you were working on your case?"

"No, I talked with the detectives," Mathews answered.

"Did you review the records or did you just talk to Kristina?"

"Just talked to Kristina."

"Did you review these records or you just talked to Manuel?"

"I don't remember."

"Detective Woodruff didn't talk to the defendant during her case," LaBorde said. "Were you aware of that?"

"No," Mathews testified.

"Is that, like, not really that important to you?" LaBorde asked.

"I worked my case," Mathews said. "We have our own caseload and I worked my case."

"So if these girls were dead—if [Leslie] were dead, [Phoebe] were dead, and [Samantha] were dead, and the same suspect was Tevin Elliott in each case, would y'all just work those separately?" LaBorde inquired.

"Well, they're not dead," answered Mathews, almost matter-of-factly.

"So it's not really important if their vaginas are hurt, just if they're dead?"

"Absolutely it is important," Mathews insisted.

"A serial killer would not be worked together; is that what you're saying?"

"Not necessarily," Mathews said. "We would work them and then we would talk to each other, but we don't work them together."

"So you don't compare notes. You don't look for patterns."

After raising serious concerns about the way Waco police investigated the sexual assault cases involving Tevin, LaBorde asked Mathews why she didn't at least send Samantha's case to the district attorney's office. "She could have testified in front of the grand jury at that point," LaBorde said. Mathews recalled doing that only one other time in a murder case.

"You made this decision on your own without ever laying eyes on her ever, is that correct?" LaBorde asked.

"My job is to take the report and then do an investigation," Mathews answered.

"And you consider this an investigation?"

"It was the best that I could do," Mathews said.

LaBorde also criticized Mathews for never meeting with Samantha face-to-face and for not trying to track her down on Baylor's campus after she changed her phone number.

"Did you go and try and find her at Baylor?" LaBorde asked.

"I don't even think she was at Baylor anymore," Mathews said.

"You don't think she graduated from Baylor a couple months after that?"

"I do not know what was going on with [Samantha]," Mathews answered.

"Because you didn't look," LaBorde said curtly. "Is that fair?"

More than two years after Tevin's trial, LaBorde still seemed dumbfounded that Waco police didn't conduct a more collaborative investigation into his behavior. If there had been more cooperation among detectives, LaBorde insisted, they might have recognized they were dealing with a serial rapist and arrested him. Getting Tevin off the streets might have at least prevented him from raping Jasmin.

"I felt like if anyone had looked at all of these things they would have noticed that there were similarities and they had a problem on their hands," LaBorde told us. "But that's not how they chose to do the work."

LaBorde also questioned whether Waco police detectives have been properly trained in how to investigate allegations of acquaintance rape: "[For them] rape is a stranger attacking someone. It's not whatever happened to [Phoebe] because nothing really happened, and it's not [Samantha] because she doesn't call you back. If she were really scared she would call you back. I think it's a real lack of awareness of what acquaintance rape looks like and how to work those."

During her testimony, Mathews said she contacted someone at the Baylor Police Department about Samantha's allegations, but she couldn't recall the person's name. LaBorde told us she didn't think there was much interaction, if any, between the departments before Tevin was arrested. "Would it occur to probably a small child that they should call Baylor PD and tell them, 'Hey, this guy now has two different events'? Yes," LaBorde said. "Honestly, do I think it occurred to Waco PD? No, I don't."

Reagan Ramsower, Baylor's senior vice president for operations and chief financial officer, said Waco police might contact the university if a student is accused of a serious crime, but the administration doesn't routinely examine jail logs or incident reports looking for students. LaBorde said she isn't aware of any formal policies between the police departments, either.

"I really think that's kind of ad hoc," LaBorde said. "It just kind of depends on the personalities involved. If the Waco cop who gets the call knows they're students and goes to coffee with someone that works at Baylor PD, he might mention it. But it's certainly not one hundred percent of the time. I don't think there's any policy. I think it really comes down to who is on the scene at the time, how well they know people, and how much they like gossiping. I don't think there's any rhyme or reason to it at all."

In closing arguments at Tevin's trial, McLennan County assistant district attorney Robert Moody told jurors: "It was girl after girl after girl. All his victims, they screamed no. They say no. Did you notice they're all little? They're small. And that big defensive end just picks them up. That's pretty common in all of them, too. He picks them up and carries them somewhere. It's a crime of opportunity. He finds a girl, and when she says no, that's a challenge. And he carries them where he wants. He throws them down and he forces himself on them.

"They all said no. Will you? It's time for somebody to tell Tevin no. You cannot do this and we're not going to tolerate it. Your verdict sends a message to him and it sends a message to this community that we will not tolerate this kind of behavior. We will not let girl after girl after girl be abused."

The jury of nine women and three men needed only about an hour to reject Tevin's defense that he and Jasmin had consensual sex and convict him of two felony counts of sexual assault. Before the jury decided Tevin's sentence, Olivia, Phoebe, Jasmin, and their mothers, as well as Samantha's mother, offered impact statements to the jury. Olivia's mother testified that her daughter felt extreme guilt for not reporting her incident to police, which might have prevented other women from being assaulted. Samantha's mother said her daughter had been treated by four different counselors and was still taking antidepressants for anxiety.

Finally, Jasmin told the jury that she felt like she was punishing her father and brothers because she wasn't comfortable when men tried to hug or touch her. "After I was raped, I just felt like there was nothing," Jasmin said. "And when you feel like nothing, it makes you think that there is nothing for you left to love."

Before Tevin was sentenced, he apologized to the women   not for raping them, but because they were mad at him. He asked the jury to sentence him to probation so that he could raise his two young sons. "Even though I don't agree with a lot of the stuff that the girls said, I do apologize," he said. "I hope they forgive me for that. I want the jurors to know that I am a great person, and I'm not a bad person like they're making me out to be."

Moody called the thought of putting him on probation "disgusting." And LaBorde told the jury that it had to reject Tevin's plea for leniency.

"The problem for Mr. Elliott and for Mr. Darling is that Tevin Elliott doesn't think he made any mistakes," LaBorde told the jury. "He's not sorry for anything. He hasn't learned anything." The jury deliberated for almost two hours before sentencing Tevin to the maximum twenty years in prison and a $10,000 fine. He was shackled and led out of the McLennan County Courthouse as his mother and other family members and friends wept.

"I wouldn't like to be locked up for twenty years," Jasmin told us. "I value my freedom very much, and I think twenty years in prison sounds terrible. But then I remember that he's a serial rapist."

Less than three months later, on April 4, 2014, more than one hundred of Tevin's family members, friends, and supporters crowded into a McLennan County courtroom for a hearing in which his new attorney, William A. Bratton III, was seeking a new trial. Many of Tevin's supporters were wearing T-shirts that read "Free Tevin Elliott," "I Am Tevin," or "Justice for Elliott." Judge Matt Johnson, who presided over his first trial, ordered his family and friends to turn their T-shirts inside out before entering his courtroom.

Bratton argued that Darling's representation in Tevin's defense at the first trial was inadequate. Bratton questioned why Darling didn't utilize the video from Tevin's cell phone and from security cameras at the Aspen Heights clubhouse in his defense. Bratton also wondered why there was a thirty-minute gap on the security footage, from 1:08 a.m. to 1:38 a.m. on April 15, 2012, around the time the assault allegedly occurred. LaBorde said her office and police didn't alter the tape and it came to them like that. Despite Bratton's arguments, Johnson denied Tevin's motion for a new trial and sent him back to prison.

For the first two years of his sentence, Tevin was incarcerated at the Preston E. Smith Unit in Lamesa, Texas. He was transferred to the James V. Allred Unit in Iowa Park, Texas, in November 2016. His projected release date is January 21, 2034, and he will be eligible for parole in 2024.

In December 2015, Tevin agreed to speak to a reporter, using a phone tethered to the wall behind an acrylic glass partition at the prison in Lamesa. In the interview, which would air a month later on ESPN's *Outside the Lines,* Tevin declined to get into specifics about

each of the accusations against him, but he again reiterated his innocence, saying he was targeted because he was an athlete.

"You know college athletes go through this all the time. Not just
myself," he said. "At the end of the day the finger is going to be pointed
at us because we are the big athletes. . . . We sittin' on a pedestal. They
trying to make us look bad, but at the end of the day, we could be
innocent. It's like we are guilty until proven innocent."

Asked what motive the women would have to lie, Tevin said, "It
could be envy. I didn't want to be in a relationship with them. They see
that I'm talking to other women. Or, 'Oh, he think he's just a big-time
football player. He think he can just do me like that? He think he can
just have sex with me, and go just leave me to the curb?'"

At that time, Tevin said he received about eight letters a week
from Baylor fans wishing him well.

CHAPTER SEVENTEEN

DIADELOSO

Waco, Texas
April 18, 2013

Like Jasmin Hernandez, Mary* traveled from far away to attend Baylor University. Mary grew up a lifelong Chicago Bears fan, about an hour outside the Windy City. As a high school student, she at first rejected Baylor when she saw the school's flier in the mail. Baylor's yellow and green colors were the same as those of the Bears' longtime rival, the Green Bay Packers. "Those are Packers colors. There's no way I'm going to go there," she said.

But as the granddaughter of a Baptist preacher—and a lifelong product of religious schools—Mary eventually had Baylor toward the top of her list of potential colleges. She also considered Wheaton College, near Chicago. It was closer to home, and less expensive. She decided on Wheaton, but five hours later flip-flopped to Baylor. Mary wanted to go to medical school, and had a long-term goal of being part of Doctors Without Borders. Baylor's premed program had a direct connection to the prestigious Baylor College of Medicine and it had an international studies track. And while she would be farther away from her parents and siblings, she was closer to extended family in Mexico. Her parents felt safe with Baylor. She was their oldest child, the organized and independent one. When she and her mom visited campus, it was springtime, the birds were singing, and someone greeted them

---

* Pseudonym

with a friendly, "Hey, y'all." So in the fall of 2010, Mary headed down to Waco, Texas, and became a Baylor Bear.

That semester, Baylor enrolled 14,900 students—the most in the school's 165-year history. Mary shared a room—"the size of a broom closet"—with two other students. She took a job as an administrative assistant checking people in and out of the school's recreation center. Even after getting a $64,000 academic scholarship, Mary still had bills to pay and had to balance her work at the rec center with studying, knowing she needed to keep at least a 3.0 GPA to maintain her scholarship. Her first semester, she had close to a 3.8. But it was more difficult her sophomore year. She couldn't meet with professors because their office hours conflicted with work. She was having trouble focusing and her grades dropped closer to a 3.0. She went to a doctor, who diagnosed her with attention-deficit/hyperactivity disorder and put her on medication, which helped get her back on track at the beginning of her junior year.

Between work and school, Mary hadn't had a lot of time to make friends, but that changed in the fall of 2012 when she joined the Baylor Bruins. The Bruins was an official organization under the Baylor Alumni Network made up of about thirty female students who greeted and entertained prospective student-athletes and their families during campus visits. It was similar to other such hostess groups at colleges with big-time athletic programs. A couple of girls in one of her classes told her about the Bruins, and it seemed like fun. She loved sports, loved talking sports, and she even liked the cool jumpsuits and jackets the Bruins wore. It seemed like the next-best thing to joining a sorority, which Mary couldn't afford. "It was nice to be invited. Nice to be recognized and considered part of the group," she said.

The Bruins were the girls she'd seen on campus talking to athletes, and she felt special to be among them. She started going to parties, and that's when she was first exposed to the seedy side of school spirit. She recalled a house party with several football players where almost everyone was drinking—including several people who were underage—and the rooms were thick with marijuana smoke. The cops came, and

Mary thought everyone was done for. They searched the rooms, and found a gun in one of them. Two male officers sat everyone down in the living room and interviewed everyone at the party. One of the officers stepped out to make a phone call. When he came back, he pointed at Mary and said, "You're sober. Take everyone home," and Mary and her friends left. The football players had to phone their coaches, but, as far as Mary knew, nothing else happened. "They were on the team for three more years after that," she said. That experience gave Mary an uneasy feeling, after which she really didn't care for house parties, instead sticking with more public venues like warehouse parties or community centers, where people were more into dancing than drugs or drinking.

It wasn't the only time Mary felt burdened to be a Bruin. She was in English class with another Baylor football player—one who more often than not skipped class. She said it reached the point where coaches had to stand outside the door to make sure he didn't leave. The professor knew Mary was a Bruin, and he asked her to tutor the player and she agreed, even though tutoring current student-athletes was not part of a Bruin's official job. She said another girl dropped the player off at her apartment, and Mary said he was so high that he fell asleep on her couch. She woke him up at 6 a.m. and forced him to watch a video that was required for class. He showed up for the final, but "I don't know how he passed the class," she said.

Mary also recalled how some Baylor football players used pit bulls as status symbols. She said they neglected the dogs by keeping them in collars that were so small they almost choked them, or by not bringing them inside when temperatures dropped below freezing. Mary said she called animal control several times, and she believed coaches were aware of the issue with the dogs as well. (A records request to the city of Waco for all animal control enforcement actions during that time did not include any offenses committed by football players. But in August 2016, Baylor receiver Ishmael Zamora was suspended for three games after a video surfaced in social media showing him repeatedly beating his dog with a belt.)

Mary was still with the Bruins in the spring of 2013, as the Baylor community readied for the school's annual Diadeloso celebration on April 18. (*Día del oso* means "day of the bear" in Spanish.) Although it's gone by different names, the annual school-sanctioned celebration has been a Baylor staple since 1932. Students get a day off from classes right before finals. On campus, the school promotes concerts, sand volleyball games, tug-of-war competitions, exhibits, and other events, and extends a welcome to the entire Waco community. Off campus, students throw parties all around town and drinking starts early. It's also a popular time to welcome football recruits to Waco so they can party with current players, and, according to Mary, the women of the Baylor Bruins. The university actually forbade Bruins from having any contact with recruits outside of official campus visits, and several Bruins we spoke with said those rules were followed, even to the point of having to block recruits from their social media accounts. Bruins weren't banned from fraternizing with current student-athletes, but organizers frowned on them dating players because of the perception it might foster, one former Bruin leader told us. Mary described a group of Bruins who she said didn't follow those rules.

Around 4:00 p.m., one of Mary's friends in the Bruins asked her to go to a barbecue, and she agreed. She brought her own drink—a thirty-six-ounce canteen of strawberry daiquiri mix and three or four shots of vodka. Mary knew how alcohol affected her, and she felt safer measuring her own drink and knowing what was in it. They ended up at Baylor defensive end Shawn Oakman's apartment. It was around 6:30 p.m. After that, Mary doesn't remember much. She was so blacked out, she wonders if someone slipped some sort of drug in her drink. She remembers bits and pieces of the night, triggered mostly by what other people have told her, told the police, told reporters, or told Baylor's Title IX investigators.

There were several other football players at Oakman's apartment: offensive lineman Pat Colbert, cornerback Xavien Howard, nickle back Kiante Griffin, defensive end Jamal Palmer, wide receiver Corey Coleman, tight end Tre'Von Armstead, and linebacker Myke

Chatman. Two of them—Howard and Coleman—would go on to play in the NFL. Several people at the party were drinking and, at one point, people were taking swigs from a bottle of Smirnoff vodka. Mary started acting flirtatious, but exactly how flirtatious depended on whom was asked. Armstead and Howard said she flashed her vagina, but they couldn't agree on what she was wearing: Armstead said shorts; Howard thought it was a skirt. But Mary said she wore black Capri leggings that night, which several of her friends and other football players verified, and none of those people remember her exposing her genitalia. Mary had been dancing suggestively, hanging on several men in the room and touching their groins, according to a few.

At one point, Mary remembered being in a bedroom at Oakman's apartment, sitting on the bed with someone, drinking from the bottle she brought, and texting on her phone. They were waiting for something. Alcohol? Maybe marijuana? Mary avoided smoking marijuana, fearing any association would hurt her chances at attending med school. The fellow Bruin who had brought her to the party, Jayme*, was in the bedroom as well. She described Mary as being all over Tre'Von—and a number of other guys—at the house party. Jayme told Baylor investigators years later, when asked about that night, that when she decided to take Mary home, Mary was really intoxicated and Jayme was unsure whether Mary was "in her right mind or not."

Jayme, and a few other partygoers, would say that Mary invited Tre'Von and Myke back to her house, although others would say the two men asked if they could come over. When Oakman realized what was about to happen, he said he told Tre'Von and Myke, "Don't go. I wouldn't go." But they left with Jayme and Mary anyway.

---

* Pseudonym

CHAPTER EIGHTEEN

WHO YOUR FRIENDS ARE

Waco, Texas
April 18, 2013

During the short drive from Shawn Oakman's party to Mary's apartment, she made out with Tre'Von Armstead in the backseat of Jayme's car. Jayme didn't think much of what might happen next. "If you're all over the guy, he's going to expect that you're cool with seeing him later as well," Jayme said.

It's unclear how Myke Chatman arrived at Mary's house. Jayme insisted she dropped off only Tre'Von and Mary, but other witnesses said Myke rode with Tre'Von. Regardless, Myke arrived at about the same time. Jayme said that Mary didn't stumble as she walked to the front door. But that's not what Mary's roommate, Emily*, remembers. She saw Mary stumbling in with Tre'Von and Myke, who stopped to talk with Emily and her friends.

Emily remembered Mary heading upstairs to her bedroom, and Tre'Von following her. Emily noticed that Tre'Von moved sluggishly and had bloodshot eyes, while Myke appeared not to be impaired at all. After a while, Emily felt uncomfortable about leaving Mary upstairs alone with Tre'Von, so she went up to check on them and found the two clothed and sitting on Mary's bed. Still, she told them it was time to get out of the bedroom. Tre'Von resisted, but Myke encouraged him to leave, so Emily thought they were on their way out. She and her

---

* Pseudonym

friends left the house—a decision Emily would say she later regretted.

Mary learned about what happened from a conversation she had with Myke the next day. She said he told her that he began making out with her after Emily left the room, and that at the same time, Tre'Von performed oral sex on her. He said Tre'Von moved on to having sex with her, but that Myke opted out because he "didn't want to share."

Myke later told a Baylor Title IX investigator a similar account, although that version included Mary having performed oral sex on Myke and that Tre'Von sexually penetrated her with his penis, from the rear, while she was on the bed and while Tre'Von was standing.

While the three were upstairs in Mary's bedroom, one of her other roommates, Caroline*, came home with her boyfriend, Jeff**. They had been at a Christian-based event on campus as part of the Diadeloso celebration. Mary figured out later that Caroline and Jeff arrived about forty-five minutes after Emily left. Jeff and Caroline found the front door open and heard footsteps upstairs, which alarmed them. Jeff, who was a concealed-handgun owner, searched the house, at one point taking his gun out and holding it behind his back. He called out for Mary, but no one responded. He heard noises, like people wrestling, coming from the bedroom Mary shared with Emily. He didn't open the door at first, thinking maybe Emily had a "guest."

When Jeff went downstairs to tell Caroline, the two heard a "big bang" and a "slap" sound, and they heard Mary loudly say, "No." To Jeff, the sound was like a body being thrown to the floor or a piece of furniture being overturned. He told Caroline, "I don't think everything is okay." He headed back upstairs and knocked on the door, asking if Mary was all right, and he received a response from a male voice that everything was fine. The door had opened and Jeff saw what he described as a very large, shirtless man—whom they later identified as Tre'Von—standing in the doorway. The room was dark and he could barely make out another person, possibly Mary, lying on the floor with

---

* Pseudonym
** Pseudonym

at least some of her clothes off. "No, she's not okay," Jeff said, while still holding the gun behind his back. "Send her out. I want to see her downstairs."

As soon as Jeff went back downstairs, Mary came running out of the bedroom. She was out of breath and shaking, her eyes were blood-shot, and it appeared she had been crying. Her clothes were on inside out. She told Jeff and Caroline that the two men were leaving, and then she ran back up into the bedroom. Jeff yelled upstairs, "You have ten seconds to come out of that room." Another man, shorter than the first and one they later believed to be Myke, walked downstairs. Jeff recalled him saying, "They are almost done up there," and then upon leaving the house, saying something to the effect of "That was whacked" or "That was crazy."

There's some difference in the sequence of events between what Waco police officers recorded in their report and what a longer, more detailed narrative from Baylor's Title IX office revealed. But at some point after Mary went back upstairs, Jeff and Caroline heard a large bang and what they described as "fist-hitting noises" and Mary say-ing, "No, no, please stop." With Mary alone in the room with Tre'Von, Jeff ran back upstairs, demanding that he leave or he was calling the police. Mary came running downstairs, collapsed at the base of the steps, and said, "I told them to leave but they wouldn't." The Waco police report indicates Jeff then carried Mary to the garage, where he told Caroline to wait with her. Baylor's Title IX report says Jeff gave Caroline his gun, telling her to take Mary into the garage and hide and call 911. Either way, after the women were in the garage, Jeff recalled Tre'Von coming down the stairs acting "big and tough" and trying to stare him down as he left the house.

Jeff was concerned for Mary. When he first saw her come out of the bedroom, her behavior made him believe that she had been flipped around and dropped on the floor. He'd never seen anyone act like she had in those moments. Jeff had some medical training, having been certified as a lifeguard. Mary's behavior—the red eyes, hysterical cry-ing, and near hyperventilating—made him wonder if she had been the victim of some sort of date-rape drug. Her behavior also made him recall what it was like to have a concussion, which he once suffered after a fall in which he hit his head and later could not even recall falling. Mary couldn't focus. She couldn't hold a conversation. She mumbled incoherently and looked off into space. That was the state Mary was in when Waco police officers arrived at the house.

Unbeknownst to Mary, Jeff, or Caroline at the time, after Myke left the house, he went to a local bar, where he ran into Jayme—the friend who had driven Mary and Tre'Von home earlier. Baylor investigators later learned that Myke asked Jayme to check on Mary, and that she and two other friends headed over to the house. When they encountered Jeff, one of them told him that she was Mary's cousin—which wasn't true—and they needed to see her right away, so Jeff allowed them upstairs. But he and Caroline quickly questioned their motives when they realized none of them were related, and especially after they heard one of the women say that Mary could "'ruin' the football career of perhaps the 'finest' back in the country," referring to Tre'Von.

Jeff said he later realized that one of Mary's friends seemed to be answering the police officers' questions on Mary's behalf, urging her to tell officers that the sex was consensual.

One of the few things Mary remembered herself was Jayme saying the same thing: to tell police that the sex was consensual. And to tell them that she'd had sex with a white male.

In an interview, Jayme denied telling Mary to say anything, and insisted that Mary told her, her roommates, and police that everything was okay that night. In retrospect, Jayme believed the entire incident got out of hand. "I've known Tre'Von since he was a freshman and he's not like that. He's a typical guy," Jayme said. "It's just an unfortunate situation." The other friend whom Jeff accused of coercing Mary's answers to police that night refused to answer questions when contacted by a reporter in 2016.

Mary and her roommates made statements indicating that because some of the Bruins were friends with football players it's possible they had incentive to protect them from any criminal accusations and to influence whatever story the police heard about Mary and the two men in her bedroom. A Title IX lawsuit Mary filed against Baylor in January 2017, alleges that coaches sent two Bruins to the hotel rooms of two recruits to have sex with them. The lawsuit said one former assistant coach, while recruiting a Dallas-area high school athlete, asked, "Do you like white women? Because we have a lot of them at Baylor and they LOVE football players." It stated coaches encouraged current players to ply recruits with alcohol, illegal drugs, and sex— even to pay for their admission to strip clubs, all of which a former assistant coach, who spoke on the condition that his name not be used, said never once happened in his nine years with the program. Several former Bruins also said they never engaged in or experienced anything like that. The university disbanded the Bruins in 2016 and replaced it with a group of coed students who offer campus tours to all students, not just student-athletes; this was after a series of scandals at other universities, including an NCAA investigation of the hostess program at Tennessee, where women were accused of having improper interactions with recruits.

Myana Johnson was one of the Waco police officers who arrived at Mary's house on the night of April 18, 2013. She noted Jeff and Caroline's description of events, but ended up not making a report because Mary "was very adamant that nothing had happened." Officer Johnson took Mary at her word, despite also noting that she was very intoxicated at the time of their conversation and elusive in her answers and that Mary had a visible bruise on her left cheek and bite marks on her neck. Officer Johnson did, however, make a point to notify Baylor officials, although her report does not indicate exactly who was contacted.

The police officers left Mary's house without collecting any evidence. Mary remembered little of her conversation with the officers, other than at one point going to her bathroom to show them her ADHD medication. When Caroline woke her up the next morning to go to work, Mary was confused. Caroline was angry with her, thinking that Mary purposely lied to police to protect Tre'Von, and so the two didn't talk much that day. In an attempt to piece together details from the night before, Mary exchanged text messages with Tre'Von and Myke, asking each of them if they had worn a condom the previous night. She initially accepted their friend requests on social media to make sure they hadn't posted any pictures or video of her from that night, and then she blocked them a week later.

Eventually, Mary remembered flashes of what happened and shared them with Baylor Title IX investigators. She remembered being forcibly penetrated by a male "trying too hard to enter her," which was similar to what she told Waco police about having pain in her stomach as if something was "pushed up into her." She remembered gasping for air from the pain, and being, at some point, on the floor near the closet on her hands and knees. Her room was also a mess, with clothes and blankets strewn on the floor, drapes torn down to the point where the rod was coming off the wall, and handles broken off a set of drawers beneath her bed.

Mary didn't realize why her roommate was angry with her and not wanting to talk. But she recalled that there was someone else wanting to talk to her that day—and desperately. She said Myke showed up at her door with a bloody leg; he had borrowed a friend's moped to come to her house but crashed it along the way. She offered him a wet paper towel, and let him come in and sit in their front living room.

Myke started to talk about the previous night. Mary said he told her that both men had sex with her, but that he knew something was wrong the second he realized how intoxicated she was, especially when she kept asking them where they went to high school—assuming they were recruits—even though they kept telling her they were Baylor football players. Mary recalled Myke saying to her that he was sorry, and that he didn't know that she wasn't "that type of girl."

"'You don't even know me,'" Mary said she told him.

She'd heard about "running a train," where several guys lined up to have sex with the same woman, but it was never something that appealed to her. Mary said Myke told her that he came over to make sure there wasn't any type of misunderstanding. He explained to her that he'd been in another situation with a woman—a student athletic trainer. The way Myke put it to her, she said, was that he and the trainer had sex and then her friends made her feel bad about it, and so she started saying it was rape. According to other sources, Myke had been accused of sexually assaulting the student athletic trainer on March 2, 2013, and that Baylor officials outside the athletic department handled the matter internally. Coaches kicked Myke off the team around the same time for an unrelated marijuana violation. Myke, through his family, declined multiple requests for comment. In spring of 2013, Myke had still been enrolled at Baylor, according to official records, but he would later tell investigators that at the time of the alleged incident he had already transferred to Sam Houston State in Huntsville, Texas, where he sat out that fall but would go on to play football for three more seasons.

CHAPTER NINETEEN

DELAYED JUSTICE

Waco, Texas
April 20, 2013

Another day passed since Tre'Von Armstead and Myke Chatman allegedly sexually assaulted Mary, and she was in a dark place. She wasn't eating and she was lying on the couch in a ball when Jeff came over to visit Caroline. That's when, Mary said, they finally realized that she didn't tell police what happened not because she wanted to protect Tre'Von, but because she was so intoxicated she couldn't remember. And Jeff, who believed her to be in shock, told her that if she wanted to go to the police department right then to make a report, he would drive her.

It was 10:15 p.m. on Saturday, April 20, 2013, when Mary arrived at the Waco Police Department and ended up speaking with Myana Johnson, the same officer who came to her house on the night of the alleged assault. According to the police report, Mary told the officer that after waking up on the morning of April 19, with bruises on her body and a feeling that she'd had sex but no memory of it, she believed that she was sexually assaulted. She told Johnson that she also found a pair of men's brown boxers and two socks, which she brought with her in case they could be used for evidence.

Mary told Johnson what little she could remember, including how Myke contacted her the next day and told her his version of what happened. She told Johnson that Myke told her that at no time did she tell them to stop. But Mary told the officer that she thought differently after hearing Caroline and Jeff's version of events. Johnson then excerpted parts of Jeff's statement from the night of the incident into the report, including his comment of hearing Mary say, "No, no, please stop."

Another Waco police officer then made a call to the McLennan County District Attorney's Office to request a sexual assault exam. Police officers also took more photos of Mary, noting bruises on her legs and arms, a bruise on her buttocks, and a scratch on her back. While at the hospital for the sexual assault exam, an officer asked Mary if she would sign a form designating her desire to prosecute. But she declined, according to the police report, and told police that she did not want to press criminal charges against Tre'Von or Myke. Nevertheless, a few days later, Waco police detective Charlotte Mathews called to follow up with Mary. Mary told her what little she remembered from the night, explaining that she doesn't drink much, but when she does drink—and gets drunk—she tends to black out but "still functions like a normal person."

Mary told the detective about the text messages she exchanged with Myke, but said that she had accidentally deleted them. Mathews offered to take Mary's phone to see if forensic experts could retrieve anything from it, and Mary agreed. The detective wrote in her report that Mary wasn't sure if she wanted to pursue the case or not. "She said she knows it looks bad because she was drinking and can't remember. She said she ended up making the report because of how her friends said she was acting and she was bruised. [Mary] said at the minimum she wants a report made in case they do this to someone else." Mary and Mathews agreed that they would see if anything could be retrieved from her phone and then go from there.

On May 22, 2013, Mathews received the CDs from forensic officers and noted that they weren't able to retrieve any text messages between Mary and Myke, only his contact information stored in her phone. She emailed Mary and asked her how she wanted to proceed.

Mary responded that since the officers weren't able to locate anything on her phone, she didn't want to pursue the case any further. Mathews wrote in the report that the case would be suspended. Officer Johnson had earlier noted in the report that she had been told to contact Baylor University, and wrote "the call notes were added and Baylor University was contacted" but she did not indicate who at Baylor police received the information.

Mary said the detective told her that Waco police officers would contact Baylor officials and that someone from the university would reach out to her. No one ever did, she said. In an interview with Showtime's *60 Minutes Sports* in November 2016, Baylor senior vice president and chief operating officer Reagan Ramsower said that although he was the administrator who oversaw the police department at the time, he was never notified of the alleged assault. He said such police reports often went no further than former police chief Jim Doak. In a later interview with us, Ramsower said the last record Baylor police has of the report is with a dispatcher who took the call from Waco police about an assault of a student (but no mention of a football player), and it's unknown what if anything happened to it after that.

Mary's police investigation began about the same time she was supposed to be studying for final exams. She missed classes. She missed quizzes and she even missed a group presentation that accounted for 25 percent of one of her class grades. She ended up with several Ds that semester, and she tried to hide her grades from her parents. "I think there was a period of just survival," she said. "Through the ongoing weeks, it got more real." She would see Tre'Von on campus and would think of him and Myke every time she saw a poster promoting Baylor football or heard people talking about the team. Her mental health didn't improve over the summer, and she started having anxiety attacks.

Mary could have used academic help, as well as counseling to help her deal with her assault. When her GPA dropped, she was offered— as was the standard at Baylor—the option to meet with an academic counselor or to take a two-hour class to help her manage her time and study skills. She took the two-hour class. On January 5, 2014, she submitted a scholarship exception request form to the financial aid office for the spring 2014 semester. She stated her GPA was 2.96. The form offered a list of exception reasons, and she checked the one that stated, "Experienced unusual family/medical/personal event, which adversely affected your academic performance and led to your scholarship cancellation/non-renewal (please explain below)."

She wrote the following:

"I was sexually assaulted by 2 Baylor football players during the Spring 2013 semester. As a result, I did not perform well in the classes I was taking at that time. Last semester I was allowed my merit scholarship back and was able to retake 1 of those classes from that semester (Bio 2401 earned a B in fall 2013). Now I ask that (I) may be able to continue my education at Baylor and retake 2 more classes from that spring 2013 semester (Bio 4401 and PSY 3301). But in order to do so, I would need and would greatly appreciate the merit scholarship Baylor has blessed me with the past 3½ years. I love Baylor and would love to continue my education at this university. I know I can do better in these classes and would be thankful for the opportunity to perform according to the best of my ability."

Baylor renewed Mary's scholarship, but no one called or emailed her regarding the assault. She initially intended to graduate in the spring of 2014, but because she had to repeat three of four classes, she stayed and graduated in December 2014. When she petitioned again for her scholarship for that semester, Baylor denied her request because she had already received it for eight semesters.

At the beginning of the 2015 fall semester, Mary's boyfriend (who would later become her fiancé) attended an on-campus workshop about Baylor's policies and procedures relating to Title IX. Baylor had hired its first full-time, dedicated Title IX director in the fall of 2014, and the presentation was part of the campus's new sexual harassment and sexual violence awareness campaign. Her boyfriend approached the new director, Patty Crawford, and told her about Mary's case, which Crawford wanted to pursue. When Mary heard about a chance to have her case investigated, even though it had happened two years earlier, she seized the opportunity. Although Myke was long gone from Baylor and playing football at Sam Houston State, Tre'Von was still in Waco. Heading into the 2015 season, he was expected to be the starting tight end and an All–Big 12 Conference performer.

Mary, who was living in Illinois by then, flew to Texas to meet with Crawford and two of her Title IX investigators in September 2015. They asked her to describe her expectations. She wrote on a piece of paper that she wanted Tre'Von suspended from the team, stripped of his scholarship, and eventually suspended from Baylor altogether. According to a former assistant football coach, the first anyone with the team knew about Mary's accusations against Myke and Tre'Von is when coach Art Briles received a call from then athletics director Ian McCaw the night before Baylor's game against Lamar University on September 12, 2015. After that, the former coach said, "(Tre'Von) was not involved in another team function, ever."

On September 18, 2015, media reported that Tre'Von was suspended from the team for a violation of team rules, with no mention of sexual assault or anything specific. Mary said no one at Baylor told her in advance about his suspension, and she found out via a friend who saw the news online.

As Baylor's investigation into her case moved forward, Mary became frustrated about a lack of communication. Halfway through the process, one of the Title IX investigators, Gabrielle Lyons, quit and Mary had to start over, retelling her story to a new one. Mary felt the investigation was taking a long time—much longer than the sixty days she'd been told it would take—and she was receiving updates maybe once a month. Her hearing was pushed from November to December and to finally January 2016. She was given a week's notice before her hearing, and three days before, she was sent an email to a Dropbox link containing records that caught Mary by surprise.

There was one set of records in particular that Mary zeroed in on: pages of partial text messages retrieved from her phone. They were the messages that Waco Police Department forensic officers were unable to recover when she reported her alleged assault almost two years earlier. Baylor Title IX officials had sent her phone to DFDR Consulting, a private digital forensics firm in Pennsylvania. They were able to retrieve portions—usually about five or six words—of the text messages Mary sent on April 19 and April 20, 2013. The records we were able to review showed Mary's texts with Myke, Tre'Von, and several of her friends who were at the party. "I know, I was too drunk," reads one. One reads, "Nah I'm good now. Just sore an" and cuts off. Another one reads, "Hey did u wear a condom last n," and cuts off. In the two pages of records, Tre'Von's name showed up three times, and Myke's name nine.

According to the Title IX adjudicator's report, Tre'Von said during the first hearing that he did not exchange text messages with Mary after the incident. At that same hearing, Tre'Von presented his own phone records, which showed only basic information, such as the date, time, and phone number but no portion of the texts themselves. Nevertheless, they, too, contradicted what Tre'Von told the adjudicator because they showed at least nine text messages exchanged between him and Mary on April 19, 2013. The report states that Tre'Von was invited back to explain how he could say he didn't exchange text messages with Mary even though his own phone records showed otherwise. The report states, "He had no explanation, except that he 'did not remember' those contacts." (He would later write in a letter to Baylor's vice president of student life that he didn't realize those texts were from Mary because he hadn't saved her as a contact in his phone and didn't recognize her number.)

According to Baylor's report, Armstead "testified he was never intoxicated, never touched (Mary) and alleged he was fully aware, with full knowledge and control of his faculties, and in his right mind, the entire night, as he believes so were both Myke and (Mary)." But Baylor investigators' reports from sixteen witnesses, multiple interviews with

Mary and Tre'Von, police reports, and the newly discovered text messages turned up information that contradicted Tre'Von.

Tre'Von's statement about the text messages was only one of a few issues the adjudicator had with his credibility, although it's worth noting that he was interviewed more than two years after the night in question—a night on which several witnesses stated he was intoxicated. He told the adjudicator that he was never alone with Mary, but the report notes that at least three witnesses—and to some degree even Myke—said he was. He said he went straight home after the encounter and did not go back out. But Mary's roommate said she saw him at a local bar. And one of his teammates, Kiante Griffin, said Tre'Von showed up at Griffin's apartment—not wearing shoes or socks and with his clothes in his hand—and said, as quoted in the report, "he (not they) were with 'that girl from Oakman's place' and had to 'run out.'"

The adjudicator noted that the "biggest single revelation" was when Myke changed his story. He initially said that he'd never had sex with Mary. But during a later interview, when asked by the adjudicator if he had told Mary that she performed oral sex on him and that Tre'Von penetrated her from behind while she was on the bed and he was standing, Myke said, "Yes." That contradicted Tre'Von's earlier claim that he never touched Mary.

The report continued, noting that the adjudicator found a "preponderance of evidence" that Mary was incapacitated at the time of the sexual acts and was, as a result, unable to give consent. It stated that "a sober, reasonable person" in that situation should have known of her incapacity and thus her inability to consent. However, it stated that if Tre'Von were intoxicated that would not constitute a defense, per university policy. It noted that Tre'Von had a "history of being on probation with Baylor University for prior misconduct." Tre'Von was, apparently, among the football players who kept dogs. According to the report, he kept a dog in his room (in violation of university policy) and the "care of the dog was called into question, as fecal matter, and urine, from the dog, were observed in his room."

The adjudicator—F. B. "Bob" McGregor Jr., a Texas district court judge with his bachelor's, master's, and law degree from Baylor—delivered his report on February 3, 2016. In this concluding paragraph, he decides to permanently expel Tre'Von from Baylor: *"Because Respondent has yet again been in breach and violation of University policy, specifically, in this instance, the Title IX policy indicated in the findings of adjudicator, and because Respondent, although most polite in hearings, has shown little or no actual remorse for his conduct, at least before the adjudicator, in the opinion of the adjudicator, and has not been accurate as to the fact recitation in his case, and has caused one or more members of the Baylor student community actual fear for personal safety, and as T.A.'s conduct involved a physical and sexual activity where bodily damage to person and property actually occurred, Respondent will be disciplined by permanent EXPULSION from Baylor University."*

Tre'Von, who was represented by Dallas attorney Willie Marsaw, appealed the ruling. Neither Tre'Von nor his attorney would talk for the purposes of this book. But in Tre'Von's appeal letter to Kevin Jackson, Baylor's vice president of student life, he stated that important information wasn't presented; the imposed sanction—expulsion—was out of line; and there was "procedural unfairness" during the disciplinary process. The letter questioned why Baylor investigators didn't reference the Waco police report or interview any of the police detectives or the nurse who conducted Mary's sexual assault exam.

In arguing why he felt the sanction was inappropriate, the letter states that he is "appealing on these grounds simply because I submit that no misconduct has been proven." Tre'Von stated there were no eyewitnesses, although Baylor's report includes information from Myke, who was present, and Caroline and Jeff, who came home during the alleged assault. Tre'Von also protested the fact that he was dismissed from the team months before Baylor finished its investigation. "It would appear to me that I was never going to receive a fair impartial hearing on this matter, since it was stated that I was dismissed for violating team rules before a single person was interviewed," the

letter stated. He argued that when the Title IX office assigned a new
investigator—because the first one had quit—she took down his
statement inaccurately; Tre'Von stated it was "full of inaccuracies and
in many cases outright lies."

Tre'Von questioned how a "university with the reputation for
Christian values" could expel him for an act that could "absolutely ruin
my reputation and my future." He wrote, "I understand that it is expe-
dient to have me gone, but to do so in a manner that demeans and
destroys my personhood relying almost solely on college kids who were
almost certainly drinking on a night from 2 and a half years ago is
wrong." He ends it by writing, "I didn't rape anyone. I didn't threaten
anyone. . . . I am not a barbarian. I didn't do this."

On April 5, 2016, Jackson wrote Tre'Von a letter denying his
appeal, stating that the facts—and Baylor policy—did not support any
of his counterarguments.

Tre'Von and Mary disagree on a lengthy list of issues about that
night, but there's one important point they both share: The investigation should have occurred in 2013, not two years later.

It took the McLennan County District Attorney's Office even longer to charge Armstead and Chatman with a crime for their alleged
actions that night. On March 22, 2017, nearly four years after Mary
claimed she was raped, Armstead was arrested and charged with three
counts of second-degree felony sexual assault. U.S. marshals arrested
Chatman the next day on the same charges. Armstead's arrest came
only nine days after he was arrested for allegedly physically assaulting
a woman, resisting arrest, and kicking out the back window of a police
car in Las Vegas.

CHAPTER TWENTY

SAM UKWUACHU

Waco, Texas
October 19, 2013

Jasmin Hernandez and the other women who were involved in Tevin Elliott's criminal trial believed his conviction for a string of sexual assaults would be a message that needed to be sent to the university. They thought, perhaps, Tevin was a worst-case scenario. What they didn't know was that even before Tevin's case went to trial in January 2014, the number of female Baylor students reporting sexual assaults—and not only those involving football players—continued to grow. Mary's case was only one example.

In May 2013, just over a year after Tevin raped Jasmin, then Boise State University football coach Chris Petersen contacted Baylor football coach Art Briles about Sam Ukwuachu, a highly talented defensive end from Pearland, Texas, near Houston. Petersen told Briles that Sam was homesick and wanted to transfer to a school closer to home.

What Petersen did or didn't tell Briles about Sam's behavior during his two seasons with the Broncos would become the subject of much debate between two of college football's most successful coaches. According to Briles, Petersen told him that Sam was kicked off the Boise State team for minor disciplinary reasons, such as being insubordinate to coaches and missing practice. Briles believed those were correctable problems and invited Sam to visit Baylor's campus. On May

20, 2013, Sam traveled to Waco, Texas, liked what he saw, and verbally committed to transfer to Baylor that summer.

News of Sam's transfer was met with much celebration by Baylor football fans. He had been named a freshman All-American at Boise State after totaling 35 tackles and four and a half quarterback sacks in 2012. He was a pass-rushing specialist the Baylor defense desperately needed. Sam enrolled in classes for fall semester 2013 but was ineligible to play for the Bears that season because of NCAA transfer rules, which require a player to sit out one full season if they transfer from one Football Bowl Subdivision program to another. So for the first two months of the 2013 season, Sam was nothing more than another spectator, watching home games at Floyd Casey Stadium and road games on TV.

On the night of October 19, 2013, only hours after the Bears blasted Big 12 Conference rival Iowa State, 71–7, at home to improve their record to 6-0, Sam celebrated the big Homecoming victory at a party at the downtown Waco Convention Center. Around two o'clock in the morning, according to court records, Sam texted Nicole*, who was an eighteen-year-old Baylor women's soccer player. After bumping into each other at the party, they had made plans to grab a late dinner and possibly attend another party. They were classmates in a religion course and attended Bible studies together. Nicole had visited his apartment on two prior occasions, spending the night the second time. But after Sam tried to make a pass at her during one of her visits, she said she asked him to stop. Nicole said she was still a virgin and wasn't interested in having sex with him.

Baylor was the only school Nicole ever wanted to attend. She'd participated in a soccer camp there during middle school and immediately fell in love with the campus and coach. She verbally committed to play for the Bears as a sophomore in high school and moved to Waco a few weeks after graduating in 2013. It didn't take Nicole long to meet a close group of friends. She met India during

---

* Pseudonym

"Welcome Week" that summer, which is when incoming freshmen are invited to campus to participate in academic orientation and other activities, and she was introduced to Brittani the night before the Homecoming game. Nicole became close friends with her soccer teammates, but her very best friend was Victoria.

Nicole's soccer career at Baylor was slow out of the gates, after she tore meniscus cartilage in her knee during the fall season in 2013. She would work on rehab and sit out games the next several months. It gave her more time to focus on her studies and adjust to college. She was a speech pathology major and hoped to work with autistic children for a nonprofit organization in an urban area.

Nicole spent much of Homecoming weekend with Victoria, India, and Brittani. On Friday night, the day before the game, Nicole and her friends attended the "Eternal Flame" pep rally and bonfire at the Fountain Mall on campus. The Flame has been a part of Baylor's Homecoming since 1947. It honors ten players from the school's first basketball team, who were killed in a bus accident while traveling to the University of Texas in Austin for a game on January 22, 1927. Just before the team reached Austin, a speeding train struck the side of the bus at a railway crossing in Round Rock, Texas, killing ten of the twenty-one passengers. Each year, Baylor freshmen hear the tragic story at Homecoming and participate in a candlelight remembrance ceremony.

On Saturday night, Nicole and her friends changed clothes after the game and got ready for the party. Around 10:30 p.m., they went to a friend's house, where Nicole had a couple of shots of liquor. By the time they left for the party, Nicole's friends said she was a little "tipsy" but not drunk. When they arrived at the convention center, there was a long line to get inside. Victoria and Brittani didn't want to wait, nor pay a twenty-dollar cover charge, so they decided to return to Nicole's apartment. They promised to come back and get the other girls when the party was over.

Around 2:00 a.m., Brittani and Victoria picked up Nicole, India, and another friend outside the convention center. Victoria noticed that

Nicole had sobered up and she assumed she hadn't been drinking during the party. The five girls returned to Nicole's apartment, and then Brittani drove Victoria and India back to their dorms. Brittani was headed back to Nicole's apartment, where she planned to spend the night, when Nicole called and said she was going to get something to eat with Sam.

After Sam picked Nicole up, he made a right-hand turn on South University Parks Drive, instead of a left-hand turn, which is the way to the myriad fast-food restaurants on the access roads near Interstate 35. Nicole texted one of her friends and told her they were headed to his place. The friend texted her back: "he probably wants to hit," which is a slang term for Sam probably wanting to have sex with her. Nicole replied with a text that said it wasn't going to happen. About thirty minutes later, however, Nicole texted the friend again: "You were right."

Once Nicole was inside Sam's apartment, she told police, he became agitated while talking with his roommate and a friend on the phone and screamed at his dog. She became worried and texted a couple of friends to come get her. No one responded. Nicole told police that she resisted Sam's initial sexual advances. She pulled down her dress as he tried to pull it up and repeatedly told him no. But then Sam grabbed her and forced her onto her stomach, according to Nicole, pushing her head against the wall. "He was using all of his strength to pull up my dress and do stuff to me," Nicole would later testify to a jury. "He had me on my stomach on the bed, and he was on top of me." Nicole told the jury that Sam pulled up her dress, forced her legs open, and then raped her from behind. After Sam was finished, according to Nicole, he told her, "This isn't rape." Then he asked if she was going to call the police.

After the assault, Nicole locked herself in Sam's bathroom. Initially, she blamed herself for what happened. She believed she'd put herself in a vulnerable position. She texted a few friends and asked them to come get her. "I am so stupid," she texted one of them. Eventually, Brittani and another friend picked her up at Sam's apartment.

She climbed into the backseat of the car and told them Sam raped her. They asked Nicole what she wanted to do, and she insisted on going home to sleep.

The next morning, after learning about what happened, Victoria and India went to Nicole's apartment and pounded on the screen door until she woke up and let them inside. Victoria told Nicole that she needed to call her parents and notify the police. A Baylor team chaplain, who had befriended Nicole through Fellowship of Christian Athletes, encouraged her to go to the hospital for a sexual assault exam.

Finally, Nicole decided to call her mother. When Nicole reached her mom, she was at the state fair with Nicole's father and younger brother. The fairgrounds were crowded and Nicole's mother struggled to hear her daughter's soft and shaky voice. Nicole told her mom she had been raped. Nicole's mom looked at her husband and mouthed the words. She didn't want Nicole's little brother to hear what she was saying.

Nicole's friends were waiting in the lobby at Baylor Scott & White Medical Center–Hillcrest when her parents arrived, and they showed them to a waiting room. Nicole walked into the room a few minutes later. "She walked in and just looked like, you know, innocent, little girl," her mother would later testify. "She looked at me, she says, 'Hi, Mom,' and that's when I just broke down. And then she started crying, and I just couldn't let go of her. Couldn't let go of her." Nicole's father stepped out of the room because he didn't want her to see him sobbing.

Hospital officials notified the police of Nicole's alleged rape, and the police contacted Michele Davis, the nurse who conducted her sexual assault exam. Davis documented vaginal redness, bleeding, and other injuries to the labia minora of Nicole's vagina. In Nicole's statement on the SANE sexual assault exam report, she wrote: "He kept trying to take my clothes off and I said no. He forced my face up against the wall, I kept screaming no, he put his private in my back private. He slid my underwear over because he couldn't get them off. He put his hands on my back private (anal area), but he put it (penis) in my front private (vagina)."

Nicole's parents persuaded her to return home with them. Her mother sent an email to Baylor's Judicial Affairs Office informing school officials that Nicole would miss classes because of the assault. Her mother received an email from a judicial affairs officer, who requested that Nicole provide the university with a written statement, which she did.

In Nicole's first week at home, she slept with her mother every night. She didn't want her brother near her and didn't want him to know what happened. She wore long pants and long-sleeved shirts. She told her mom, "I don't want anybody to see my skin." She was easily startled by men—she nearly jumped out of a chair when her grandfather snuck up behind her in a dark den in their house. To stop Nicole from being so anxious, her father announced when he was coming down a hallway, or he called and told her when he was coming home from work. "I would have to say, 'Uh, [Nicole], I'm coming back there,' so I just wouldn't startle [her]," he testified. "I would always say that. I even do that now when she's around just out of habit."

Nicole returned to school after a week at home, and Baylor officials arranged for her to see Dr. Cheryl Wooten, a clinical psychologist in the Baylor Counseling Center. Wooten was familiar with the trauma of sexual assault. She'd attended annual meetings of the International Society for Traumatic Stress Studies, where she collaborated with nationally recognized experts in posttraumatic stress disorder. Wooten studied PTSD in combat veterans and sexual assault victims. "As we all know many veterans return from the battlefield with posttraumatic stress disorder," Wooten later testified. "But we also know that more women develop posttraumatic stress disorder following a sexual assault than do veterans returning from combat."

According to Wooten's studies, combat soldiers are more equipped to cope with traumatic events than an eighteen-year-old freshman because soldiers might have anticipated something bad happening to them at war. "One of the main theories regarding trauma is that part of what causes us to have such adverse reactions to a traumatic event is that typically as human beings we have this belief in what we call the just world hypothesis," Wooten explained.

"We teach little kids that if you do the right thing, good things happen to you; if you do bad things, bad things happen to you. And part of what's so difficult about something like sexual assault and interpersonal violence, if you're eighteen, is that you don't have any thought about the fact that that could happen to you. It's like outside of our normal concept that you could be in an environment that appears to be safe, and then there could be a person there who's not safe but who looks just like everyone else."

Wooten also believes that freshmen on college campuses, like Nicole, are more vulnerable to sexual assault and interpersonal violence than older women because they have less experience in the real world. Freshmen are at the greatest risk because they're still building a social support system and don't know whom they can trust and whom they can't. Conversely, female seniors are at the lowest risk because they know whom they can get in the car with and where they should and shouldn't go. They've experienced a lot more than younger women who might be living on their own for the first time.

Wooten, who has a doctorate in clinical psychology from Wheaton College in Wheaton, Illinois, started working at Baylor as a staff psychologist in 2011. Shortly after Wooten was hired, a female freshman student who said she'd been sexually assaulted came to her office. The woman told Wooten, "I wish I had known. If only I had known that this was a possibility, I would have made different choices."

"I was so mad," Wooten recalled during testimony. "Not at her, but I was like, 'You're right. You need to know. That's only fair.' We have students come in and we tell them about what's gonna happen if they cheat, right? The consequences of that, they need to be aware of that, and the risk of that. But sometimes in the past, schools haven't talked about the risk of sexual assault."

In August 2015, Wooten was treating six female Baylor students who were dealing with posttraumatic stress disorder from sexual assaults. She estimated that 80 percent of women who are sexually assaulted develop PTSD. Nicole was one of the women Wooten was treating. Nicole had eighteen weekly individual sessions with Wooten and also participated in fourteen group sessions. Wooten testified that Nicole was suffering from flashbacks, inability to sleep, feeling unsafe, emotional mood swings, and an inappropriate feeling of guilt and shame.

"There were multiple times that she questions herself and said that she felt she was being stupid and that if she had only done this or only done that, she wouldn't have been in the situation she was in and that she was stupid to trust this person and wished that she could do the whole situation over again," Wooten testified. "Blamed herself for it."

On at least two occasions, Nicole was traumatized when she randomly encountered Sam on campus. When she saw him in the Student Union Building, she frantically called her mother. "I don't know what to do," Nicole told her mom. "I just saw him. Mom, why did he do this to me? Why did he do this to me?" Her mother called Victoria, who found Nicole and calmed her down enough to go to class. Another time, Nicole saw Sam in a Baylor dining hall on a Sunday after church. When she noticed him sitting at a table, she froze and asked her friends to leave with her.

Other times, Nicole said she hid from Sam in stairwells in campus buildings and behind soda fountains. When Nicole and her parents asked Baylor officials to make accommodations so she wouldn't bump into Sam on campus, they moved her—instead of him—out of classes and tutoring sessions they shared. Eventually, Baylor officials did agree to prohibit Sam from eating in certain dining halls to avoid her.

During the Thanksgiving holiday in November 2013, Nicole, her parents, and her brother stayed in a hotel while visiting out-of-town relatives. Her parents noticed that she was staying up all night. Nicole told Wooten that she was suffering from recurring nightmares in which she was being chased by a monster with Sam's eyes.

CHAPTER TWENTY-ONE

INSUFFICIENT EVIDENCE

Waco, Texas
October 20, 2013

Sergeant Stephanie Gibson was the first Waco police officer to meet Nicole at Baylor Scott & White Medical Center–Hillcrest. Immediately, Nicole told Gibson that Sam Ukwuachu sexually assaulted her and she wanted to pursue criminal charges. Nicole told the officer he'd raped her in his apartment in Building 10 at The Grove, a gated community on South University Parks Drive, but she wasn't sure of the apartment number.

Before becoming a patrol officer, Gibson spent six months at the McLennan County Police Academy and she'd had another three or four months of training with the Waco Police Department. She'd worked numerous sexual assault cases involving children during her six-year career, but before meeting Nicole had investigated only one other incident involving an adult victim. After talking with Nicole and her parents, Gibson left the hospital and tried to locate Sam's apartment. Since it was a Sunday, there wasn't a resident manager on duty at The Grove, which consists of ten three-story buildings, as well as a clubhouse, swimming pool, and recreation area. Without anyone to help, Gibson was unable to locate Sam's apartment.

Since Gibson didn't make contact with Sam that day, crime scene technicians weren't able to secure the sheets and blankets from his bed. They weren't able to photograph his apartment or process other evidence, either. In fact, the only evidence police obtained on the day after Nicole's alleged sexual assault was her black dress and under-wear, her written statement, and her rape kit exam from the hospital.

For whatever reason, Gibson never called police dispatch to try to obtain Sam's address or telephone number. Gibson would later say she didn't try because she only had a phonetic spelling of his last name. Gibson might have just as easily called Baylor police to ask for the identity of a football player named Sam or a player whose last name started with *U* to get the correct spelling. She also didn't think to use her cell phone to search Google for a Baylor player with that name, and she didn't contact a police officer who lived at The Grove to see if he was familiar with Sam.

"It's just an unusual name from what I've had," Gibson later testi-fied. "So, um, if we try to run somebody through our dispatch, if we've never dealt with them before, we don't have a locale on them, there's no way for me to find an address."

Detective Manuel Chavez was assigned to handle Nicole's case. He was the same detective who investigated Tevin Elliott when Phoebe accused him of trapping her in her bedroom and poking her with a broomstick. Chavez interviewed Nicole for the first time on Novem-ber 4, 2013, more than two weeks after she reported the alleged assault. After hearing Nicole's allegations, Chavez called Sam and advised him that he was mentioned in an investigation and they needed to talk. Sam said he didn't want to talk to police and referred him to his attorney, George Reul III of Houston.

In a statement provided to police, Reul wrote that Sam and Nicole had previously performed oral sex on each other and had consensual sex on the night of the alleged assault. Reul alleged that Nicole did not "say no or stop or resist in any way" and "she was very vocally into it," according to police records. Sam said the two talked after having sex and then he rolled over to sleep while she texted friends. Sam sent her a text a day or two later and she responded, "Leave me alone." Sam asked her, "What the hell is the problem?" She did not answer. Several days later, according to Reul, one of Sam's coaches told him that Nicole was filing criminal charges against him. "He [Sam] was completely dumb-founded," Reul wrote. "Samuel adamantly denied these allegations from day one. Mr. Samuel Ukwuachu maintains that he and [Nicole] engaged in completely mutually consensual sexual intercourse."

At some point during the investigation, Chavez suggested to Sam that he might want to take a polygraph exam to prove his innocence. Sam said he had nothing to hide and agreed to do it. On January 9, 2014, Stephen Cabler, a polygraph examiner in Houston, administered Sam a lie detector test. The exam consisted of four questions:

"Did [Nicole] ever tell you she did not want to have sex with you?"

"No," Sam answered.

"Did [Nicole] ever tell you to stop your sexual advances towards her?"

"No."

"Did [Nicole] ever physically resist your sexual advances towards her?"

"No."

"Did you have sexual intercourse with [Nicole] without her consent?"

"No."

Cabler, according to his company's website, had conducted polygraph exams in criminal and internal affairs cases for the Harris County Sheriff's Office in Houston for nearly a decade. He is a member of the American Polygraph Association and the Texas Association of Polygraph Examiners. In Cabler's opinion, "there was no deceptive criteria present" during the exam, and Sam was "considered to be truthful as the listed relevant questions were answered."

On January 30, Chavez met with Nicole and told her that Sam passed the polygraph test. Nicole told Chavez "at no time was there implied consent to having sex." Nonetheless, based on Sam's cooperation and the polygraph exam, which is rarely admitted as evidence in a criminal trial under Texas law, Chavez suspended Nicole's case and referred it to the McLennan County District Attorney's Office for grand jury consideration.

"[Chavez] had eight years in social crimes and four hours of training in sexual assaults—in his career," McLennan County assistant district attorney Hilary LaBorde said. "He had literally no idea what he
was doing at all."

LaBorde told us that Chavez later admitted to her that since Nicole
and Sam were both Baylor athletes, he couldn't decide who was telling
the truth. "He didn't understand the medical piece and didn't know
the significance of it," LaBorde said. "He didn't talk to the nurse. He
didn't talk to her counselor. Sam passed a polygraph and he didn't
understand how that could happen."

Waco police weren't the only ones who didn't believe Sam sexually assaulted Nicole. After Nicole emailed a statement to Baylor chief
judicial officer Bethany McCraw shortly after the alleged attack, the
university opened a Title IX investigation.

After Baylor received the Dear Colleague letter from the U.S.
Department of Education's Office for Civil Rights, McCraw was given
the added responsibility of overseeing Title IX investigations and hearings, even though she wasn't technically a Title IX coordinator. In
preparation for her new duties, McCraw took an eight-week, online
course through the National Association of College and University
Attorneys, a Washington, D.C.–based group that educates attorneys
and academic administrators in campus legal issues. The Title IX
course that McCraw completed wasn't solely focused on sexual assault
and interpersonal violence; it also included guidance in gender equity
in athletics, sexual harassment, and other issues.

McCraw received Nicole's Title IX complaint about eight months
after she was certified by the NACUA. As part of her investigation,
she interviewed Nicole and Sam and agreed to speak to one witness
from each side. McCraw interviewed Sam's roommate, Peni Tagive,
who was a former professional rugby player in his native Australia
before enrolling at Baylor and joining the football team in the summer of 2013. Tagive told McCraw he was asleep in their apartment
on the night of the alleged rape and didn't hear Nicole screaming or
fighting back, as she'd told police. Celine Antwi, a member of Baylor's

women's track-and-field team, was also interviewed as Nicole's chosen witness and, according to McCraw's notes, stated "there had been previous penetration in one of the prior meetings between the two and that the complainant was concerned she might get pregnant because a condom had not been used." McCraw also examined multiple text messages between Nicole and Celine, Sam's phone records, and the results of Sam's independent polygraph exam.

After a four-month investigation, McCraw ruled on January 21, 2014, that Nicole's sexual assault allegations couldn't be proved by a "preponderance of evidence." Basically, McCraw didn't believe there was a 51 percent chance that Sam sexually assaulted Nicole. "While sexual intercourse is believed to have occurred, there was not sufficient evidence to prove that it was non-consensual," McCraw wrote in her ruling. "As a result, student conduct charges will not be filed against the accused."

McCraw wrote that she based her ruling on several factors, including the fact that Nicole wasn't forthcoming about her earlier visits to Sam's apartment. "Complainant's initial report of the incident, in my opinion, gave the impression that she did not know this individual well and felt uncomfortable almost immediately when she arrived at the apartment," McCraw wrote in her ruling. "Later evidence obtained showed that she had been over to the accused's apartment at least two other times and only a week before the reported assault, she had spent the night with the accused." McCraw wrote that she also had "special concern" about Nicole not turning over all of her text messages with Celine from the night of the alleged assault. Multiple sources have told us that McCraw did eventually get access to all of the text messages. She questioned Celine about a message she sent that read, "Okay be careful, wrap it up this time," which Celine said was in reference to Nicole and Sam's prior encounter when Nicole was "freaking out because he 'put it in' a couple and he didn't have a condom on." "She was saying how she had to forcefully push him off of her," Celine told McCraw. The report notes that Nicole responded to that text with Celine from the night of the alleged assault. One of them from Nicole read, "I'm not going to do anything" before arriving at Sam's apartment.

McCraw sent her decision to Nicole and Sam in a joint email, which also notified them that the protective order prohibiting Sam from using certain dining halls on campus was being lifted. Already cleared by police and now Baylor's Office of Judicial Affairs, Sam was allowed to return to football activities and begin his preparations for the 2014 season.

McCraw's ruling left Nicole and her parents crestfallen. How could Nicole continue to attend Baylor if she didn't feel safe? She'd already had chance encounters with Sam on campus, and she didn't want to spend the next three years looking over her shoulder. Plus, Nicole's teammates and closest friends weren't the only ones who were aware of the alleged sexual assault anymore. Rumors of a football player allegedly raping a women's soccer player had made their way around the close-knit campus. Making matters worse, Baylor women's soccer coach Chuck Codd informed Nicole that he was reducing her athletics scholarship for the 2014–15 season. She'd struggled to recover from the knee injury that sidelined her the previous fall, and she admittedly wasn't playing well. It didn't help that she was reliving the alleged assault in weekly therapy sessions and couldn't focus on her sport and studies.

"She wasn't playing well and she's a black cloud," LaBorde told us. "They all have to deal with her emotional problems. What would be a lot easier? Not having her there."

When LaBorde received Nicole's case file from Waco police in March 2014, she was surprised by what she read. When LaBorde studied her sexual assault exam, she saw injuries that were consistent with a violent rape. LaBorde also noted that Nicole immediately reported the assault to friends and never changed her story.

"I thought it arrived with enough evidence," LaBorde told us. "It arrived with injuries on her SANE exam, and those happen in like five to ten percent of adult rapes because that part of the body is meant to deal with that kind of contact. It was a violent rape and from day one everyone knew that. I have no idea why he wasn't arrested."

LaBorde requested an interview with Nicole and her parents. She quickly realized the tragic toll the alleged assault had taken on Nicole's family. Nicole was being forced to leave Baylor for another school— the same young woman who left home with big dreams only months earlier was now returning with her life completely shattered.

Over the next few months, LaBorde, Assistant District Attorney Robert Moody, and their investigators took a closer look at Nicole's case. They requested a copy of Baylor's Title IX investigation, and LaBorde immediately recognized it was flawed. LaBorde discovered that McCraw reached her decision without examining Nicole's sexual assault exam, without talking to the friends who picked her up from Sam's apartment and drove her to the hospital, and without talking to her parents.

"[The investigation] was terrible," LaBorde said. "From the moment [Nicole] opens her mouth, it's 'How can I destroy what she's saying? I don't like that she's drinking. I don't like that she's at his house. I don't like that she's been over there. How can I catch her in a lie?' That's what I felt was the focus from the moment it began."

What bothered LaBorde the most, however, was that McCraw didn't interview Dr. Cheryl Wooten, the psychologist who was treating Nicole for posttraumatic stress disorder at the Baylor Counseling Center. McCraw would later say she didn't speak with Wooten because Baylor officials didn't like to pry into student counseling issues, especially those that might involve mental health problems.

"[McCraw] has a degree in educational psychology," LaBorde told us. "That would make me think that she should have been able to get her counselor in the office and talk with her about all the problems [Nicole] was having as a result of what occurred. Anyone with that kind of education should have realized that you don't develop PTSD from a lie; you develop PTSD from a traumatic event."

During the Title IX investigation, Nicole's mother informed McCraw that another Baylor female student-athlete told Nicole that Sam was dismissed from Boise State University due to violence against

a female student. McCraw wrote in her report that she contacted Boise
State's dean of students and that Baylor police chief Jim Doak reached
out to Boise State police and neither had records of an accusation of
assault. When Sam transferred, Baylor officials had relied on what
Boise State director of compliance Jenny Bellomy told them: Boise
State hadn't disciplined him while he was enrolled, he left in good
standing, and was free to transfer to another institution. But LaBorde
and Moody believed there must have been another reason for Sam
leaving and coaches letting him go so easily. "No one ever thought that
a freshman All-American was kicked off for being late for practice,"
LaBorde said. "It had to be pretty significant."

Abdon Rodriguez, one of the investigators in the district attorney's office, reached out to Boise State officials, who told him they
had no record of discipline issues involving Sam. But someone in the
Boise State athletics department suggested Rodriguez subpoena Sam's
health and student records. The Ada County Prosecutor's Office in
Boise helped facilitate the request, and Boise State officials turned
over a 238-page file that was extremely revealing. In fact, the records
showed Sam was suffering from serious psychological problems,
including suicidal thoughts, and had previously checked himself into
a mental health facility. A Boise State athletics director also suspected
Sam of physically and mentally abusing his live-in girlfriend.

The records showed that Boise State officials tolerated Sam's problems for a while, but eventually cut him loose once he became too
unpredictable. On April 8, 2013, Sam met with Boise State football
coach Chris Petersen and assistant athletics director for sports medicine Marc Paul after he tested positive for Spice, a form of synthetic
marijuana. According to the records, Sam told Petersen and Paul
that he was smoking Spice to cope with anxiety, which was caused
by his lifelong stuttering problem. The records showed Sam was also
being treated with Zoloft, an antidepressant, and Risperidone, an anti-
psychotic medication. Four days after the meeting, Sam voluntarily
checked himself into the Intermountain Hospital, a psychiatric and
substance abuse treatment center in Boise, after experiencing suicidal

thoughts. According to Paul's handwritten notes, Sam was with his girlfriend at the time and talked about hanging himself. Sam spent three days at the facility.

Paul met with Sam's girlfriend, Beth*, a Boise State female student-athlete, on April 25 to discuss their relationship. She told Paul they'd been in an argument before his latest episode, but believed the situation was improving. Paul wrote in his notes that Beth "wishes he would retake anger management classes," and added that their relationship was scary for a number of reasons. "We know there [are] issues [including] verbal abuse," Paul wrote. "She acknowledged arguments & name calling/yelling, etc., but refused to elaborate further. When asked if [she] would admit if physical violence occurs, stated '[probably] not' & quickly added 'but he's much better now & has it under control.'" At the bottom of his notes, Paul wrote: "NOT Healthy Relationship!"

On May 2, 2013, Sam and his girlfriend argued again after she accidentally spilled a glass of Kool-Aid. He left their apartment and said he was going to kill himself. Sam called Paul later that night and said he wasn't suicidal, but admitted he and Beth shouldn't be together "right now." The next day, Boise State medical director Vincent Serio evaluated Sam and diagnosed him with "major depressive disorder, recurrent, moderate," according to the records.

Two days later, Sam's roommate, Broncos defensive lineman Elliot Hoyte, called a Boise State coach and said Sam was drinking and talking about suicide. After Sam cut his wrist as a result of having punched a window, Paul contacted Boise police and asked them to go to his apartment. Sam told a police officer that he was probably going to be kicked off the team and have to return to Texas. On May 6, Petersen dismissed Sam from the team and called Baylor coach Art Briles on his behalf.

On May 20, 2013, only sixteen days after Sam violently punched a window and cut his wrist, he visited Baylor's campus and verbally

---

* Pseudonym

committed to play for the Bears. Briles would later say that Petersen told him only that Sam was homesick and depressed. But Petersen said in a statement that he "thoroughly apprised Coach Briles of the circumstances surrounding Sam's disciplinary record and dismissal."

In another statement, Briles said: "I know and respect Coach Petersen and he would never recommend a student-athlete to Baylor that he didn't believe in. In our discussion, he did not disclose that there had been violence toward women, but he did tell me of a rocky relationship with his girlfriend which contributed to his depression. The only disciplinary action I was aware of were team-related issues, insubordination of coaches, and missing practice."

Regardless of which coach was telling the truth, Baylor officials now agree that the university should have examined Sam's background more closely before so readily accepting him as a transfer student.

"I think they had a practice of not doing much vetting," LaBorde said. "They get this one page that asks, 'Can you re-enroll?' They think they're golden and move on. They might not even have any natural curiosity about it. They just want to know if he can play."

Armed with the rape exam and damning documents from Boise State, LaBorde presented Sam's case to a McLennan County grand jury on June 25, 2014. He was indicted on two felony counts of sexual assault for raping Nicole. He was arrested and released on $30,000 bond. The indictment had been sealed and LaBorde secured a gag order, which prevented either side from talking to media. LaBorde struggled with the impact of that decision, but said she was concerned about Sam's attorney publicizing the polygraph test results, which are not admissible as evidence in a trial but could taint any potential jury pool. News of Sam's arrest remained quiet and his criminal charges weren't reported until August 5, 2015—only twelve days before the start of his criminal trial.

CHAPTER TWENTY-TWO

"SHAME ON BAYLOR"

McLennan County Courthouse, Waco, Texas
August 18, 2015

In June 2015, about two months before Sam Ukwuachu's trial, Baylor defensive coordinator Phil Bennett spoke at a luncheon for the Baylor Sports Network in Fort Worth, where he told people in attendance that he expected Sam to make his long-anticipated debut that coming season. In fairness, Bennett might have thought he had every reason to believe Sam would be back on the field: Sam had pleaded not guilty to felony charges of raping Nicole; Waco police had previously suspended the criminal case against him without an arrest; and Baylor's Title IX investigation didn't find enough evidence to even present the case to an adjudicator.

In opening statements at the start of Sam's criminal trial at McLennan County Courthouse on August 18, 2015, Assistant District Attorney Robert Moody told jurors that Nicole immediately made an outcry for help. "She immediately goes to the bathroom, locks herself in the bathroom, and begins texting and calling friends for help to get her out of there. She immediately says she's been raped."

Sam's new defense attorney, Jonathan Sibley of Waco, was a seventh-generation Texan who had deep connections to Baylor. His grandfather, Jack Patterson, was the school's former track coach and athletics director (he hired legendary football coach Grant Teaff), and his father, David Sibley, was a Baylor basketball captain and onetime

Waco mayor and Texas state senator. Sibley told jurors that Nicole wasn't even the victim in the case. She made false allegations of rape, Sibley insisted, after she and Sam had consensual sex. "You heard that the state used the word *victim* several times, and I think the facts in this case are gonna show that the victim in this case is sitting next to me in that chair, and he'll be there all week," Sibley said.

In fact, Sibley told jurors Nicole's allegations of rape were a "classic case of buyer's remorse."

"I really didn't mean to go that far. I didn't mean for this to happen. He must have raped me," Sibley said. "And then it ballooned and the snowball is rolling down the hill."

Heading into Sam's trial, Assistant District Attorney Hilary LaBorde wasn't sure how Nicole would react to having to testify. During their initial interviews and preparations for trial, Nicole wept each time she had to recall details of the alleged assault. She took the stand at the end of the first day, after her friend Brittani had testified about what happened the night she picked her up from Sam's apartment, and after her mother and therapist described her behavior immediately after the assault and during her recovery.

After providing jurors a blow-by-blow account of what led to her ending up in Sam's bedroom in the early morning hours of October 20, 2013, Nicole told them his flirting started off in a playful way. "He kind of was stopping if I said stop," she testified. "Then it got to the point where he wasn't stopping. He was using all of his strength to pull up my dress and try to do stuff to me." She described Sam forcing her onto her stomach on his bed, pushing her head into the wall, and then hitting her head on the desk as he violated her. Nicole also testified she believed Sam planned to assault her because she noticed a condom sitting on the desk while he was having sex with her.

"Do you think he should have realized when he had to force you into that position, and your head is hitting the desk every time he's doing something, that this was not something that you wanted to do?" LaBorde asked her.

"Yes," Nicole answered.

"How else do you think the defendant knew this was not something you wanted to do?"

"Because I was screaming, stop and no."

"Were you trying to keep your clothes on?"

"Yes."

"Did you try and keep him from getting on top of you?"

"Yes."

"Did you try and keep your legs together?"

"Yes."

"Was your private area hurt?"

"Oh, yes. Yes. I lost my virginity to him."

During Nicole's testimony, she described what it was like seeing Sam on campus in the weeks and months after the assault, hiding in stairwells in buildings on campus, behind soda fountains, and frantically calling her mother and friends for help when she encountered him. As part of her therapy, she wrote Sam three or four letters but never sent them.

"Every time that I saw him, my heart would just sink," she said. "And it was just like this overpowering feeling that it was like he had control again. Even after the rape, he still had control every time I saw him."

Sibley's cross examination of Nicole focused on why she went to Sam's apartment at 2:15 in the morning if she knew he was romantically interested in her. Sibley also questioned why she didn't immediately reveal to police investigators that she was there on two previous occasions, including one visit in which she spent the night.

"You were aware that he had an interest in you physically?" Sibley asked her.

"Yes," Nicole answered.

"And knowing that he had an interest in you physically, you still chose to have him come pick you up at 2:15 in the morning after Homecoming, correct?"

"Yes."

"After you had been drinking?"

"Yes."

Sibley also questioned why Nicole told Michele Davis, the nurse who administered her sexual assault exam, that she wasn't scared or frightened during the attack. She'd also told Davis that she didn't experience any pain while being raped, according to the SANE report. Davis documented redness and bleeding in Nicole's vagina the day after the alleged rape and decided not to use an invasive speculum to examine her genitalia because she feared it would be too painful. Sibley also wondered why there weren't any bruises or scratches on her body if she fought back, as she'd told Davis and the police.

"A second ago, you said that you did experience pain during the sexual assault," Sibley said. "Why did you tell the nurse that you did not experience pain?"

"I don't remember specifically," Nicole answered.

Once the prosecution rested, Sibley opened Sam's defense by re-calling Nicole to the stand. Having a victim testify a second time rarely happens in criminal trials. Sibley asked her to go to a whiteboard and draw a diagram of Sam's apartment. As Nicole drew the living room, kitchen, bedroom, and bathroom, she talked about how she sat on his bed and played with his dog, until Sam took the puppy and put it in his roommate's room. Then she described how he lay next to her on the bed, and then pulled her over on her stomach and raped her.

"Is that when you started screaming or did you scream prior to that?" Sibley asked.

"I started screaming once he was on top of me, because at one point . . . he was just laying behind me," she answered. "And then it turned into he pulling me back here and his body was on top of me. At that point was when I started screaming."

"And were you screaming loudly?"

"Yes."

"Okay, if Peni had been in his room do you think he would have been able to hear you?" Sibley asked her, referring to Sam's roommate, Peni Tagive.

"Yes, the rooms are not that far apart. I think he would have been able to."

"Do you believe it would have been loud enough where even if somebody was asleep they could have woken up?"

"Yes."

Tagive previously told police and Baylor officials that he was asleep in his bedroom when Nicole was allegedly raped. Nicole repeatedly told investigators that she didn't believe Tagive was there, and Sam couldn't recall if he saw his roommate in bed when he put their dog in his room. For whatever reason, according to Sam, Tagive didn't inform him that he was there until several weeks after the alleged assault. Even when Sam told Tagive that he'd had sex with Nicole on the morning after the incident, Tagive didn't mention that he'd been in his bedroom.

The confusion and delay raised red flags with the prosecution, so Moody scheduled an interview with Tagive. But Tagive failed to show up and informed Moody he didn't want to talk because Sam told him not to cooperate. Moody obtained a subpoena that required Tagive to testify to a grand jury, but he didn't show again. Moody secured a writ of attachment and sheriff's deputies found Tagive and escorted him to grand jury proceedings. Tagive was wearing an ankle monitor to ensure he would appear at Sam's trial.

According to LaBorde, Tagive's cell phone records indicated he was on the other side of Waco making phone calls at the time he claimed he was sleeping. (The prosecution mistakenly believed the cell phone records were recorded in Central Time, but they were actually documented in Universal Time. LaBorde said even with the differences, the phone records still contradicted Tagive's story.)

"He never told the same version about when he got picked up and when he got dropped off," LaBorde said to us. "His phone records didn't line up with anything he told. He waited six weeks to tell Baylor that he was there. If your roommate has been accused of rape and you slept through it because she can't be telling the truth about screaming no, like she's saying, if you know that's not true, why do you not want to tell the people who are prosecuting him? It just didn't make any sense."

Morgan Reed, a Baylor volleyball player, testified she picked Tagive up at the Waco Convention Center around 12:30 that morning, after he called her asking for a ride. They went through the drive-thru at Whataburger to get him something to eat, and then they let Sam's dog use the restroom outside his apartment before she left between 1:00 and 1:30 a.m., according to her testimony.

Tagive told jurors he went to bed and then was awakened by the sound of the front door opening. Tagive testified he heard Sam's voice and a woman's voice enter the apartment and went back to sleep. He said he didn't hear Nicole screaming the rest of the night. When Moody asked him if he thought he'd be able to hear a woman screaming into a pillow, he said he wasn't sure. When Moody switched up the question and asked if he would have heard a woman screaming in pleasure—as Ukwuachu had said she was "vocally into it"—Tagive said yes.

Before Baylor chief judicial officer Bethany McCraw testified, the prosecution requested a gatekeeping hearing with the judge because Sibley was trying to introduce her as an expert witness. After reading McCraw's Title IX report, LaBorde wasn't convinced she was even qualified to investigate a sexual assault, let alone be an expert on the subject. In a hearing, LaBorde told Judge Matt Johnson the prosecution was going to challenge "her being an educated or qualified investigator in any way whatsoever. She has a master's in education. We challenge her qualifications. We challenge the fit between her qualifications as to what her job has been, which was to do these Title IX investigations. I think if you hear the basis of her investigation and how limited it was, I think any findings that she had are flawed."

During the hearing, which was not in front of the jury, McCraw testified that her office investigated thirteen alleged sexual assaults in the 2013–14 academic year. In fifteen years of working in Baylor's Judicial Affairs Office, McCraw said she could recall only one instance in which a student was expelled for sexual assault.

"You have never been to any kind of law enforcement investigation school or anything put on by law enforcement?" LaBorde asked her.

"No," McCraw answered.

"You did not have a copy of the SANE report in this case, is that right?"

"That's correct, yeah."

"You do not have Mr. Tagive's cell phone records, is that correct?"

"No, I do not."

"You did not talk to Cheryl Wooten about any of [Nicole's] issues in therapy?"

"They can't release that information, so . . ."

"Can you ask for a release?"

"From [Nicole]?" McCraw asked. "Yes, I could. Yes."

Later, LaBorde asked McCraw if Baylor had requested and received any of Sam's medical or student records from Boise State University.

"Are you aware that the athletic department had records of violence against a woman?" LaBorde asked her.

"Uh, no," McCraw answered.

"So that would, again, not have been something that you considered in your investigation."

"Right, I had no knowledge of that."

"Were you aware that the defendant was ordered to go through anger management through the athletic department at Boise State because of his relationship with his girlfriend?"

"No, because we didn't have the records sent to us," McCraw admitted.

Johnson ruled McCraw could testify, but not as an expert. She was prohibited from testifying about her investigation, its findings, and the fact that Sam had passed an independent polygraph examination. However, she would be allowed to talk about her interview with Nicole on December 12, 2013.

During McCraw's testimony at court, Sibley asked her: "Do you remember her telling you that she had kissed Samuel Ukwuachu on the first time they went over to [his] apartment?"

"Yes, I do recall her telling me that they had kissed," McCraw answered.

"Do you also remember her telling you that Sam had tried to have oral sex with her and she refused?"

"I don't remember her saying the last part that you just said, that she refused. I just remember her saying from these notes on the twelfth that they had oral sex."

Moody and LaBorde immediately jumped from their chairs and objected. "We would ask that it be struck, as it's not true, and it's not part of her notes," LaBorde insisted.

"And the jury be asked to disregard that," Moody added.

Johnson instructed jurors to disregard McCraw's statement that Nicole had oral sex with Sam. Sibley asked her again: "When [Nicole's] talking about the first time that she's over there, did she tell you that the first time he tried to have oral sex with her?"

"I remember her telling me he tried to have oral sex," McCraw answered.

During cross-examination, LaBorde attempted to allow McCraw to clarify her remarks for the jury since Nicole had never said she and Sam had oral sex.

"Ma'am, I'm confused," LaBorde said. "Why did you just testify that they had oral sex if she never told you that?"

"I'm sorry," McCraw said. "I don't recall saying that."

"I recall quite clearly you just saying they had oral sex. Please show me in your notes with your conversation with [Nicole] where she ever said such a thing."

"She said, 'He tried to have oral sex.'"

"Ma'am, they had oral sex; he tried to have oral sex. Are those the same?"

"No, they're not," McCraw admitted.

"So when you said that earlier, you were completely, absolutely, utterly wrong?"

"Yeah, I apologize," McCraw said. "I'm certainly not trying to say anything that's not truthful."

"And you're not in here trying to trash [Nicole], are you?"

"Absolutely not," McCraw insisted.

When McCraw was finished with her testimony, LaBorde followed her into the hallway outside the courtroom and confronted her about what she'd said on the stand.

"I was livid after that," LaBorde told us. "She was putting words in her [Nicole's] mouth, and I felt like she did it deliberately. She was like, 'Oh, right, I misspoke.' That's a pretty big thing to misspeak about it, and we had just talked in chambers about what she was going to be able to testify about, which was one sentence, and she screwed it up. She screwed it up to make her [Nicole] look bad."

In the hallway, LaBorde recalled telling McCraw: "You know, you really ought to be ashamed of yourself for doing that— and for the whole thing, too. For not taking her seriously and not doing a decent investigation, to where [Nicole] had to be on campus with her rapist and she ended up not being able to stay. You cost [Nicole] her Baylor dream and he got to keep his. I don't know how you can live with that. You should be ashamed."

LaBorde said McCraw only looked at her in disbelief and didn't say a word before hurrying out the door. During closing arguments, Moody told the jury McCraw didn't "know her head from a hole in the ground" and that it was "disgusting that she was involved in this case."

"Shame on Baylor," Moody said.

"I can't say that she was untrained," LaBorde told us. "I can just say that she seemed determined to do a bad job."

McCraw has never agreed to be interviewed by the media. She is still employed at Baylor, and the university declined to answer any questions pertaining to what she did or did not do in relation to any sexual assault case.

Karla Leeper worked with McCraw at Baylor for more than two decades before leaving for a position at Augusta University in Augusta, Georgia, in April 2014. Leeper described McCraw as someone who was more than qualified to work in student conduct.

"She was very by-the-book and wasn't the kind of person who

would overlook conduct violations because of who a student was or the role they had, whether it was an athlete or student body officer or something like that," Leeper told us. "That wasn't Bethany. I found her to be very conscientious and very professional. The materials that we received from her office were very well done." Another source with Baylor told us that McCraw wasn't one to give athletes any favors, and was among those concerned that the athletic department was dodging the rules when it came to student conduct issues and student-athletes.

But Leeper said investigating Title IX cases involving allegations of sexual assault was entirely new ground for McCraw. It was something she'd never been asked to do before Baylor received the Dear Colleague letter in 2011.

"I perceived her as being very objective and very fair," Leeper said. "But I think this was a very different kind of area of student conduct, and I don't believe she was adequately trained. I think everything that made her effective in the other areas of student conduct created challenges in this area." She followed rigid rules, another source said, which was good in some areas, but not when it came to the complex and sensitive issues involved in Title IX cases.

CHAPTER TWENTY-THREE

REAL MEN DON'T RAPE

McLennan County Courthouse, Waco, Texas
August 20, 2015

Sam Ukwuachu's version of what happened in his bedroom in the early morning hours of Sunday, October 20, 2013, remained pretty consistent throughout the investigation. Sam said he and Nicole had consensual sex after he picked her up from her apartment. He said she'd spent the night with him one other time, six days earlier, and that they'd had oral sex during an even earlier visit.

But when Sam took the witness stand on the last day of his trial on August 20, 2015, his story changed dramatically, according to prosecutors. He told the jury Nicole spent the night with him two previous times, and he'd kissed her breasts and penetrated her vagina with his fingers. He also said she'd masturbated his penis. On the night of the alleged rape, Sam testified, they kissed and touched each other before having consensual sex.

"You heard [Nicole] accuse you of sexual assault," Sam's attorney, Jonathan Sibley, said. "Did you sexually assault [Nicole]?"

"Absolutely not."

"Did you have consensual sex with [Nicole]?"

"Yes, sir, I did."

"Had you had prior sexual relations with [Nicole]?"

"Yes, sir, I did."

"On the night that she's accusing you, did she consent and have sex with you voluntarily?"

"Yes, sir, she did."

Assistant District Attorney Robert Moody knew Sam's story didn't add up. The prosecution recovered text messages between Nicole and Sam from the iCloud account on her cell phone. On October 14, 2013, a few days after Nicole's first visit to his apartment, Sam texted her the following: "Wyd? [What are you doing?]" She replied: "Just finished working out, wbu [what about you]?" Sam texted that he was "chillin" and suggested, "we got unfinished business . . . haha." Later, Nicole replied: "I don't think we need [to] finish any 'business' . . . lol . . . lets just chill." Nicole went to his apartment later that day to study and ended up spending the night.

The next morning, Sam texted Nicole again: "Goodmorning. Sorry if I made you late or tired this morning. see ya lataz." She responded: "U didn't. I'm always tired lol. The grind never ends." Sam told her: "I told you all we would do was chill . . . lol. . . silly willy walnut head." She replied: "Lol . . . you tried to do more!"

Based on those text messages and Nicole's testimony, the prosecution believed Sam tried to have oral sex with her during the previous visit and nothing more happened. But now Sam was testifying that she'd masturbated his penis and he'd kissed her breasts and fingered her vagina.

First, Moody asked Sam about a photograph he'd posted on his Instagram account. It was a photo of a woman covering her face with her arms. The words REAL MEN DON'T RAPE were written on her forearms. At the bottom of the photo were the words I'M NO MAN, BABY.

"My friend from Boise posted that picture on his Instagram and I just reposted it," Sam said. "I didn't think anything of it. It was a joke. He thought it was a joke. . . . That's not the way I feel about it."

Moody's line of questioning with Sam over why he said the two had oral sex, when Nicole said they'd only kissed, turned into a battle of semantics when Sam said, "I thought oral was everything but penetration by the penis and vagina." Moody responded, "What does the word *oral* mean? Not in relation to sex, what does the word *oral* mean?"

"I don't know, sir."

"You have a college degree and you don't know what the word *oral* means?"

"It's my understanding that the word *oral* meant anything but actual sex, sir." Sam said he thought that sucking on Nicole's breast constituted oral sex.

Sam told jurors that on the night of the alleged rape, he and Nicole had sexual intercourse in the missionary position, with him on top and them lying face-to-face on his bed. Nicole testified that he'd forced her on her stomach, held her head against the wall, and penetrated her from behind. Then Moody referenced her screaming.

"Sir, she never screamed," Sam responded. "I would never be on a woman if she was screaming, sir. I would never do that. I have four sisters. I respect women, sir."

"You respect women?" Moody asked him.

"Yes, sir," Sam answered.

Much like in the criminal trial against Baylor football player Tevin Elliott more than a year earlier, in which he was accused of raping Jasmin Hernandez, Sam had opened the door for prosecutors to introduce evidence he'd abused women in the past.

LaBorde told us, "I think it showed not only that [Sam] was a liar, it also let us bring another victim in and another time that he used violence against a woman. It showed the jury he is the kind of person who will lose his mind and do something violent."

LaBorde knew she had documents from Boise State that suggested Sam had a tempestuous relationship with his live-in girlfriend, Beth. Beth confirmed to Boise State officials that she and Sam argued, but she wouldn't admit he physically assaulted her. Still, Boise State assistant athletics director Marc Paul suspected that was indeed the case. Nicole's mother figured out Beth's identity by searching the rosters of women's sports teams on Boise State's website.

When Moody contacted Beth about her relationship with Sam, she was unwilling to participate in his prosecution and wouldn't come to Waco. Moody obtained a subpoena from Judge Matt Johnson, and a judge in Boise, Idaho, signed off on it. Beth flew to Dallas the day before Sam testified, and she was waiting outside the courtroom as he testified.

"You said you respect women," Moody said.

"Yes, sir," Sam answered.

"You ever hit a woman before?"

"Never, sir."

"So you never hit [Beth] up at Boise State?"

"Absolutely not," Sam insisted. "I love [Beth], sir."

"Did you have to go to anger management at Boise State?" Moody asked.

"Yes, sir, I did."

"And that was following beating her, wasn't it?"

"No, sir, it was not."

"She is here to testify, so she is gonna come testify in here. Do you want to be truthful to this jury?"

"Yes, sir. I'm being truthful."

"Have you ever struck [Beth]?"

"Absolutely not."

But Beth testified that before they moved in together, Sam punched her in the head more than once and choked her with one hand during an argument. She said Sam's roommate, football player Elliot Hoyte, broke up the altercation. She didn't call the police, didn't tell Boise State officials, and didn't take photographs of the bruises on her head. She also testified that she'd hit Sam in the face during another incident when they were living together. Another time, she kicked in the door of his bedroom and he broke her laptop computer in anger. Beth said she had consensual sex with Sam and he never forced himself on her. She also testified she'd suffered vaginal bleeding and having sex with Sam was sometimes painful because of the size of his penis. She admitted they had an "unhealthy relationship."

"You did not want to come?" LaBorde asked her.

"I did not want to come," Beth answered.

"But you realize that there are records of things you have said to people in the athletic department about your relationship with the defendant?"

"Yes."

"Did the defendant ever hit you?"

"Yes."

"Did that happen one time or more than one time?"

"I only consider it a one-time thing, so just that once."

"Did he ever keep you from leaving the apartment when you wanted to leave?"

"Yes."

"Did he put both of his hands around your neck and squeeze?"

"Just one hand."

"Did that keep you from breathing?"

"Um, it was a very brief moment."

"Would you say that he has a problem with his anger, the defendant?"

"Yes."

"Did he go to anger management?"

"Yes."

Beth told the jury that she'd grown up in an abusive home and witnessed her father striking her mother. "I know what's right and wrong," she said. After Beth testified, according to LaBorde, Sam's parents, Roseline and Felix Ukwuachu, confronted her in the hallway. They wanted to know why she'd said bad things about their son. She fled to the front lawn outside the courthouse.

"In the end, like most people, she wasn't going to lie about it," LaBorde told us. "But she did not want to come and talk about it. I think it weighed really heavily on her that she was some part of getting him in trouble. I think she loved him at one point. She told us whatever happened to her mom growing up was much worse than what happened to her. She kind of accepted the violence as part of life and it wasn't nearly as bad as what she'd grown up with."

The jury deliberated for more than five hours before finding Sam guilty of one felony count of sexually assaulting Nicole (the state had waived the second count). During punishment phase the next day, Baylor director of sports ministries Wes Yeary testified that he'd worked closely with Sam the past two years. Sam attended a Fellowship of Christian Athletes mission trip to Zambia, where he worked with orphans. Sam attended church with Yeary and his family and had been to their home several times.

"Would you still be comfortable with him being around your children?" Sibley asked him.

"Yes," Yeary answered.

"Even knowing that he's been found guilty, you wouldn't feel threatened by him at this point at all?"

"No, not at all."

At that point, Nicole left the courtroom. She was upset because she felt like she had a close relationship with Yeary as well. She attended his wedding and fiftieth birthday party. She worked with FCA at homeless shelters and juvenile centers and attended a winter retreat.

"She had to leave," LaBorde told us. "She had not cried in court all week, and then seeing that he was there for Sam was terrible. That's the one thing that brought her to tears."

What made it worse for Nicole was she had shared her darkest secret with Yeary. When Nicole returned to Baylor about a week after the alleged attack, Yeary was the first person she told. Yeary told her that he would have picked her up from Sam's apartment if she'd called him that night.

"Do you recall what you told her?" LaBorde asked Yeary.

"I listened to her," Yeary answered. "I just remember listening to her and telling her I cared about her and wanted to help in any way."

Near the end of Yeary's testimony, LaBorde asked him: "How many students have told you they were raped?"

"This is the only one ever," Yeary said.

"I was appalled," LaBorde said. "I think she really looked at him like a chaplain and a spiritual advisor. For whatever reason, I don't know if he didn't believe her, but he took Sam under his wing and it appeared very orchestrated."

In fall 2013, a woman would report telling "Baylor's football chaplain" about having been gang raped by football players, according to a 2017 lawsuit. A suit filed in 2016 would name Yeary as one of the people another woman said she told about being physically assaulted by her football-player boyfriend. Yeary never responded to requests for an interview. On March 7, 2017, Baylor officials announced that Yeary was leaving the school after nine years of employment because of a "restructuring of positions."

As for Sam, even though he was facing a possible prison sentence of two to twenty years, under Texas law the jury was allowed to recommend that his punishment be served through probation.

The jury sentenced him to eight years in prison, but recommended the sentence be probated. Johnson sentenced him to ten years of probation and 180 days in the McLennan County Jail, which was the maximum incarceration allowed under Texas law when a jury recommends probation. Johnson also ordered Sam to complete four hundred hours of community service and register as a sex offender. Sam was released from jail in October 2015 on a $100,000 appeal bond. Baylor officials reached an undisclosed financial settlement with Nicole in December 2015, and no Title IX lawsuit was ever filed.

On March 22, 2017, a three-judge panel from a Texas court of appeals overturned Ukwuachu's conviction and granted him a new trial. The judges determined that the trial judge should have allowed into evidence the entire series of text messages Nicole exchanged with a friend before she went to Sam's apartment on the night of the alleged assault. McLennan County district attorney Abel Reyna appealed the ruling to the Texas Court of Criminal Appeals. If Ukwuachu receives a new trial and is convicted a second time, a different jury could sentence him to twenty years in prison.

Sam declined to be interviewed for this book, but he did send us several emails, many of which were titled "TRUTH WILL SET YOU FREE." They included references to court testimony, Tagive's phone records, and an affidavit from a forensic expert, who examined Tagive's phone records. "Here are all the important facts regarding my appeal and how I will win my case and get justice in my case," Ukwuachu wrote in an email. "I am innocent. You can write whatever you want about Baylor. . . . I have informed you about this information and have proven that she lied about 'screaming' because she didn't know my roommate was home. She lied on me but my case is NOT over yet."

A former Baylor assistant coach we spoke to said he still doesn't believe Sam is guilty, but rather thinks that he was the victim of a vengeful woman and overzealous prosecutor. And he defended the football team's actions, implying that they were hamstrung in what to do with Sam once he was accused of rape. The Title IX office cleared Sam in January 2014, yet he was still not playing that fall while his criminal case was ongoing, and coaches were ordered by the university not to talk about it. If there was anything he could change about how Sam was handled, he said it would have been in public relations.

"As soon as they thought that Sam could be convicted, they should have hired a crisis team immediately to get in front of it," he said. "I think the program got way too big too fast, and I just think that nobody caught up with the Alabamas of the world, the Auburns of the world, the Florida States, who know how to deal with crisis media situations."

CHAPTER TWENTY-FOUR

THE OUTSIDE INVESTIGATION

Waco, Texas
August 28, 2015

There were many parties to Baylor's sexual assault scandal. The women. The accused students and student-athletes. The coaches. The administrators. The regents. The police and prosecutors. The alumni. And they would disagree, distrust, and discount each other's stories—and likely still do. But they have one point of consensus: The conviction of Sam Ukwuachu was the beginning of the end.

In January 2014, news of Tevin Elliott's conviction seemed confined to Waco media, and barely was even mentioned on Twitter and other social media. Even within the Baylor community, the case didn't seem to raise many eyebrows. Elliott was suspended and dismissed shortly after his arrest, and there was no internal Title IX investigation that involved reaching out to all of the women. There was a view, one regent told us, that while Tevin's behavior itself seemed to be a pattern, it didn't point to a larger problem within the football program. He was described as a "predator" and one "really bad guy." But when Ukwuachu popped up more than a year later, "That's when people said, 'Uh oh. How deep is this?'"

Ukwuachu's conviction made national news—networks such as CNN, ESPN, and others broadcast stories. It was all over social media, in large part due to an August 20, 2015, story written by Jessica Luther and Dan Solomon in the newsmagazine *Texas Monthly*.

Its story, "Silence at Baylor," took the university, law enforcement, and even Waco media to task for what seemed to be a purposeful silencing of Ukwuachu's alleged crimes even though it was all splayed out on online fan boards.

It took eight months for Ukwuachu to be indicted, but that indictment *also* went unreported for more than a year. That's significant when you consider that Waco is a city with a population smaller than 130,000, and the man accused of felony sexual assault is a football player for one of the nation's top programs. Local sports media seemed curiously incurious about Ukwuachu's suspension for a violation of team rules, though rumors certainly indicated that some people on the school's campus knew which team rule Ukwuachu violated.

The article publicized Ukwuachu's violent past at Boise State and questioned what Baylor coaches knew. It drew attention to what were characterized as shortcomings in Baylor's own internal investigation that found him not responsible, and the school's treatment of the female soccer player, noting she lost some of her scholarship and transferred to another university. The story led with a description of the Baylor Sports Network luncheon in June 2015, at which defensive coordinator Phil Bennett told the crowd that he expected Ukwuachu to take the field that season. The story ended with a quote from Coach Art Briles taken from the *Waco Tribune-Herald* prior to the conviction: "I like the way we've handled it as a university, an athletic department, and a football program."

But even as the case went to trial, Baylor's senior leadership knew they might have a major problem on their hands. "We had not found Ukwuachu responsible from our system, and we were aware that if the trial—the verdict—went and found him guilty, that was going to pose a problem of explaining our situation," said Baylor's senior vice president for operations, Reagan Ramsower.

Baylor's Judicial Affairs Office didn't have the same evidence as the district attorney's office—namely the allegations of past abuse. And there was a great deal of confusion surrounding what Briles had known about that incident from Boise State football coach Chris Petersen.

But there were other concerns out of the handling of Ukwuachu's case, and the board of regents had a hastily arranged conference call with President Ken Starr to discuss their options. Starr suggested that Baylor law professor Jeremy Counseller, who happened to be the school's faculty athletic representative to the Big 12 Conference, conduct an internal review. Only seventy-two hours later, Counseller went to Starr and told him that based on what he found, the school needed to hire someone externally to do the review. Board members we interviewed said they didn't see the report from Counseller, but according to one senior administrator, the law professor's brief investigation had already stumbled upon allegations of a gang rape involving football players.

Several regents and Starr discussed their options, and the name of Philadelphia law firm Pepper Hamilton quickly climbed to the top. They saw Pepper Hamilton as the "gold standard" in working with colleges and universities on Title IX compliance. Baylor administrators had been to conferences where Pepper Hamilton attorneys presented, and they received references from the University of Virginia, which hired Pepper Hamilton earlier that year in the wake of allegations in a controversial—and later retracted—*Rolling Stone* story about a fraternity gang rape.

Two attorneys, Gina Maisto Smith and Leslie Gomez, directed Pepper Hamilton's work in this area, and both were former sex crimes prosecutors and worked closely with the U.S. Department of Education. Smith's bio noted that she spent two decades in the Philadelphia state district attorney's office handling cases of child abuse, sex assault, and domestic violence, and she was hired by the Archdiocese of Philadelphia to review their cases after several priests were indicted for sex abuse. Gomez spent fourteen years in the Philadelphia DA's office, where she was the senior prosecutor for child abuse and sex crimes and supervised more than one hundred prosecutors.

Smith and Gomez had been recently criticized by sexual assault advocacy groups that their work was too favorable to school administrators, with one *Huffington Post* article from October 2014 stating,

"Among many sexual assault survivors and advocates, Smith and Gomez have developed a reputation for glossing over the shortcomings of the schools that hire them." The same article stated, "The attorneys concede in their report that some on campus felt the 'very fact that the college engaged us meant that we could not be viewed as objective.'"

Baylor regent J. Cary Gray, a Houston attorney, felt that the current public scrutiny warranted an external review, and there was a sense among regents that Baylor would be vindicated. "I actually still—obviously incorrectly—still believed that it would conclude that we didn't have these kinds of problems that were being suggested we had," Gray said to us. On a conference call in late August, the regents and Starr agreed that Pepper Hamilton was the way to go, and Starr announced the decision publicly on September 2, 2015.

Regents were also aware that the U.S. Department of Education might want to take a look at Baylor's actions. Knowing that the department was already tied up in investigating hundreds of schools for alleged Title IX compliance issues, they figured if Baylor commissioned a review by Pepper Hamilton—which had close ties to the Education Department—and the school committed to the law firm's recommendations to improve, that would satisfy federal regulators and the government would look favorably on what Baylor had already done.

The board also created a three-person special committee to oversee their investigation, chaired by regent David Harper along with regents Jerry Clements and Chris Howard. It was a diverse group—a white man, a white woman, and an African-American man. Harper was a graduate of Baylor and Harvard Law School and was a partner at Haynes and Boone, an international corporate law firm with offices in Dallas. Clements received her law degree from Baylor and was the chair of Locke Lord, a Texas-based global law firm. She was the first woman in fifty-three years to be named Baylor Lawyer of the Year. Howard was an anomaly on the board; he had no degrees from Baylor. He was a graduate of the U.S. Air Force Academy, where he played football and in 1990 received the Campbell Trophy, the highest academic award in the sport. He served as an air force helicopter pilot and earned a Bronze

Star for his service in Afghanistan. In September 2015, he was named president of Robert Morris University in Pittsburgh.

The committee's job was to make sure Smith and Gomez had support and cooperation from the administration and to define the scope of their investigation. When they were hired, the regents thought they'd be focused on the Ukwuachu case, but once they started, the attorneys and the committee members realized there were far more issues. So after the regents met again with Gomez and Smith in Waco and then discussed the investigation over the phone, the question the two attorneys were tasked with answering was: Using the lens of specific cases, did Baylor respond correctly to Title IX regulations? And if not, why not?

The time frame was of some concern, because, as some of the regents pointed out, the university was already making changes—albeit slowly—and many of those had been recently implemented. Because long before Pepper Hamilton was hired, a different consulting firm told Baylor it had problems in Title IX compliance.

In February 2014, a male student—and one who had ties to a member of the board of regents—was mugged on his front porch only a couple of blocks from campus. He reportedly called Baylor police and they told him there was nothing they could do (although a records request to the department turned up no documentation of such a call). When the administration was asked about the incident, regents said they were told, "Oh, we can't take care of all the kids who live two blocks off campus." When most of Baylor's students live within a six-block radius of campus, that answer didn't sit well with the regents, they said. And so they started asking questions, mostly directed at Baylor police and campus safety.

"Their perspective on the world was that their job was to give students parking tickets," one regent said, adding that regents had a different perspective about what role the campus police should serve by then. "They were security for the students. And they were supposed to be taking care of the students, not causing them to get in trouble, and they needed a whole different mentality about the relationship they had with the students and that was sort of at the heart of what was happening at the beginning of 2014."

The Baylor police chief at the time, Jim Doak, was brought in to talk to regents, and they were sorely disappointed by what they heard. When he told them the campus had about a dozen security cameras, they were stunned, because they estimated it should have in excess of one thousand, based on its size. In an era where schools were facing active-shooter situations, like the 2007 Virginia Tech massacre, in which a student shot and killed thirty-two people on campus, they determined that Baylor had a police chief who was the equivalent of—as one regent phrased it—"Barney Fife," alluding to the goofy, befuddled deputy sheriff on *The Andy Griffith Show* played by Don Knotts. (Doak did not respond to multiple requests for an interview.)

That spring, the regents decided to hire Vermont-based consulting firm Margolis Healy, which specializes in campus safety and security. Margolis Healy produced a report that summer that told the regents a lot of what they had assumed: They needed a more sophisticated police department. Millennials are different. The campus footprint had changed. And the safety and security response should change along with them.

Doak, who had worked at Baylor's police department for twenty-eight years, retired in September 2014. A senior administrator said that one of the report authors who had known Doak in the 1990s and found him to be incredibly competent then, noted, "I don't know what's happened. He just let things go." The school promoted assistant police chief Brad Wigtil to chief, and he reported to the newly created assistant vice president of campus safety and security position, filled by Mark Childers, a former member of the U.S. Secret Service.

Baylor received another bit of feedback from Margolis Healy as well: It wasn't doing Title IX the way it was supposed to be doing it. That, according to Gray, was a bit of a surprise to the regents, because they thought Baylor had someone in charge of Title IX. And it did, technically, but not in the way it was supposed to be.

CHAPTER TWENTY-FIVE

IN TITLE ONLY

When the U.S. Department of Education sent out its Dear Colleague letter in 2011, Baylor president Ken Starr assigned Title IX compliance to John Whelan, because he handled other compliance oversight. But Whelan was also vice president of human resources, which was a full-time job whose duties didn't really coincide with what the U.S. government expected out of a dedicated, full-time Title IX coordinator.

There was also a concern among Baylor leaders that having a human resource officer in charge of compliance issues like Title IX would give the impression that it was an employment function, and not something applicable to students. In fall 2013, the Title IX duties began to transition from Whelan to Chief of Staff Karla Leeper. Whatever the upper directive was on Title IX compliance, some of Baylor's top administrators said it was never passed on to them. It's unclear what Whelan did to address Title IX issues at Baylor; he has since moved on to a job at Indiana University and has not responded to requests for an interview.

Baylor's senior vice president for operations, Reagan Ramsower, said that in 2011 his understanding of Title IX was that the university had to have enough sports programs for women. "That was the only thing I'd ever dealt with in Title IX," he said. "That was my own fault for not being more informed about that. I just didn't know."

Kevin Jackson, vice president for student life, said he and Charles Beckenhauer, Baylor's general counsel and chief legal officer (who passed away in July 2016), began talking in the fall of 2012 about the changes needed to comply with the 2011 Dear Colleague letter. They met in the summer of 2013 with President Starr—whom Jackson described as supportive—to launch a task force "specifically charged with reviewing our administrative processes related to Title IX."

Jackson said during that time frame, Baylor and many other colleges were grappling to understand and implement what the U.S. Department of Education recommended. Could they adapt their student conduct process to handle sexual assault cases? One problem: They couldn't have students on the hearing panel. Another issue: They had to share information with each side, but also protect confidentiality. Women or men complaining of assaults shouldn't be forced to be in a hearing with their alleged perpetrator. But then they were required to make sure each side had equal access to information presented at the hearing. It was all very complex.

"We were slow to get our heads around the complexity of the changes to Title IX. This is not an excuse, just a reality," Jackson said. "I would say ninety-eight percent of the colleges and universities that I was in contact with were also slow."

On December 5, 2013, the student newspaper the *Baylor Lariat* published a story specifically about Baylor's compliance with the 2011 Dear Colleague letter that stated, "Baylor takes proactive steps when looking into a complaint on behalf of the victims." It quoted Whelan as saying, "Our desire would be to have every single one reported. If we don't know about it, we can't do anything about it. We try to educate campus so that people will report." The story laid out the steps that Whelan and chief judicial officer Bethany McCraw would take in addressing sexual assault complaints and it noted that Judicial Affairs worked closely with Baylor police and the counseling center.

The story noted several steps—such as adjusting class schedules—that Baylor was taking to accommodate students who reported acts of sexual violence, and said that students shouldn't worry about reporting a sexual assault out of fear they'd be punished for drinking or for sexual behavior the university would typically frown on. But there were already contradictions. The story came out only a few months after football player Sam Ukwuachu's victim reported her assault, and one of her main complaints was that she was forced to change her schedule to get out of classes and tutoring sessions that she shared with him, not the other way around. And there was a very telling passage from Cheryl Wooten, staff psychologist with the Baylor Counseling Center (who would also end up diagnosing Ukwuachu's victim with posttraumatic stress disorder):

> There are numerous people at Baylor right now in positions of authority who are running at this as hard as they can. We are all very concerned about it and there are a large number of professionals here on campus working at this behind the scenes even as we speak, very hard. And I think that we are all hoping to have something very different in place by next fall. But it's really complicated because we're talking about money, time, public relations, and legal statutes.

In October 2013, within months of launching the task force, Karla Leeper was assigned to oversee all of Baylor's compliance duties. She was Starr's chief of staff and vice president for executive affairs, making her the point person with the board of regents. And although she had been at Baylor since 1992, starting as professor of communications studies, she attended public universities in Iowa, Kansas, and Texas and had no historical ties to the school or Waco.

Leeper described the state of Baylor's compliance with Title IX as far more incomplete than the December 2013 *Baylor Lariat* article would lead one to believe. On paper, Baylor's policies weren't much different from those at other colleges; in practice, they didn't hold up, she said. She blamed much of Baylor's struggle with Title IX on its culture, one deeply rooted in Baptist values that admonished drinking alcohol and premarital sex.

"There were some who understood it was happening and they were struggling for a way to address it," she said. "Remember, you're talking about a campus that didn't dance until the nineties, and it wasn't that people weren't dancing."

But drinking, even if a student was twenty-one or older, could still be grounds for expulsion, as could illegal drug use. And other forms of behavior the university felt compromised its Baptist values—such as gambling, cohabitation, and using weapons—were punishable. In 2002, Baylor suspended fraternity Sigma Phi Epsilon after about fifty members posed fully clothed with four bikini-clad women for *Playboy* magazine's "Women of the Big 12 Conference" feature; the individual men and women also faced unspecified sanctions.

And then there was Baylor's stance on homosexuality, which made headlines in a big way in May 2013 when women's basketball star Brittney Griner spoke out against her former coach, Kim Mulkey, who Griner said asked her and other players not to talk publicly about their sexuality, out of fear it would deter recruits, and that she was asked by a Baylor official to remove a tweet that referenced her sexuality.

Griner, who has come out as gay, was the top pick in the WNBA draft a month earlier, and was recounting her experience at Baylor in an interview with ESPN when she said, "The coaches thought that if it seemed like they condoned it, people wouldn't let their kids come play for Baylor."

In Baylor's sexual misconduct policy, "homosexual acts" were listed as a violation—or "misuse of God's gift"—along with sexual assault, sexual harassment, sexual abuse, incest, adultery, and fornication. (In the summer of 2015, that reference would be dropped and the entire policy shortened to "Baylor will be guided by the biblical understanding that human sexuality is a gift from God and that physical sexual intimacy is to be expressed in the context of marital fidelity," with no reference to any misbehavior.)

Sex, in all its forms, had been simply taboo. One woman we interviewed, who said she was raped in 2012, recalled going to chapel—a requirement of Baylor students—and sitting through lectures on alcohol, domestic violence, suicide, and pornography, but not recalling a single time anyone ever spoke about sexual assault. "They would never say the words *sexual assault* or *rape*," she said.

One female student who attended Baylor from 2005 to 2010, and who said she had unwanted sexual encounters with football players and their friends, described Baylor as a "summer camp for rich kids."

"We'd participate in all these planned activities during the day—chapel, religion—and at night we'd all go crazy and wild like we had only two months of summer camp left, even though we had four years," she said. It started with drinking, then binge drinking, and then on to "cocaine-fueled threesomes," all the while Baylor was projecting this outward image of a bunch of "nerdy, religious kids," she said.

"I don't think these guys came to Baylor with the mindset that they're going to be raping women. I think that Baylor was in such denial that students drank, and [Baylor leaders] did not like things that were against their mission so they just were in denial about it," the former female student said. "The more you ignore it and the more you just pretend it doesn't happen the more people think they can get away with things."

Patty Crawford, Baylor's former Title IX coordinator, who would leave the university in the wake of the scandal that would break months later, described what she saw as the university's pervasive silence on controversial issues.

"Baylor administrators were mainly older white men who had historically not discussed or openly chose to listen to the real issues at Baylor, including drugs, alcohol, and sex, not to mention any violence relative to these three factors," she said. "To sum it up, the Baylor way is to look the other way until the media may expose something and then have a PR firm write a statement asking for prayers and deny knowledge of such cases."

In a lawsuit that was filed in June 2016, one woman alleged she went to Judicial Affairs in 2014 to report a sexual assault and claimed the investigator didn't take down details about her assault, but did take interest in her alcohol consumption. "(She) left the Judicial Affairs Office with only a lecture on drinking," the lawsuit stated.

Michele Davis, the countywide sexual assault nurse examiner in Waco, said many women didn't even report their rapes because they feared they would be judged by anyone they told at Baylor.

They'd face questions like, "Why were they out at midnight? Why did she go to his apartment to begin with? Why did she eat with him the day before? Why did she call him on his cell phone? And she was dating him, they were girlfriend and boyfriend," Davis said. "So that activity, in their thought process, from the victim's perspective means that she consented to some sort of sexual activity."

The regents we interviewed said they understood how women might see the university's actions as "victim blaming," but they said there likely was no intent to do harm. Those Baylor employees were good people, trying to do the right thing, but they simply weren't trained to know what the right thing really was. Many of them had a 1950s view of Baylor, that "this doesn't happen at Baylor. This is not our culture."

Regent Kim Stevens, who was among the regents who spoke to us about the board's actions, is a mother of four children—all but one of whom is out of the house—and is CEO of Blue Scout Media, a Waco-based company that streams live events, including concerts and corporate conferences. She's one of the few regents who live in Waco, and said the mentality at the college is not unlike what's reflected in the community.

"It's a little bit like raising kids right now, and that's kind of like what we're doing at Baylor," she said. "You have a segment, and it's usually in Christian populations, that you don't want to acknowledge that things exist. Then I don't have to think that my kid might be doing it. Versus, going to your child to say, 'Hey, I know these things are out there. Let's have a conversation about them. I am not endorsing that you go do them.'"

When judicial affairs investigators, or whoever else at Baylor, ended up talking to a woman to discuss what they should do, they would say things like, "It's really hard. Do you really want to go through this?" Those comments would end up deterring women from taking any action.

"They are not trying to cover it up. They are not trying *not* to be helpful," said regent David Harper. "In their way, they think they are being helpful."

Among Baylor's top leadership, there was a clash between people who held on to that 1950s view and those who had a more modern approach. There was a convergence of a lack of training, a lack of understanding, a lack of resources, and a lack of awareness on campus. Women were confused, and they thought, *Gosh if I report that, and I say I was drinking, will I get in trouble?*

One woman, who alleged in a lawsuit that she was raped by a fraternity member in April 2014, said nothing came of her report to Judicial Affairs and that she was discouraged from telling her story to others. Later, when the woman called 911 to report a male student who was beating a friend of hers at a party, Waco police didn't take action against the male student, the lawsuit states. But they did inform Baylor officials that the woman had been drinking, and Judicial Affairs disciplined her for a student code of conduct violation. Baylor's attorneys responded in a court filing in June 2017 that their records showed that none of the women in that lawsuit were charged with an honor code violation in retaliation for reporting sexual assault. (We asked Baylor officials over a period of six months for Baylor to provide statistics on the number of students who were suspended or expelled for violations but were never provided with that information.)

Davis said she'd heard of women who chose to stay out all night—making a ripe situation for a sexual assault—instead of finding a ride back to their residence hall because they were afraid of being caught intoxicated and have the school punish them and/or tell their parents. Crawford, the former Title IX coordinator, said she'd heard the same from women who told her that Baylor police hung out at residence halls on Friday and Saturday nights checking for students who smelled of alcohol. "There is a culture that exists that women at Baylor should be virgins, that they don't drink alcohol," Crawford said.

These issues were appearing at the very top levels of Baylor leadership. Neal T. "Buddy" Jones, former chairman of the board of regents, in emails on October 14, 2009, wrote to then chief of staff Tommye Lou Davis, about trying to get a female Baylor student expelled from the university for drinking alcohol at a party. He referred to the girl and her friends as "perverted little tarts," and wrote, "It is plain to see that alcohol was present and right in front of them. If you tell me I have to prove it was consumed by medical evidence I might go berserk. Get this [name redacted] girl dealt with. Please. She should be expelled." When asked about the email, Jones declined to comment, saying only, "Your story will just have to be incomplete."

Leeper said some of those reservations women had to tell anyone at Baylor, or the police, about their assault likely also stemmed from the women's own background, considering the university draws a substantial population of students from Christian families who sent their children to religious schools all their lives. Many women likely feared their parents finding out they were drinking or having sex. Leeper said the university technically had an amnesty policy at the time for sexual assault complainants, but did not widely publicize it. Or, according to many women's experiences, did not practice it.

One of those was a woman at Baylor who reported being raped by a classmate. She said she strongly believed that Baylor draws a certain type of man—a man of white privilege and entitlement—from families where men are still the head of the household. "Sexism is still alive and well on the Baylor campus," she said. She said some will view her assault as a woman who shouldn't have been at a boy's house after 6:00 p.m. and that she made bad choices, and not that someone was hurting her. "'Stand up for yourself' is not a virtue that you are taught as a Christian woman, and 'fight back' is definitely not one," she said.

Leeper's transition to Title IX coordinator happened shortly before football player Tevin Elliott was convicted in January 2014, and even if others weren't talking about it, she said the case made her realize there was urgency in her work. In February 2014, she and a handful of Baylor attorneys went to the National Association of College and University Attorneys workshop in Miami on "Sexual Assault: Addressing Institutional Culture and Compliance."

From that seminar Leeper knew Baylor had to step up its efforts. She sought out training programs to educate students, faculty, and staff on sexual violence, but she received pushback. "Some voices in the Baylor community" didn't like the programs because they included assumptions that students drank in college or they were having sex or intimate relationships. "When you see off-the-shelf training that has language in it like, 'When you drink . . . ,' there were some people who said, 'That's not us,'" she said.

As a tenured professor with protected employment, Leeper had no issues being candid with the board of regents, and she advised the university go with one of those programs immediately and that everyone at Baylor needed to be more realistic about the nature of its students. "That's a tough conversation for that institution to have and I think that contributed in part [to what happened]," she said.

Leeper said she also thought cultural attitudes about alcohol and sex were getting in the way of properly investigating Title IX cases, including the beliefs that women who were intoxicated made poor witnesses and that certain sexual behavior damaged someone's credibility. In an interview in November 2016 with the newsmagazine 60 Minutes Sports on Showtime, Ramsower admitted the university's culture led to assaults not being reported.

"I think it's probably true at other places, but certainly our problem, and we own it, people have blamed victims," Ramsower said. "People have done victim blaming and they have excused bad behavior and I think that's some of the failures that happened. And as a result it didn't get reported."

Leeper also touched on a more nuanced, but important, view of what was happening. McCraw and her Judicial Affairs Office were charged with handling student conduct cases for several years—typical college problems such as drinking alcohol, smoking marijuana, cheating, plagiarism, vandalism, and so on. Those issues are more black-and-white and often backed up by solid evidence. It was a mistake for people with those investigative skills and background to try to adapt that format to investigating sexual assault cases, which are far more complex. "If you look at the accounts on paper, they are just so dramatically different, how do you assess that?" Leeper said of the parties in sexual assault cases. "Someone might look at that and say, 'Everyone was so intoxicated, we'll never get to the bottom of this.'"

Leeper said judicial affairs investigators weren't using "trauma-informed" methods to investigate sexual assault cases, which might call for asking different types of questions or altering the timing of questions and weighing evidence in a different manner than in a typical student conduct case. It's the type of training recommended by the U.S. Department of Education and U.S. Department of Justice for any agency—including law enforcement—investigating sex crimes. And Baylor's judicial affairs investigators were still holding Title IX complaints to a higher standard of proof—closer to beyond a reasonable doubt—than the recommended preponderance of evidence, despite what was being said or posted publicly.

Jackson, the vice president of student life, said that as soon as he and others recognized that its existing student conduct setup wasn't going to work—and that taking on Title IX was too much for the three staff members in Judicial Affairs—they went to work on building a new program from the ground up.

Another problem Leeper recognized in some cases was the delay caused by a pending criminal case. Even though the Dear Colleague letter explicitly stated that schools should not wait on a criminal investigation while proceeding with their own Title IX investigation, in the Ukwuachu case Leeper said they were "in limbo" waiting on the district attorney's office. (But the district attorney's office claimed the opposite—it was waiting on Baylor. In a story assistant prosecutors Hilary LaBorde and Robert Moody wrote for the Texas District & County Attorneys Association website in 2016, they stated the delay was caused in part by Baylor, which took several months and many emails to turn over records and that it took "no fewer than forty emails" to arrange a meeting with a university counselor.)

In direct contradiction to what Whelan and McCraw said in the December 2013 *Baylor Lariat* article, Leeper admitted there wasn't a great deal of communication among the agencies involved—law enforcement, the district attorney's office, and other local players. "What I discovered early on, all of those units aren't talking to each other. We needed to all be on a similar page," Leeper said.

Administrators claimed they were not always being informed by Baylor police, especially if there was no arrest. As Ramsower detailed what happened in the case involving football player Tre'Von Armstead: A call from Waco police came into the Baylor police dispatcher that specifically said, "We have a young woman here that reports of sexual assault. . . . She doesn't want to report it. She doesn't want to go forward." There was no mention of a football player or a name. Ramsower said he had no information of anyone doing anything after that, or whether or not anyone at Baylor police actually received the report.

Most assaults happened off campus, under the jurisdiction of Waco police, and Ramsower said he had no direct connections to the agency and that he relied on Baylor police to maintain those ties. As an aside from Baylor's problems, the Waco Police Department's role in how student sexual assault cases were handled would emerge to be its own quagmire. Their responsiveness and skill in handling sex assault cases—according to the women who reported assaults to them—was a crapshoot that simply depended on which detective was assigned.

Another aspect of Baylor's response to sexual assaults was the need for academic and mental health support for students who reported assaults, which campus leaders said they thought at the time was adequate. They had a counseling center. They had academic advisors. The consensus among regents and administrators is that they weren't trained in this particular area, nor did they, like many others, realize the scope of the problem. Counselors were not informing women of their right to file a complaint with Judicial Affairs, and many sexual assault victims used up their allotment of free sessions and were left without continued therapy, unable to afford or otherwise attend counseling off campus.

"I don't think [Title IX] was overlooked," Leeper said. "It's a question as to whether people had the right level of energy and urgency in looking at the issue." She said it isn't fair to say the board or the administration was uninterested in Title IX, but "they had maybe been slower than they should have been."

"I did not meet with anyone who suggested to me that we should whitewash these issues or hide them or cover them up," Leeper said. "And I was pretty direct with them about what I expected to happen in terms of (sexual assault) reports. And it was all just based on data. You look at the federal government, you look at what other institutions' experiences have been: We need to prepare for additional reports."

Leeper's number-one recommendation as she was leaving was that the university hire a full-time, properly trained Title IX coordinator and investigators. She said the administration supported the budget she proposed for both, and the board also wanted to move forward, especially after the report from Margolis Healy advocated the same. "The culture change at Baylor certainly started in the fall of 2014," regent David Harper said.

To reflect that change in its handling of sexual assaults, Ramsower said the university needed a full-time, dedicated Title IX coordinator who was a true outsider.

"We had difficulty at Baylor understanding how to reconcile, 'How do we train people with regards to sex outside of marriage . . . and drugs and alcohol when both of those were outside our code of conduct?'" he said. "We needed someone that wasn't sort of within that Baylor perspective to come in and help us understand, 'How do we do this Title IX training? How do we do this?'"

And they found someone: Patty Crawford. She was an Ohio State–educated, midwestern, Roman Catholic young woman with Title IX experience at a small state school in Indiana.

Shortly before she arrived in November 2014, Baylor released its 2013 Clery Act report. The federal Jeanne Clery Act requires all colleges and universities that receive federal funds to make public statistics of crime on campus and immediately surrounding campus and in buildings off campus owned or controlled by the institution.

From 2008 through 2011, Baylor reported zero forcible sex offenses. In 2012, Baylor reported two forcible sex offenses. It reported six in 2013 and six in 2014, according to the U.S. Department of Education's online Campus Safety and Security database. (Those figures don't include incidents at off-campus, private housing, where about 64 percent of Baylor students live—and, because Baylor is a dry campus, almost entirely where they party.) In comparison, two other private religious Texas colleges, Texas Christian University and Southern Methodist University, reported 13 and 15 sexual assaults, respectively, from 2008 to 2011, according to an Associated Press story in February 2016, which also noted there was only one other private school in the nation with an enrollment similar to Baylor's that reported no sexual assaults during that time, Wilmington University in New Castle, Delaware.

While it has been well known and reported for years that Clery Act statistics often underrepresent reality at college campuses, Crawford would soon find out exactly how far off the mark they were at Baylor.

CHAPTER TWENTY-SIX

THE WHISTLEBLOWER

I n the months to come, there would end up being a great deal of debate about Patty Crawford's effectiveness as Baylor's Title IX coordinator, but one thing that her superiors at least agreed upon was that she was passionate—and compassionate—in her work.

Crawford has roots in Ohio but experience that spans the globe, working for a time in 2005–06 on a microfinance program in the war-torn African nation of Sierra Leone, where she rode a motorcycle into bush country to help impoverished and oppressed women start small businesses. She described a passion for work that helped empower women, and in 2009 she started working at Indiana University East, a regional school with about 4,500 students in Richmond, Indiana, where she worked to help students graduate from college and find jobs in the state.

Along the way, an opportunity opened for her to expand her role into the type of human rights work she enjoyed by taking on affirmative action, diversity and inclusion, equal opportunity—and Title IX, which became a more pressing issue after the U.S. Department of Education's Office for Civil Rights released its Dear Colleague letter. She said that summer that she and her colleagues on the main Indiana University campus in Bloomington worked on new policies and procedures to bring campuses into compliance.

When a recruiting firm first contacted her in August 2014 about the Title IX coordinator job at Baylor, her first question was, Where's

Baylor? She wasn't terribly interested; she had concerns about the school's stance toward gender identity issues and current compliance. And it would be difficult to take her husband away from his job and move their three children—all under the age of six—to Texas, where they had no family ties. But the recruiter contacted her again in September and told her that Baylor's board, which had transitioned to more businesspeople than pastors, recognized sexual assault was an important social issue, so she agreed to travel to Waco for an interview. She met with nine groups of Baylor leaders who all seemed committed to the new position and asked good questions. She accepted the offer, believing it would be a way to focus her efforts on gender-based compliance and incorporate her own Christian faith into her passion to address sexual and dating violence and to "build a program from scratch with God's love at the center of that effort."

She started in a temporary office in the Clifton Robinson Tower just off campus and soon realized that her view of a Title IX office was different than the audit and compliance view of the department. And there were immediate hurdles: One of the first requests she made was to have a statement from Baylor president Ken Starr posted on a newly created Title IX page on Baylor's website. She said Baylor's marketing and communication department denied her request for the statement from Starr, with no real explanation.

Crawford arrived a semester after a jury had convicted Tevin Elliott, and the school's Judicial Affairs Office had cleared Sam Ukwuachu, but while he was still under indictment. When Crawford asked for files from the previous three years, she received a disorganized and seemingly incomplete stack of records, almost entirely from the last five months, and the records included no names. Baylor practice had been not to record anyone's name in a sexual assault complaint, she said, which is contrary to what the U.S. Department of Education requires. Cases ended up not being tracked or followed up. In fact, in one of the lawsuits that would end up being filed against Baylor, a former female student, who was seventeen at the time of her alleged attack, said that even Baylor police didn't take down her name or the names of witnesses, telling her that if they kept her alleged assailant's name off the report as well, they wouldn't have to tell her parents. (A June 2017 filing by Baylor attorneys would include a redacted copy of her police report, noting that she refused to identify her alleged assailant or provide witness information.) Crawford said she had enough information to determine that, up until then, Baylor's treatment of Title IX was "minimal and noncompliant." But Crawford said she put most of her focus on moving forward—writing a compliance policy, building a judicial process, creating centralized complaint reporting, and building her office. "I didn't even have my own trash can for two months into the job," she said. "So I wasn't able to sit and spend time on closed cases from the past." That would come later.

In her first weeks on the job, Crawford met with student groups, mostly in small group settings, trying to get word out about her office and what she could do for sexual assault survivors. She started receiving reports the second day on the job. By six months, she had received seventy-seven reports. Most of them were rapes. The rest were a mix of sexual harassment, stalking, domestic violence, and other acts of sexual violence. She would end up working seventy- to eighty-hour weeks.

"The narratives were heart-wrenching and were more and more complicated as each hour came and went. It was as though these narratives had been suppressed for over a hundred years of Baylor's history and our little team were the first to hear about violence at Baylor," she said in an email. "We felt as though we were opening Baylor's version of Pandora's Box."

By the start of the next semester she had a permanent office and had hired two investigators—one in February 2015 and the other in April, which Crawford said took quite a bit of persuading to her supervisors despite the volume of reports they were getting. She said there was also still resistance to acknowledge the problem, adding that she wasn't allowed to use the word *consent* or talk about alcohol in her training sessions with students because it was against the university's Christian mission.

"It was me explaining to executive leaders and select board members that students are having sex at Baylor and they're drinking alcohol and even saying that was almost explosive. And I said, 'But it's worse because there are students having nonconsensual sex and there's abuse happening,'" she said.

Later on, Crawford would assert that the ignorance on display was only a ruse, and that several administrators knew that sexual violence was a problem long before the university decided to act on it.

During that first year, Crawford also started working to bring "It's on Us"—an awareness campaign to address sexual assault on college campuses launched by the Obama White House in 2014—to the Baylor campus. And she had taken over a sexual assault advisory board, which included several people who represented various aspects of the Baylor community—counseling, the health center, student life, and, later on, fraternities and sororities—but few outsiders, save for Michele Davis, who was the sexual assault nurse who worked with local hospitals. The board, which operated under Baylor's Office of Student Life, was an opportunity to share what each person knew about sexual assaults at Baylor. Its primary purpose was to create educational materials for freshman orientation sessions, and it had no role in student judicial proceedings or individual cases. All the awareness raising was great, but Davis wanted to see practical things done, such as letting women get rape exams at the campus health center. At the time, the health center didn't perform exams and instead referred women to local hospitals, which Davis said was sometimes enough of a hurdle to discourage someone from reporting. Davis said she asked Crawford about that, and her response was "no." Crawford said she doesn't remember Davis asking her that, and she said she never had the authority to make such a decision anyhow.

Davis said there was a notable absence on the board: There was no one from Baylor Athletics. Davis made a point of sharing two things with the board: The number of Baylor students reporting rapes was going up, and an alarming number of alleged perpetrators were student-athletes. In fact, Davis said that at least 25 percent of her cases involved a student-athlete who was accused of rape (Crawford would note that 10 percent of her cases were from football athletes alone), which would certainly stand out at a campus where male student-athletes make up about 4 percent of the undergraduate male population. Davis said she never received a good answer for why no one on athletics was on the board, which would later be disbanded and reorganized. (Crawford noted that the board existed before her arrival at Baylor and that she did invite athletics to send someone to the board meetings during her last eight months there after she was given permission to do so by administrators.) It struck Davis as curious why statistically so many alleged perpetrators were student-athletes.

"I don't know if it was an environment that was tolerable to it, or if it was the players themselves that thought it was tolerable to do because they came from different environments that were abusive to women," Davis said. "I don't know if it's because if they did do it, nobody did anything about it or if there was a general tolerance to parties or using women sexually. I don't know what their environment was."

Crawford may not have discussed her concerns at the board meeting about what was happening with student-athletes, but she said she certainly had them. Within her first two months on the job, she heard about a gang rape allegation from 2012 and a dating violence report from 2013 involving football players.

The January 10, 2013, report named a prominent player still on the team, All–Big 12 Conference defensive end Shawn Oakman, who only months earlier announced he would return to Baylor for the 2015 season, despite being projected as a possible high-round pick in the NFL draft. The report indicated Oakman and his girlfriend were arguing about the status of their relationship and at one point Oakman "shoved her into the brick walls and cabinets" and was calling her a "slut and a whore." She told police he shoved her face into some clutter on her bed, hurting her lip, which an officer noted was swollen. Police also took pictures of bruises near her biceps. The woman didn't want to press charges, and no charges were ever filed.

Crawford said that the very day she learned of the two reports, she went to her boss, Juan Alejandro, vice president for governance, compliance, and risk, and told him she thought there might be "cultural issues" within the football program. Crawford wanted to investigate right away, and Alejandro gave his approval. On February 4, 2015, Crawford said she was called into a meeting with Alejandro, Senior Vice President Reagan Ramsower, athletics director Ian McCaw, and university attorney Christopher Holmes to discuss what Crawford found. Crawford laid out what she needed to investigate the allegations, including getting an interview with a current football player. She asked McCaw if he had been aware of any gang rapes, and McCaw said no—even though it would be revealed later that he had been involved in discussions in 2013 about yet another gang rape involving a former volleyball player. Although Crawford's and McCaw's versions of what happened next differ slightly, McCaw claims he asked whether the student-athlete was "at risk or whether he would be provided any type of immunity." Crawford said she immediately protested and said the student-athlete would not receive immunity, and she said university attorney Holmes only looked down at his hands; McCaw and Baylor regents would later say in separate documents that Holmes refused McCaw's request. Crawford was stunned. She thought: *How was she to give immunity to anyone without knowing any of the details first, whether someone was an accomplice or part of the very culture she wanted to investigate?* She said it took clearance from three vice presidents before she was able to interview the athlete three weeks later.

"I think it was clear that they didn't like the fact that this information had come to my attention so quickly in my tenure at the university," she said. "It became very clear that they were monitoring everything I was doing," and they were trying to protect their student-athletes.

One of Crawford's investigators was Gabrielle Lyons, who was new to Title IX but was an experienced investigator, having worked several years for the federal government, including four years investigating employment discrimination with the U.S. Equal Employment Opportunity Commission in Chicago. Her first day on the job, April 1, 2015, four women came in to report a gang rape that they said happened over spring break. She would end up fielding about 80 cases, of which 25 called for an investigation, during her seven months at the university.

"The violence is what took me aback," Lyons said. "My limited understanding was that it was a great Baptist institution. Me, being a Christian myself, I was just appalled at the level of violence taking place so rampantly at the institution."

Lyons first started getting indications of serious noncompliance when women would tell her that they reported their assault to a dean or to someone in athletics and nothing was done to address it. "I was scratching my head and saying, 'This isn't right,'" she said.

Lyons said she had no trouble investigating the spring break gang rape allegations, which she said did not involve any student-athletes. But when an allegation involved a football player, she said she received resistance. At first, she said she couldn't get a copy of the police report. Then when she asked to interview football players, she had no trouble reaching some of them, but the ones who were identified as being star players were nowhere to be found. A coach gave her a phone number, but it was disconnected and no one seemed to have an alternate. She said it had been made clear that she shouldn't just approach students on campus, including during sports practices. "I got the impression that they did not want me to interview them," she said.

The final straw came when she described a meeting with top Baylor police and public safety officials who she said told her it was not safe for her to interview certain alleged perpetrators by herself because they have "a potential for violence," which she said she saw as a means to intimidate her and prevent her from doing her job. Baylor has since disputed that characterization, stating instead that Lyons was the one who initially expressed concern for her safety, and she was offered an escort to accompany her if it would make her feel more comfortable. (Nevertheless, it wouldn't be the first time Baylor football players made employees uncomfortable on campus. In June 2009, Bears lineman Phil Taylor, six feet, four inches and 330 pounds, was cited with misdemeanor assault after he was seen pushing a parking service officer away from Taylor's yellow Dodge Charger as Taylor grabbed a parking violation sticker out of the officer's hands and ripped it up.

He allegedly said to the officer, "Don't let me catch you on the moth-
erfucking streets." That parking service officer and two others filed
complaints with campus police about repeated harassment from football players and strength coach Kaz Kazadi who the officers said were
mocking them or calling them names and being belligerent until
police officers arrived to intervene. One officer who asked for a disciplinary report on Kazadi wrote it was his second run-in with the
coach, who the officer said that during a previous altercation gave an
eye gesture that the officer took to mean "I better watch my back.")

Problems extended beyond case investigations for the fledgling Title IX staff. Crawford started training sessions with university administrators, faculty, coaches, and resident hall advisors—all
people designated to be mandatory reporters of sexual violence incidents under U.S. Department of Education guidelines. A few attorneys and administrators had previously been training people at Baylor
to not put names in a sexual assault file, but Crawford said that was
incorrect and hindered the university's ability to act. She said it took a
great deal of work to correct those practices.

Her problems extended into her efforts to get police records from
Waco and Baylor police. Crawford said she wasn't even allowed to talk
to anyone at Waco police—that communication was supposed to go
through the vice president in charge of campus safety. Baylor police,
who had copies of Waco police reports, refused to turn them over to
the Title IX office because of an agreement the campus police had
with their municipal counterparts. Instead, Crawford said she was
allowed to ask officers questions about specific cases and they would
give her information verbally, which she said posed a risk for missing a
lot of vital details.

Crawford cited an email exchange from June 2015 (almost
a full academic year into her job) in which Baylor police chief
Brad Wigtil notified Mark Childers, associate vice president of public
safety and security, about what Waco police described as an arrest of
a Baylor football player for misdemeanor assault. Baylor's media relations contact was copied on the email, but not Crawford. She found

out four hours later and only after McCaw forwarded her an email he received from the chief marketing officer about the incident, and wrote, "This email is the first I have heard about this incident. I'll keep you informed as I learn more." According to the police report, the football player—who had been before judicial affairs twice before— was actually not arrested or charged after police doubted the credibility of his girlfriend.

The media never reported about the incident. Yet at the time, there was concern among Baylor leaders. In that email to McCaw from John Barry, chief marketing officer, Barry wrote, "Obviously the issue of athletes and domestic abuse is very hot right now," and he included a link to a *USA Today* story about protecting student-athletes accused of domestic violence or sexual assaults and allowing athletic departments to have oversight of their discipline. "We need to be very careful about how our response to these situations is characterized in the national discussion," he wrote. The email exchange occurred about two weeks after Baylor defensive coordinator Phil Bennett told the crowd of Baylor fans in Fort Worth that he expected the fall roster to include Sam Ukwuachu, who was preparing to stand trial for sexual assault, unbeknownst to the public at large.

Around the time of the Ukwuachu trial, Crawford said Starr asked her in private whether she thought there was a problem at Baylor. She said her response was, "I think the fact that you have not even talked about even consensual sex for the entire history of this university that there are things that have gone on here that were violent that need to be talked about." She advocated an awareness campaign and more publicity of the fact that students reporting assault would have amnesty from getting in trouble with drinking or sex in general. "Because of that, I think there is a culture here," she told him.

Within weeks after Ukwuachu's conviction on August 20, 2015, Crawford said she was summoned to a meeting in the president's conference room with senior Baylor administrators and asked about every case involving athletes over the past five years. She said they appeared shocked and were quiet until one of the executives broke the silence by saying Crawford was describing allegations, and that these accounts were not fact. "I said, 'I investigate every report I get to the extent that I can and their credibility is not in question here.'" At that point, she said Reagan Ramsower spoke up and said, "Well, these women are mentally ill." Ramsower denies saying that. A statement from Baylor addressing Crawford's allegation notes that someone at the meeting may have spoken about mental illness but that it was referenced "out of concern for the victim's wellbeing and recovery" after Crawford herself described the fragile emotional and mental state of a particular victim who had been suicidal.

But Crawford still stands behind her account. "I understood the mentality of how they see victims and how they see the reality of these cases," she told us. "They did say this is a person's professional career at stake, we cannot affect the career that this person has in front of them. And that was their rationalization of the football player."

The 2013 domestic violence incident involving Oakman came up—the same one Crawford brought to administrators' attention almost seven months earlier—and they discussed how to address it. Oakman would end up being suspended for the opener against Southern Methodist University at the start of the 2015 season, although the university later stated it was because of "an unrelated incident involving his disrespectful conduct" during a Title IX training session. Board chairman Richard S. Willis joined the conversation via conference call. Reporters were asking for police records, and Crawford said there was fear of more bad publicity. She asked them what they would do if media got hold of a police report and were about to report on a situation, and she said they responded, "That's an entirely different story."

During that meeting, Crawford said administrators were interested only in cases involving football players—not any of the other cases involving, even by then, hundreds of students on campus. She said that concerned her. She wondered whether Baylor was worried about doing the right thing, or if it was only worried about *looking* like it was doing the right thing in the media.

CHAPTER TWENTY-SEVEN

REPORTS OF GANG RAPES

O n September 3, 2015, the day after Baylor's media communications office issued the press release announcing the hiring of Pepper Hamilton, it issued another press release with a statement from president Ken Starr that said in part:

> Pepper Hamilton's independent investigation will proceed even as we continue vigorously to support the work and essential student services of our Title IX Office. Federal regulations and recommendations with respect to the proper handling of allegations of campus sexual assault have evolved significantly—and rapidly—over the last few years. Baylor has been among the universities across the nation responding swiftly to these emerging mandates and seeking to ensure the safety of our campus.

Among the thirty-two voting members of Baylor's board of regents—living in various places with different careers and ties to the university—it was obvious that some were more aware of what was happening than others. After football player Sam Ukwuachu's conviction, it became apparent to more of the board that administrators had been battling with Title IX policies for some time.

Regent David Harper, who was chairman of the board committee overseeing the Pepper Hamilton investigation, said he first learned of some of the allegations from Baylor administrators around the time Pepper Hamilton was hired. "I felt the weight of there's a lot here," he said. Pepper Hamilton's attorneys started their investigation by interviewing people from Judicial Affairs and Baylor's legal office, and they gave weekly updates to three regents on the special committee— Harper, attorney Jerry Clements, and Robert Morris University president Chris Howard. The committee members vowed not to share details of those conversations with the rest of the board, lest that get back to employees who might end up being questioned later and jeopardize the investigation.

Pepper Hamilton attorneys Leslie Gomez and Gina Maisto Smith were instructed to go where the evidence led them. They were not asked to adjudicate cases or determine anyone's guilt or innocence. They were asked to examine how the university responded when an allegation of sexual violence arose. Pepper Hamilton attorneys were not directed to focus on the football program—although that's where the evidence first led them. It was during a conference call one evening in October 2015 with Gomez and Smith that special committee members learned details of one of the alleged gang rapes. Part of it involved Jennifer's* story. It's unclear what specifics the regents heard, but she told us the following details.

In the summer of 2012, Jennifer kept ignoring her parents' requests to see her grades. For a while, she tried to convince them she couldn't log in to the Baylor website where they were posted, because someone changed her password. Finally, out of excuses, she sat down with her parents, pulled out her laptop, and called up her grades. They were not good: two Fs, two Ds, and a C. After ending her first semester as a freshman at Baylor with a 3.31 GPA, the downfall by spring was a shock to her parents. They accused her of partying too much and not paying attention in her classes. They were spending good money to send her to a private school, and she wasn't taking it seriously. Jennifer knew that wasn't why, but she couldn't bring herself to tell them the real reason. She grew depressed. She went days without sleeping.

---

* Pseudonym

When Jennifer told her parents she wasn't going back to Baylor that fall, they knew something was wrong. She still wouldn't tell them why, but she agreed to go to a therapist. She really hadn't planned on telling the therapist, either, but five minutes after she walked into the office, the therapist asked: "Why are you here?" Jennifer says she blurted out what happened and started sobbing on the couch.

It was the first time she told anyone—aside from a friend—about the two nights on which she said several Baylor football players assaulted her in the spring of 2012. One of the alleged assaults would happen, amazingly, at what has been described, most likely, as the very same party in April 2012 where Jasmin Hernandez said she was raped by then Baylor defensive end Tevin Elliott. Jennifer's alleged assaults were among the four alleged gang rapes that Baylor officials would reference in late 2016 when discussing the investigation of the school's handling of sexual violence.

Yet to this day, Jennifer has never reported the alleged assaults to police. She didn't tell anyone at Baylor what happened until she was contacted in the spring of 2015 by a Title IX investigator who heard about Jennifer's experience from her friend. As far as Jennifer knows, no professor, no administrator, no coach, no one at Baylor can be faulted for not investigating her case or reaching out to help her when it happened. But her story is an important one for Baylor. Jennifer faults university officials for what they knew—or should have known— about the risks for female Baylor students *before* her alleged assault, more than she does for what they did, or didn't, do after.

* * *

As a high school senior from San Antonio, Jennifer didn't have any really strong attraction to the Baptist college, but her parents valued its religious ties and her older siblings had a positive experience attending another private religious college in Texas, so the family felt safe with Baylor. "They had the idea that there was a higher moral standard," Jennifer said.

When Jennifer arrived in Waco in the fall of 2011, she reconnected with a friend she'd met that summer during Baylor Line Camp, an orientation program for incoming freshmen. One day that fall, Jennifer and her friend met two Baylor football players when another friend of theirs went to the players' house to purchase marijuana. "Then they were starting to want to hang out with us and we were like, cool. You know, I think at that age it's like, 'Oh, these hot football players want to hang out with us,'" she said.

For several months, she and her friends hung out with the football players and their buddies, whether it was studying at their house or going to parties, and she trusted them. Then came a party in late February or early March—Jennifer can't remember the exact date—when she and her friend ended up at a different player's house with about six of his teammates. People were drinking and smoking marijuana, but at one point, something struck Jennifer as odd. None of the football players had a drink in their hands, but they kept giving her and her friend more to drink. She acknowledges now that then-eighteen-year-old Jennifer didn't recognize that as the red flag it should have been. But, still, these were guys she knew and she had no reason to fear them.

The last thing Jennifer said she clearly remembers is sitting on the living room floor and having a drink. She has a vague memory of being in a bedroom. It's dark, but she can see the lights of cell phones around her. She would wake up in her dorm room the next morning—unsure of how she got there—and she immediately had a feeling that something bad had happened the previous night. She knew someone had penetrated her vaginally, as she felt a definite soreness and pain. Her friend didn't remember any more than she did, Jennifer said, so they reached out to the one player they knew best among those who were there.

The player met them outside his dorm. Jennifer asked him, "What happened last night?" At first, he seemed as though he didn't want to tell them. "He said, 'You know, you guys were really drunk,'" she recalled him saying, almost jokingly. He told Jennifer and her friend that they had their clothes off even before his teammates took them upstairs. Jennifer said he continued, telling them they were so drunk that guys were dragging them, limp and unresponsive, up the stairs and into a bedroom.

And then the player revealed he had much of the incident on video. He pulled out his smartphone and played the clip for the two women. Here's what Jennifer said she saw: A pitch-black room lit by the glow of cell phone lights. She and her friend were lying on the same bed. Naked. Facedown. Motionless. There were two men behind them. Each woman was being penetrated vaginally. Jennifer didn't recognize the two men having sex with them. But she did recognize several of the Baylor football players who were standing around, cheering the two men on. She heard indistinguishable, muffled noises coming from her and her friend. Jennifer said the lineman showing them the video indicated the guys were taking turns having sex with the two women.

The video was about thirty seconds long, from what Jennifer can remember. She said the football player claimed he wasn't in the room and someone had sent him the video, and she did not see him on the video either. She never saw the video again and doesn't know what happened with it, although there were rumors it was passed around among members of the football team and their friends. She doesn't recall if she and her friend said anything to the football player before they walked away that day.

Jennifer felt shocked, disgusted, horrified, and incredibly guilty. What she saw on that video was so much worse than she ever expected. But she didn't even think about reporting it to anyone, and she didn't want to talk about it, not even with the friend who was there. "I don't think I realized at that age that that was necessarily assault. I knew it made me feel really bad. I knew I didn't like it. I don't think I realized that, oh, when you're that drunk you obviously can't consent. I don't think I really understood that at eighteen," she said. "I think we just kind of tried to forget about it. At least I did."

Her account—not surprisingly—would differ greatly from the account of the football player who showed her the video. When they came over, he said everyone was down with what was going to happen. The women did drink excessively at the party, he said, but they were "fully awake and comprehending" when they went upstairs where the alleged sexual encounter occurred. "I don't understand them going around telling people they got gang raped." The football player recalled showing them the video, and he said their reaction was one of, "'Aw, man,'" but that they did not respond with disgust. He said it would be years later before he heard the women claimed they were raped. He, and another football player who spoke to us on the condition they not be named, said that the football players assumed that the women were okay with group sex.

Jennifer went on to describe another party that would lead to her winding up in a similar situation. At the time, Jennifer rationalized it for three reasons: There would be hundreds of people there, they clearly wouldn't be the only women, and it would be a different group of athletes. The party was at Baylor running back Glasco Martin's house, and based on her description and of two football players we interviewed, it was described as likely the same party on April 14, 2012, at which Tevin Elliott would be accused—and eventually convicted— of twice raping Jasmin, on a grassy slope and against a swimming pool fence behind the apartment complex.

At the party, Jennifer and her friend were separated, and Jennifer found herself the only woman in a room with several football players. She said she was sitting on the floor talking to one of them and she responded jokingly to something he said by saying, "Oh, that's just mean." She said he responded, "Oh, I can be mean to you," and then he immediately pushed her on the ground, ripped off her pants— breaking the metal clasp at the waist and the zipper—and started having sex with her in front of the other men in the room.

Jennifer said she was intoxicated but aware of what was happening, and she yelled—exactly what, she can't remember. She said he pinned her down and she struggled to get out. As soon as he finished, several of the other men, who Jennifer said were all football players or recruits, dragged her into a large adjoining bathroom and put her on her knees on the tile floor. They also sat her on the bathroom counter by a sink, all the while either taking turns having vaginal sex with her or trying to get her to give them oral sex. On the floor, one guy was penetrating her from behind while others forced her to give them oral sex. When two guys tried to simultaneously put their penises in her mouth, Jennifer said she looked up to see someone recording her with a smartphone camera. That moment, above all, is emblazoned in her memory.

"I kept asking, 'I want to leave. I want to leave,' and I was crying," Jennifer said. "I tried to get up and they threw me back to the ground. I was all bruised up because of that."

Although there were five or six men in the room originally, Jennifer said between ten and fifteen assaulted her in the bathroom and she only knew about four of them by name. "I feel like they invite people when something like this is happening," she said. She didn't recall any of them using condoms.

Through the bathroom door, Jennifer said she saw her friend walk into the room and call out for her, but someone tried to grab her friend by her hair and she quickly fled out into the hallway. Everyone left. Jennifer found her shirt on the floor in the bathroom and her pants with the broken clasp by the bed. She ran out, holding them up with one hand, and she found her friend and they both left.

One football player who she says was a part of the alleged assault contradicted her version of events. "Everything for me on my end was consensual. I didn't do anything in there that was not welcome and allowed," he said. "If you want to say I was part of a fuck-around, I was part of a fuck-around for sure. But I've never been a part of anything where I've heard somebody say, 'Oh my God, no, stop. Don't,'" he said, "I've never been a part of anything that somebody never wanted me to do to them. That's not how I get down. That's just not how I was raised. That's not even my character." The former football player who showed the women the video from the earlier encounter wasn't at the party at Martin's house in April, but he said he heard conflicting stories about what happened, and noted that there was some indication it might have gotten out of hand, but he said no one described it as rape.

"I think what happened was, after the fact, they kind of regretted what they had done. And I believe so many people had caught wind of

what they had done," he said. He and Jennifer ended up briefly corre-
sponding online years later about the incidents in 2012. "Again, maybe
they weren't those type of girls and that was just a one-time thing on
their bucket list that they wanted to do. I don't know, but some people
are going to look down on them. I never looked down on them."

The football players often gathered outside between the student
union and the buildings where Jennifer had many of her English
classes. As she walked by, they would shout catcalls at her like, "Oh,
you're looking fine today."

"It was like a power play," she said. "It just made me feel very vulnerable." It unnerved her, and she stopped going to class.

Jennifer told no one. She thought she could handle it. But the aftermath of what she described as two assaults quickly started to manifest
itself.

After going home for the summer and seeing a therapist in San
Antonio that fall, Jennifer said she felt ready to return to Baylor in
the spring of 2013. The catcalls and comments from the football players continued, though. One time as Jennifer was walking to class, a
woman standing with the athletes muttered "whore" as she walked by.

"Every day I had to prop myself up so I could walk by them," she
said. "You know, like it's fine, it's going to be fine, and just tune out
whatever they said."

Jennifer tried to plow through, but it was rocky. She wouldn't sleep
for two or three days at a time. She felt stressed and anxious. She ended
leaving Baylor for another stint in 2014, and temporarily enrolled at
a different private, religious college in Texas in the spring, which is
when she had her worst breakdown. She picked aggressively at the
skin on her chest and knees to the point that she had large bloody
and wide-open sores. (Pathological skin picking is what's considered
an impulse control disorder often associated with stress and trauma.)
Medication helped, and by spring 2015, Jennifer again returned to Baylor. She wasn't thrilled about coming back, but she realized going to
another school would only prolong her degree requirements by several
more semesters because credits wouldn't easily transfer.

Jennifer was in class on Monday, March 23, 2015, when she received an email that sent her into full panic mode. It was from Ian McRary, a newly hired Title IX investigator at Baylor. The email, which Jennifer provided to us, read in part:

> . . . I recently heard from an anonymous football player about an incident involving the football team, during which there may have been an unwanted sexual experience. I want to make clear that you're NOT under investigation or in trouble for anything. But, I was wondering whether you would talk with me about the football team in general. If you had an unwanted sexual experience, you don't have to share it with me. We could, however, talk about available resources and options to support you, personally and academically, if you're interested in that.
>
> I have reason to believe this incident may be part of a larger culture. If you're willing to talk with me, I can keep your name anonymous and our conversation private. Also, if there was underage drinking or soft drug use involved, you will not get in trouble for that either. Our main concern is our students' well-being and safety, so anything you share would be helpful toward addressing this problem and protecting students. Some students have already spoken with us about this, but I need to learn more.

Jennifer learned later that her friend—the one who went with her to both parties in 2012—reported a different and later run-in with a football player to the Title IX office, and through investigating that case, they learned of Jennifer.

Jennifer told her story to McRary but left the meeting confused about what to do. Most of the guys she remembered from those nights had left Baylor. But there was one player who was in a class with her, and she asked McRary if she could switch classes or find another way to avoid him. In response, she received an email from

Title IX coordinator Patty Crawford offering her details on how to contact someone for academic support, tutoring, and counseling—and advising her to reach out directly to her professors—but not addressing her concern about being in the same class with one of the men she said assaulted her.

"It was just a very cold email, and it made me feel like they don't want to talk about this," she said.

If Crawford and McRary intended the email to be supportive, Jennifer didn't take it that way. By that time, her view on Baylor was already jaded. She declined to pursue a Title IX case any further.

"I didn't really ever expect anyone to help me, because of the love affair they had with the football team," she said.

In November 2016, Baylor reached an undisclosed financial settlement with the two women and no lawsuit was ever filed regarding their allegations. The two alleged gang rapes that Jennifer described were referenced in a February 2017 legal filing by three members of the board of regents. It noted that the Title IX office—in reviewing those and other alleged gang rapes—had identified six players in particular, but "by the time the Title IX office pieced together the information in late March 2015, all six of those players were no longer at Baylor."

CHAPTER TWENTY-EIGHT

THE SILENCE

Baylor regent David Harper had two words for what he heard from Pepper Hamilton attorneys about Jennifer's alleged gang rape by football players: sickening and sad.

"It was the kind of thing that you can't imagine would go on anywhere, let alone at Baylor," Harper told us.

Harper said it was also clear that it wasn't an isolated case and that he had heard parties of that sort were happening. How often, he didn't know. But they were happening. Right then, the Pepper Hamilton lawyers didn't know the details of when it was reported, who reported it, or who knew, and Title IX coordinator Patty Crawford had concluded her investigation. Most of the players involved had left Baylor. But the special committee members knew the magnitude of such allegations would call for consequences. They didn't know what they were. But there would be consequences.

That's when Harper prepared a speech he would routinely give the board over the next several months. He couldn't give them details, but he could prepare them. His speech had three parts: "We are going to do the right thing, no matter how hard it is. We are going to protect and care for our students at the highest level. Football is important, but it's never more important than the mission of the university."

Pepper Hamilton attorneys Gina Maisto Smith and Leslie Gomez continued their work, gathering documents, emails, recordings, and other records from 52 laptops and 62 mobile devices—more than 26.5

terabytes of data. (One terabyte is estimated to hold about 344 million pages of Microsoft Word documents.) A private forensics firm hired by the university retrieved emails, text messages, and other data from computers and mobile devices of faculty, staff, and students or former students. In the ensuing months, the attorneys pored through those documents and started to conduct interviews of employees, coaches, and women who reported having been assaulted. They did not, however, interview the accused students or student-athletes, noting they were not tasked to determine whether or not a violation occurred but whether the university responded to and investigated it properly—a point that would subject them to much criticism in the months to come.

Administrators and regents braced themselves for the results, and Crawford's Title IX office was flooded with new reports. One of her two investigators, Gabrielle Lyons, found the weight and frustration too much. "At night, I was having nightmares about rape," Lyons said. One female student recalled how Lyons seemed incredibly distraught during her interview. She quit on November 1, 2015, after what she and Crawford described as a particularly frustrating meeting with senior Baylor officials, including Reagan Ramsower, during which they said they needed support and help in dealing with the emotional stress. On November 10, according to Baylor officials, Crawford sent an email to Vice President for Governance Juan Alejandro, writing, "I am struggling with maintaining my momentum in this position. Every day there are issues that go beyond my scope, and in this climate I do need some forgiveness and sensitivity."

Despite the tensions between Crawford and her supervisors, she says the university added something else to her plate: public relations. In mid-December 2015, ESPN's *Outside the Lines* requested an interview with someone at Baylor—specifically asking for President Ken Starr or football coach Art Briles. But Crawford said she was told that speaking to the media was part of her job, which made her uncomfortable because she felt she didn't have enough information to speak accurately about what happened at Baylor in the past. In the interview, Crawford spoke positively of the progress Baylor was making on Title

IX—bringing along pamphlets, fliers, and pens bearing the "It's on Us" logo—but she would not answer questions about past cases, deferring instead to the ongoing Pepper Hamilton investigation.

No one else at the university who was contacted by *Outside the Lines* would talk. Some cited privacy laws they said prevented them from talking about certain cases, even though ESPN had obtained signed letters from women waiving their rights under those laws and giving Baylor officials permission to talk about them. Baylor and Waco police refused requests for police records. On January 31, 2016, *Outside the Lines* aired its story, in which, for the first time, three of the women involved in the Tevin Elliott case spoke out. It included Jasmin Hernandez, who went by the pseudonym Tanya at the time and was interviewed in shadow to disguise her face, as did the other two women.

They spoke not only about what happened with Elliott, but about how they felt Baylor officials treated them. The report included information about what Baylor officials knew about Elliott's behavior long before he was arrested in April 2012. In the story, McLennan County assistant district attorney Hilary LaBorde also criticized Baylor for its investigation of the Sam Ukwuachu case, saying, "I wouldn't call it an investigation." She accused Baylor officials of having an almost "1940s idea of how women should behave" and not knowing anything about how college rape occurs. "If they're sitting around and waiting for a victim who has been pulled off the jogging path and raped by a stranger wearing a trench coat, they're going to be waiting for a long time," she said. It was a very public airing for a university that preferred to keep its business private; only a month earlier, Baylor had reached an undisclosed financial settlement with Nicole, Ukwuachu's alleged victim, and neither the university nor her attorney would publicly discuss details. No lawsuit was ever filed.

The *Outside the Lines* story also referenced a letter that Olivia—the woman who said Tevin raped her in 2009—sent to Starr on November 3, 2015. She also sent copies to several other Baylor officials, including Briles, athletics director Ian McCaw, and Crawford, as well as a few non-Baylor officials, such as a Texas state legislator. Her subject line was: *I was raped at Baylor.*

Despite the graphic start, the letter was written in a kind and considerate tone. The former student described herself as being "a proud alum of Baylor University and also a former student-athlete." She wrote that after Elliott assaulted her on October 31, 2009, she didn't report the incident to anyone because of what she knew about "the lack of support and the stories of unsuccessful prosecutions of sexual assault charges." She was not among those who could make a claim that Baylor officials or police didn't respond to her alleged assault— simply because there's no way they would have known—but she believed things would have been different had she received more education about her options.

> This negative event changed my life and taints all other experiences during my time at Baylor. In fact it was this experience that motivated me to rush my final semester by taking 20 hours of classes, separate myself from my sport, Baylor teammates and friends, and ultimately spend numerous years in counseling after college.

In a very organized and straightforward manner, she outlined four steps she hoped the university would take, concluding with making sure the "entire student body is aware of university efforts to support assault victims and follow through with disciplinary actions for the perpetrators." She included a verse from scripture, Jeremiah 29:11: "'For I know the plans that I have for you,' declares the LORD, 'plans for welfare and not for calamity to give you a future and a hope.'" And she closed by writing, "I would love the opportunity to talk with you further and hope to hear from you soon. Thank you for your time."

The Texas congressman she emailed responded with a very detailed email within a day. Six days later, she received an email from

Crawford. It was very kind and encouraging, laying out steps Baylor had taken, and in it Crawford noted, "I joined Baylor a year ago and have seen first-hand that Baylor does not tolerate sexual violence of any kind." The former student-athlete would never hear from Briles or McCaw. And she would never hear from Starr.

ESPN's *Outside the Lines* story sparked national outrage, especially coming on the heels of Ukwuachu's conviction five months earlier. The *Dallas Morning News* editorial board called for a U.S. Department of Education investigation into Baylor's lack of action. CBS Sports senior writer Jon Solomon wrote what he called "an open letter to Ken Starr" asking him to "stop hiding behind privacy laws and Baylor's status as a private university. Explain fully what mistakes occurred and why your students and alumni should believe they won't happen again." Another hit at Baylor's secrecy came from *Fort Worth Star-Telegram* sports columnist Mac Engel, who wrote about his trip to campus during which he was met with "Sorry, can't help you" from students, professors, and employees. He wrote that one professor told him, "Knowing this school, no one is going to talk to you."

On February 3, 2016, Starr sent an email to students that addressed the *Outside the Lines* report, outlined what the university was doing to comply with Title IX, and stated repeatedly that university officials couldn't comment about specific cases because of federal student privacy laws and the ongoing Pepper Hamilton investigation. He sent another one to the larger "Baylor Nation" on February 7, 2016, noting the frustration being expressed about the university's lack of response on certain instances and again citing federal student privacy laws and the pending Pepper Hamilton investigation.

"We were deeply saddened to learn about these instances of interpersonal violence; we acknowledge and commend the great courage these survivors demonstrated by coming forward to share their experiences. Their stories continue to raise consciousness and awareness about these critically important issues," he wrote in the email that was sent Sunday afternoon, only a couple of hours before Super Bowl 50.

The letters and media coverage created an awakening on campus among a group of students who decided to value advocacy over privacy. On Monday morning, there were—written in white chalk—nine questions about Baylor's handling of sexual assault, phrased more like accusations, on the concrete in front of Pat Neff Hall, the campus building that houses administrative offices. No. 9 was "WHERE IS OUR APOLOGY?" A group of Baylor alumni gathered more than 1,700 signatures on a letter to Starr calling for reform and stating:

> Baylor's failure to adequately serve survivors of sexual assault compromises the University's Christian identity. Parents must know that their children will be safe at Baylor, and students must be assured that should the unthinkable happen, their decision to report sexual assault will be met with the University's full support and resources. We can and must do better, for the sake of Baylor students, and for the sake of faithful Christian witness to the world.

A public Facebook page called "Survivors' Stand" was created and spread through the Baylor student body, calling for a candlelight vigil at Starr's house the evening of Monday, February 8, 2016. Temperatures dropped close to freezing as bundled up students headed to Albritton House, the Southern Colonial mansion that serves as the official residence of the Baylor president. Starr was reportedly out of town that evening. Media estimated that upwards of two hundred people huddled in front of the four stately pillars shielding their small candles as they prayed, sang—at one point breaking into "This Little Light of Mine"—and spoke about the need for Baylor to support sexual assault survivors, some of whom came up individually to tell their own stories. Many of the students then went to a prayer service at the George W. Truett Theological Seminary on campus.

The catalyst was a blog post by a senior philosophy major who wrote almost eight thousand words about the night in March 2015 when she said she was raped by a fellow student and then the following ordeal she went through at Baylor when she reported him:

I wasn't at a party. I wasn't drinking. I hadn't been drugged. I wasn't kidnapped in the dark. I fully admit that I willingly went over to his house that night. But it wasn't to have sex— it was to do homework. When I resisted his sexual advances, he resisted taking "No" for an answer. He raped me twice that night, instructing me to shower to wash the blood off my thighs in between the two instances.

I didn't do a rape kit. I didn't go to the hospital. I didn't call a crisis line or even 911. I went home to my little apartment, alone. The next day, I woke up and went to work at the law firm I worked at as if nothing had happened. I didn't report it, and I didn't seek counseling. My story didn't make the local news and my case didn't go to trial. I spontaneously adopted a puppy, and went on about my life, even managing to convince myself, on the good days, that it hadn't really happened that way.

CHAPTER TWENTY-NINE

"I FELT UNHEARD"

Amber* never publicly named her alleged perpetrator. Right or wrong, there's a certain social stereotype about Baylor women: They're rich with daddy's money, they wear designer jeans, and they have (often bleached) long blond hair. That was not Amber.

For most of her time in Waco, she paid for school by working in Baylor's philosophy department, serving as a teacher's aide in the honors program, clerking for a local law firm, and waiting tables at a restaurant nights and weekends. She took eighteen credit hours each semester so she could finish in three years, which would save on housing. She bought the cheapest Baylor meal plan, and remembered once running out of meals early.

"I hadn't eaten in three days," she recalled. "I was sitting on the curb outside my honors dorm at Baylor, crying because I was hungry."

She may not have fit the reality of Baylor students, but in some ways she fit the ideal—at least in terms of the university's stated Christian mission—because it was, literally, her background. Her parents were Christian missionaries, and Amber had mostly grown up in a southwestern Pacific island nation, in rural villages without electricity or running water, where houses were built of tied-together palm trees and elevated on stilts to avoid frequent floods. They had supplies flown in every three months and if their communications radio went out, they'd have no way to call for help.

---

* Pseudonym

She didn't relate much to kids her age back in Texas—the pop culture references, the fashion. "I remember walking into Wal-Mart the first time," she said. "I could not fathom how anybody could ever need that much stuff."

Amber's family returned to the United States for her senior year, which she completed in a small, central Texas town. She wanted to be a missionary doctor, and her dream school was Baylor. She applied, "just for fun. Just to say that I had gotten in. There was really no belief on my part I could ever afford anything like private school." But when she was admitted into the honors program and offered an academic scholarship, she enrolled, allowing herself what she called her one extravagant luxury, knowing she'd be in debt with student loans to pay off the balance. After being disappointed with the B-plus grades she received her first semester, and falling out of love with the idea of becoming a doctor, she transitioned to prelaw.

One day in February 2015, she went to the house of one of her classmates to watch movies, and at one point he asked to kiss her. She laughed it off, she said, feeling as though she couldn't risk angering him. She laughed it off again when, as she tried to walk out the door, he pushed her up against the wall and started kissing her.

She said her classmate texted her several times to apologize, and she ignored him up to a point. "I said, 'You know what? I believe that somebody should always respond in kindness and love even when someone is unkind to you. I didn't know how to respond in kindness and in love and so I didn't respond at all, and maybe that was wrong and I'm sorry. I accept your apology and I forgive you.'" She thought that everyone deserves a second chance.

On March 12, 2015, Amber accepted his invitation to come over and work on their take-home midterm. He started to get flirtatious with her, but she deflected his talk, insisting that the only intimacy they shared was as friends. When he kept trying to touch her, that's when she said she got upset and tried to leave. That's when she said he raped her. She remembers him being on top of her. It hurt, and she was crying and begging him to stop.

"After he got off, I remember looking down at my legs and see-ing there was blood on them and I remember thinking to myself, 'I'm not on my period. Where is this coming from?'" She washed off in the shower. As she came out wearing a towel, she said he raped her again. She said she has no memory now of what happened after that or how she got home.

Calling the police never crossed her mind. She said she was in a daze. "I didn't wake up thinking I was raped last night. I woke up thinking that something bad happened last night."

Amber didn't report it to authorities; she had, however, told two people: a male friend of hers and her roommate, who took the news pretty hard and actually broke down and told her thesis advisor, a Baylor professor, who notified the Title IX office. Someone from the office reached out to Amber via her roommate in April 2015, but at the time she didn't want anything to do with making a report. She believed she just had to hold out until May, when both she and her classmate would graduate and after which she'd never see him again.

But then Amber learned that he might be staying on campus over the summer. That's when she knew she had to report the assault, and so sometime in June she dug up the email from a couple of months ago from the Title IX office and typed a reply, asking to set up a meeting.

Amber met with Title IX Coordinator Patty Crawford, a meeting that left her feeling better than she'd had in months because she felt as if someone heard her and cared. Crawford gave Amber options: She could report the assault to Baylor police and pursue a Title IX investigation, and if her alleged attacker was found responsible, he would not be allowed back on campus. "I was like, 'That, that's what I want,'" she said. In June, she gave Baylor officials a sixteen-page document in which she explained what happened to her. But she ran into a problem when the male friend she first told of the rape—someone who could be used as her "outcry witness"—refused to show up for his interview with the Baylor police department, later telling her brother that he didn't believe her anymore, she said.

At that point, Amber said it seemed in conversations with Baylor police that she didn't have much of a case. She said the police report noted that their relationship was "Boyfriend/Girlfriend," which she had vehemently denied and could only assume had come from her teammate. "I felt unheard," she wrote in her blog. "They had heard my abuser loud and clear, 'We kind of had a "thing," but they hadn't heard my voice saying, 'I wasn't interested in him at all. That's not how it was.'"

Amber wrote in her blog that she'd also sought counseling at Baylor. It took weeks for someone from the counseling center to call her back, and when they did, she said they told her that she should seek outside counseling because her problems were beyond the scope of what Baylor counselors could handle in ten free sessions. They helped her find an outside counselor, "but nobody told me how to handle the $100 (an) hour that every outside counselor charged." After Amber said she was led to believe that the criminal process couldn't help her, she instead focused on pursuing her complaint with Baylor. Because both students were employees, she said she started with human resources.

Amber was asked to provide a list of witnesses—although no one else was present for the alleged assault—but she gave them more than a dozen names of people they both knew. They were people who she said could vouch for her character, how she avoided her alleged perpetrator, and how she was found crying in the bathroom many times, she wrote. A week later she heard from someone with the university stating that the department "was in need of their employee. They asked me if it would be 'alright with you if we gave him his job back, pending the resolution of this case?'"

Amber said she pleaded with them not to bring him back. A couple of days later, she was called into a meeting with human resources. "They sat me down in a chair. Offered me a drink of water," she wrote in her blog. "I knew what they were going to say when they silently placed a box of tissues in front of my face prior to speaking." The HR woman told her that they didn't have enough information to support terminating her former classmate's employment, and that he would be reinstated as an employee. Amber said she pointed out that she had no motive for lying. She described the rest of the interaction in her blog:

> Frustrated, I beat the table with my fist. "I want to know what's more important than me. He's an at-will, temporary summer employee. You can fire him for wearing a blue shirt on Tuesday, if you so choose. I don't see why you wouldn't say 'Better safe than sorry.' There's a reason you won't fire him, and I want to know what it is—what the reason is, that supersedes my well-being as a student AND employee of Baylor University."
>
> Her response was short: "Consistency in terms of employment." I burst out, "So I'm not even supposed to be mad at you? I'm supposed to be mad at . . . at bureaucracy?" Curtly, she said, "Sure, be mad at bureaucracy."
>
> I stared at her. She continued, "He gets his due process, (Amber)."

A Title IX investigation had been Amber's last option at Baylor. Because neither of them was a student anymore, the only relief she could possibly get then was to bar him from coming back in the fall to help with activities on campus. In her blog post, Amber wrote that the Title IX investigator said because the Title IX office was so backed up—and it would take months for her to get a normal hearing with a panel of adjudicators—she could opt for a decision by what's known as a single adjudicator, meaning having one person decide her case instead. She reluctantly agreed, and the case was assigned to a retired Waco judge.

Amber recalled how on the day of her hearing she spent most of the day in the bathroom throwing up, and that she changed outfits five times. "Because how do you dress when you're hoping that someone will believe that you are a victim?" She walked into a little room with the judge and an attorney who was taking notes.

She was asked if there was anything she wanted to explain to him, and she said she fell into her "law student groove," pointing out what she said were discrepancies in her former classsmate's statement. She wrote in her blog:

> After I explained the inconsistencies, I leaned forward, wiped the tears off of my chin, and calmly looked him in the eyes. I said, "Sir, either I am lying, or he is lying. But I have no reason to lie. None. My rapist graduated in May. He's in law school now. The only thing this will do is send a message to him that says 'Hey, you didn't get away with this.' He has many, many reasons to lie."

Several weeks later in October, Amber was about to go into a classroom at the private high school in Waco where she helped teach sixth-grade civics when she received the email: The judge had ruled against her. In reading his decision, she believed that he "completely misunderstood the concept of consent."

Amber said she was denied another appeal—which would have been to President Starr—because neither she nor the alleged perpetrator was a student anymore, even though that was the same situation as when the investigation started.

So, sometime in November, Amber said she emailed Starr directly. She said she didn't ask him to intervene in her case. She didn't ask for any sort of personal compensation. But she had seen some of the recent stories about Baylor and sexual assault, in light of Sam Ukwuachu's conviction. And she said she felt that Starr could use—as she put it—an insider's perspective. They scheduled a date in December to meet in his office.

Amber found Starr to be incredibly nice and complimentary. He asked her about her story—even though she said she wasn't there to tell it. After telling him, she said Starr told her that he thought there had been a misadjudication of justice in her case and he would look into it and email her after Christmas break.

Then the ESPN *Outside the Lines* program aired, and she felt compelled to write on her blog post "I was raped at Baylor and this is my story," which was on a site using her real name. She'd written about her rape before, in fact multiple times on her blog, which had a collection of posts about love, loss, anxiety, Christianity, and even poems. Amber thought at first only her Facebook friends would see it and find it relevant. But it went viral. Television stations reached out to her. Her story was in national newspapers. Social media responded—at least at first—with encouragement. *Sports Illustrated* writer Richard Deitsch wrote, "The written word is a powerful tool. What you wrote will have true impact beyond you. Keep fighting for you."

Amber never intended to be a public face for sexual assault survivors, but women kept emailing her, and she willingly kept responding. "My sort of thing is if at least one girl reads one of my blog posts . . . and feels less alone, then this is worth it," she said.

A few weeks later, another sexual assault survivor would come forward with her real name—and Baylor would have no choice but to respond to her.

CHAPTER THIRTY

USE MY NAME

Ever since the night of April 14, 2012, Jasmin Hernandez's life had taken an uncharted course. She went in for interviews with Waco police detectives. She testified at trial. She felt as though the assault would always be a part of her life, and she never knew when something would trigger a reaction.

She recalled one afternoon when she was out in the yard with her two brothers and one of them, Elijah, was bugging her about joining them on the trampoline. She declined. She wasn't in the mood. Although Elijah was five years younger, he was bigger and stronger than she was, and despite her protests, he scooped her up in his arms and tried to carry her to the trampoline.

Jasmin had a meltdown. She screamed at him. She swore. She clawed at him. She made such a scene. It was the same way Tevin carried her before he assaulted her. It upset her parents, and it wasn't her only outburst. She again sought therapy, and was regularly seeing a therapist in the fall of 2015, and attending classes at a community college. "Every time I think it's done, something comes back," she said.

This time, it was Baylor football player Sam Ukwuachu's conviction, which was the first indication to her that maybe Baylor's problem was bigger than Elliott. Then Olivia—the woman who testified that Tevin raped her in 2009—reached out and asked Jasmin if she'd be interested in talking to a reporter from ESPN for a story about Baylor's handling of sexual assaults.

At first, Jasmin didn't want to be involved. She didn't want to bring it all up again. "But at the same time, I have the choice and the opportunity to allow my actions to be more impactful than myself," she said. "And you know, I just feel like it's the cultural awareness, if you don't speak about it, it won't be spoken. And I can't count on other people to fight my battles."

Jasmin agreed to the interview. Her real name wasn't used in the story. Living so far away in California, she wasn't worried about retaliation; she was worried about being embarrassed. "I don't want people to know what happened to me. I don't want pity. I hardly want sympathy. I just want to be myself," she said.

The interview was difficult. At one point—just as she was about to describe the actual assault—she stopped the interview. Her father, Ostes, had been filming with a handheld recorder, and she asked him to stop. He needed to leave the room, to not even be in earshot. Even though he knew his daughter's story, she could not—and still can't—talk about it in front of him. She spoke for almost two hours. Her mother, Candice, started crying while being interviewed, stopping at one point to grab a tissue.

As difficult as it was for the Hernandez family, it was eye-opening. Despite everything they'd been through, they didn't know much—if anything—about Title IX. Her parents were upset at Baylor officials for not helping. When they found out Baylor didn't help their daughter despite being legally required to, they were livid. "It shocks me. They just don't want to be responsible for what happened and I feel they should be held responsible," her mother said. Her father cut in, "How could they not want to help somebody?"

"There was no compassion, no help," her mother continued. "They're telling the public that they're a Christ-centered university. That is the furthest thing from what they're thinking. Football is their center. Their revenue is their center."

As Jasmin and her parents learned more about what Baylor was supposed to be doing, they were curious about their legal options. They knew about such things because the attorney who represented the female soccer player in the Ukwuachu case had called them for information about their case. That attorney, Colorado-based John Clune, told them that he was unable to represent Jasmin, but he referred her to a firm in San Diego that also handled Title IX cases. It wasn't long before Jasmin and her parents were sitting at their dining room table talking to attorneys Alexander Zalkin and Ryan Cohen about filing a Title IX lawsuit.

It was a big move, and in doing it, Jasmin said Zalkin was also asking something more of her. "He says, 'Jasmin, you can remain a Jane Doe. But it would help the case a lot if you came forward.'" They told her that putting her name on the case would generate more attention, and that would put more pressure on the school. "So that people can have someone to identify that this did happen to a person, it's not just some nameless figure kind of in the shadows. It's like, no, this is this person and this is what happens," she said.

Jasmin's parents wanted her to think about it, but she didn't hesitate. "All right. Let's do it. Why not?" Jasmin said. "Like, what are they going to do to me from here? I just said, 'All right, you can use my name.'"

On March 30, 2016, Jasmin's attorneys filed a federal Title IX lawsuit against the Baylor board of regents, football coach Art Briles, and athletics director Ian McCaw in the U.S. District Court for the Western District of Texas in Waco, and Jasmin was named as the plaintiff. Her case would be the first of many Baylor sexual assault filings assigned to U.S. District Judge Robert Pitman, whose appointment as U.S. attorney in 2011 made news in part because at the time he was the first openly gay U.S. attorney in Texas and one of only a few nationwide, and upon his judicial confirmation in 2014, he would become Texas' first openly gay federal judge. The next day, Jasmin appeared on national television, in an interview with ESPN's Bob Ley on *Outside the Lines*, to talk about what happened to her. She spoke of Baylor's culture, and of Baylor's knowledge of Elliott's past. Ley asked her, "Do you think things could be better now at Baylor?" Her response:

I think they could if the school was true to their word, which there are a lot of words that come out of that school. And the words tend to be, "This is important to us." And it talks about policies and procedures, but in regards to how they're actually treating people. People keep coming out, especially young women, keep coming out of that school saying, "Oh, by the way, a similar situation happened to me when I went to that school."

Baylor officials refused to comment, and instead released a statement in response to the lawsuit, stating, "Individual incidents are deeply personal matters that do not benefit from our public statements." Even if students themselves chose to speak out publicly, the statement read, "We must not publicly comment in a way that could compromise student confidentiality or inadvertently discourage future students from coming forward."

It would be the first of many such statements Baylor would be forced to release in the coming months.

CHAPTER THIRTY-ONE

MOUNTING PRESSURE

Publicly, in the spring of 2016, it seemed as though Baylor officials were responding to one sexual assault incident after another. And despite all the training Title IX coordinator Patty Crawford and her staff members were doing on campus, some students weren't getting the message.

On March 3, 2016 the *Waco Tribune-Herald* reported that twenty-year-old Jacob Anderson was arrested on a sexual assault charge in connection with an incident at a fraternity party on February 21. Anderson was a junior and president of Phi Delta Theta. According to the arrest affidavit and court documents, the woman said she was handed a glass of punch and told, "Drink this," and shortly after she consumed the beverage, she became disoriented. She reported that Anderson then led her outside to a secluded area behind a tent, where he allegedly sexually assaulted her. He was indicted May 11 by a McLennan County grand jury on four counts of sexual assault. The university suspended the fraternity, and wouldn't comment to the Waco newspaper about the incident—even reportedly sending an email to several Baylor sororities instructing members not to talk to the media and to refer all questions to the university's media relations department.

On April 13, 2016, ESPN's *Outside the Lines* reported on the 2013 case involving football players Tre'Von Armstead and Myke Chatman—the first time those allegations were made public. The very same day the public learned about the allegations against Armstead and Chatman, there was yet another incident involving a football player. Waco police arrested former Bears All-American defensive end Shawn Oakman for a sexual assault alleged to have occurred April 3. Oakman, the school's all-time sack leader, was awaiting the NFL Draft, only two weeks away. The woman was a Baylor graduate student who went back to Oakman's duplex with him after meeting him at a Waco nightclub, and she was not the same woman who had reported the domestic violence incident against Oakman two years earlier. She told police that Oakman "forcibly removed" her clothes, forced her onto his bed, and sexually assaulted her. She reportedly ran out, leaving her underwear and an earring, which police later seized as evidence. Oakman told police the sex had been consensual, and several of his former teammates would say that he and the woman had an ongoing sexual relationship and that she was upset that Oakman, who was headed for the NFL, did not want her as his girlfriend.

Oakman had arrived at Baylor with already a bit of a troubled past. He was dismissed from Penn State in 2012 after an incident in which he allegedly tried to steal a sandwich from a convenience store and was aggressive with a female store clerk by grabbing her wrist. Baylor athletic department staff would know of that incident, but wouldn't request his full Penn State student file. They relied instead on Penn State head coach Bill O'Brien's email in which O'Brien said that Oakman's name was one of the five or six players who kept showing up on disciplinary lists, including police matters, which is why he had to dismiss him, Penn State was under heavy public scrutiny in light of former assistant coach Jerry Sandusky's sexual abuse conviction and firing of coach Joe Paterno amid accusations that he took no action despite knowing about Sandusky's suspected molestation of children. But O'Brien wrote, "I believe that Shawn is a decent kid that should be allowed to play this season. I am sure that he has learned his lesson," in an email that Baylor coach Art Briles forwarded to the compliance office, with Briles writing, "Here we go." Only a couple of weeks after Oakman was arrested in Waco—and days before the

NFL Draft—Rivals.com reporter Alex Dunlap posted on Twitter copies of the 2013 Waco police report showing the domestic violence accusation from the other woman.

Public reaction was putting pressure on Baylor's administration, and players were already feeling the heat. Running back Terence Williams tweeted out, "Can't even get with a girl at Baylor [sic] with out fearing for my future now." Defensive end Jamal Palmer's tweet was, "I gotta keep it 100 not every girl but some of these girls out here just trying to come up but people only see one side to it." The NFL Draft came and went with no team selecting Oakman.

As local and national media piled on Baylor, as social media waged a war of defenders and accusers, and rumors heated up message boards, university spokeswomen Lori Fogleman and Tonya Lewis issued statement after statement indicating Baylor could not comment on specific cases of sexual assault because of federal privacy laws, even when the women involved had chosen to share their stories. They routinely deferred to the ongoing Pepper Hamilton investigation. One email Lewis sent with a statement from president Ken Starr concluded with, "We must let [Pepper Hamilton's] comprehensive work best inform of us any actions we take to improve our efforts to prevent and respond to incidents of sexual violence and provide support for those involved."

Behind the scenes, Pepper Hamilton's attorneys were sharing details of their investigation with the regents on the special committee—and it wasn't looking good. Regents were shocked by allegations of gang rapes and the sheer number of incidents. Woman after woman said she'd told someone but nothing happened. There was an insensitive conversation between the police chief and an alleged victim. One of the most worrisome issues—and the one that led the regents to hire Pepper Hamilton—was whether anyone at Baylor knew about Sam Ukwuachu abusing his girlfriend at Boise State before he came to Waco. Ironically, that was decided in Baylor's favor and presented at the board's regular meeting in February 2016. The attorneys determined that no one at Baylor knew about the abuse until the woman testified at his trial in August 2015, although they had been told that there were some concerns about his mental health. That bit of news, however, would end up being a tiny silver lining on a big cloud.

Some of the regents then learned about an issue with the football team's drug testing policy that seemed to exemplify the ongoing clash between the athletic department and—as one regent put it— "1950s folks," who had a different and unrealistic view of modern-day students.

They said that Baylor was not properly testing its student-athletes for marijuana—in contrast to the practice at most other Division I universities, and Big 12 Conference rules. Athletics avoided random testing because of the university's overall strict policy against marijuana use, in which one reported incident could lead to suspension for a semester and a second incident could result in expulsion. Such a strict rule would derail a student-athlete on scholarship. As such, athletic officials didn't feel it was fair to test student-athletes because routine testing made them more vulnerable to being caught than regular students who might get caught smoking a joint in a residence hall.

The regents understood the athletics department's issue that being severely punished because of positive results on a routine, required test—compared to a law enforcement situation—wasn't fair to student-athletes, but to only avoid marijuana testing altogether wasn't the answer. "What was really happening was the underlying message to them is, 'Hey, the rules don't apply to you,'" one regent said. "You know, and they have been hearing that since the seventh grade anyway. Some rules do apply to everybody, and telling them they don't apply is not calculated to make them productive citizens."

The National Collegiate Athletic Association doesn't require its member institutions to drug-test its student-athletes. But if a school has a written drug policy it is required to follow it under NCAA rules. The NCAA penalized Syracuse University in March 2015 for lack of institutional control, which included failure to comply with its written drug policy. Not testing student-athletes for street drugs such as marijuana might have given the Bears a competitive advantage, though, since players who might have been smoking marijuana weren't subject to penalties that could have included missing games. Other Big 12 Conference schools tested their student-athletes for using street drugs. The University of Texas, for example, conducted 188 drug tests of its football players in the first eight months of former coach Charlie Strong's tenure in 2014. The Longhorns' drug policy included a suspension for 10 percent of the football season after a second positive test for marijuana; a suspension for 50 percent of the season after a third; and dismissal from the team after a fourth. A player who tested positive was subject to more random testing as well.

Another regent said there was a concern that the no-testing policy drew recruits to Baylor who wanted to smoke marijuana, and contributed to the football program's problems of "getting bad guys." It also kept players who had addiction problems from getting help, with one regent referencing the 2010 arrest and subsequent suspension of Baylor football players Josh Gordon and Willie Jefferson, who were found asleep in a local Taco Bell drive-thru lane and charged with misdemeanor marijuana possession. Multiple failed drug tests would derail Gordon's NFL career. "We didn't do anything to help him apparently," the regent said.

A former Baylor assistant football coach, who wanted to remain anonymous, agreed the athletics department policy on drug testing conflicted with university policy, but he said football players who were caught with marijuana by police or university officials were subjected to ongoing testing and those tests were in conjunction with Judicial Affairs, which had strict punishment for violators. "It was the absolute opposite of it being lenient. It was the hardest place in America to go without getting caught," he said. And a former player who said he was kicked off the team in 2012 after failing more than one drug test for marijuana said that his punishment was handled concurrently by the coaches and by Judicial Affairs. He said even though Briles wanted to keep him, he adhered to the policy, and assistant coaches helped the football player transfer to another university. "Coach B kept it very strict," he said.

Baylor funded two airplanes full of Baylor administrators and regents to fly to South Bend, Indiana, to meet with officials at Notre Dame who had come up with a solution for the student-athlete drug-testing problem there. In 2016, Baylor adopted the same drug policy that Notre Dame uses. It calls for a six-month probationary period for the first positive test for marijuana; one year of probation and ban for 33 percent of competition for a second; one-year ban and probation for a third; and dismissal from the team for a fourth. There are more severe penalties for using street drugs other than marijuana, including a one-year ban for a second positive test and dismissal from team after a third.

Regents J. Cary Gray and David Harper were at an Association of Governing Boards national conference in Washington, D.C., in mid-April 2016, and Gray said he was standing in the lobby, talking to Harper, when he learned about the drug policy issue and the administrative tug-of-war around it. "That was my first realization that this was likely to not end up well," Gray said.

Harper, who was Pepper Hamilton's main contact and knew more than almost anyone on the board by then, already feared where the investigation was leading. He said he was made aware of incidents, including the 2013 domestic violence situation with Oakman, that had been reported within athletics but not to anyone outside the department. "There was some point where I started praying every day, 'Please, Lord, don't make me have to fire Art Briles,'" he said. Harper kept giving his three-point speech to the board, hoping to brace them for what was to come. "You knew, at least, that had to be on the table," he said. "And in a certain sense, as a board, you had to be prepared to do whatever you needed to do."

But Pepper Hamilton's lawyers still had a lot of work to do. They were reviewing select cases from three academic years: 2012–13, 2013–14, and 2014–15. By their presentation to the board of regents in February, they had a list of people yet to interview, including Briles and his coaching staff. The regents wanted them done by the end of April so they could present their findings to the full board in May.

On Sunday, May 1, 2016, board chairman Richard Willis and regents Ron Murff, Christopher Howard, Jerry Clements, Dan Hord, Ken Carlile, Jeff Reeter, and Harper, along with Baylor attorney Chris Holmes, flew to Philadelphia, where they met up with Gray, who was coming from his son's engagement party in Houston. The collective group was about a quarter of the full board of regents. On Monday morning, they met at the downtown headquarters of Pepper Hamilton. They gathered in a large, stark conference room around a table on which attorneys Leslie Gomez and Gina Maisto Smith placed a stack of three-ring binders full of printouts of text messages, emails, interviews, and other documentation. They started with a prayer. They stayed in that conference room from 8:00 a.m. well into the evening, listening to what the attorneys found. The attorneys reviewed about six cases, all involving football players.

The regents were informed of an interview one regent said came "straight out of a script of victim blaming," between the former Baylor police chief Jim Doak and a woman reporting an assault. There were statements like, "Honey, don't you know that if you wouldn't have been out drinking, this wouldn't have happened to you? What are your parents going to say?" The regents heard about a woman who showed the attorneys a list of the twenty-seven people she had to recount her assault to in order to switch majors to the business school so as to avoid encountering her alleged perpetrator. They heard about the alleged gang rapes. Every story left them shaking.

"The briefing was when I learned the full depth of the information and my reaction was one of profound shock and sadness," Murff said. "I was sad for the victims, first of all. It was horrific to hear of how some of these women were treated along the way, from the initial acts of violation and then when they tried to get help. We didn't help them the way we should have. It was very disturbing."

During the meeting, one of the regents started crying and pounded the table, saying, "Not my Baylor," and "Why do we have to listen to any more of this? Don't we know what we have to do?" Every one of the nine regents ended the meeting completely emotionally drained.

Some were in shock. Some would cry the next day. "For me, it felt like I'd been run over by a truck," Gray said.

They learned from the attorneys how difficult it had been for some of the women who participated in the interviews, with one such woman in particular only able to talk to them if she was curled up in a fetal position on the floor. At that point, none of the women who talked to Gomez and Smith had asked for anything. They weren't making demands through lawyers. "They all talked to [the investigators] on the basis of they wanted Baylor to be a better place and that was always impactful to me," Gray said.

Most of the regents traveled back to Texas, debating during the trip how best to inform the rest of the board on what they had heard. They discussed a written report, which they were told might take months for Gomez and Smith to prepare. Then there was the concern about putting that much private information into a written report, and what risk releasing such a report would pose to the university's liability insurance coverage as well. Jasmin Hernandez, who did not speak with the Pepper Hamilton attorneys, had already filed her lawsuit and others were likely coming. As one regent put it, if releasing too much detail in a report is determined to have compromised the university's defense, an insurance company could refuse to pay out for any legal fees, settlements, or judgments. They said they believed it was their fiduciary duty to Baylor to take that into account, despite what they knew would be a likely demand for information. The regents weighed all those considerations in light of the weight of what they had heard. There was a sense of urgency and a discussion about needing to have Gomez and Smith give their presentation at the next board meeting and then decide what to do.

Over ten hours on Monday, May 11 and Tuesday, May 12, Gomez and Smith gave their presentation to the full board in Waco, and Starr was present for all of it but the discussions the board had about him. We were told, in the interest of time—and possible liability—that the Pepper Hamilton attorneys were instructed not to put together a comprehensive written report. Instead, they had a lengthy Microsoft

PowerPoint presentation that included their observations, excerpts of emails, and text messages and other documents, as well as highlights of interviews with more than sixty-five people, including current and former employees and students. This is when the full board heard of the many troubling findings coming from the football program. During those meetings, it was made clear there were problems at the highest level of the administration—poor communication and coordination and, a word Pepper Hamilton attorneys used, "dysfunctionality."

They heard that in the case of the woman who reported the 2013 domestic violence incident against Oakman, she had taken her police report to director of football operations Colin Shillinglaw. Every football program has people who step in when its players get in trouble with the law, and at Baylor, one of those was Shillinglaw, a friend of Briles for almost three decades—and a colleague, as the coach hired Shillinglaw everywhere he went, from Stephenville High School to the University of Houston and then to Baylor.

The woman decided she didn't want to press criminal charges against Oakman, but met with Shillinglaw and two other people in the football program to see if there was some way they could address it. As to that incident, Briles said in an interview on ESPN's *College GameDay* in September 2016 that Oakman received counseling for the alleged domestic violence at the time. (Briles's attorney Mark Lanier said in an email in June 2017 that Briles didn't remember saying that, and actually doesn't remember sending Oakman to counseling.) But none of them—or anyone with athletics—ever reported the incident to Judicial Affairs, according to what the Pepper Hamilton attorneys found in their investigation. The woman left Baylor that spring, and tried to return in the summer and fall, but withdrew after more encounters with Oakman. Lanier wrote that Briles remembered one of his assistants coming to him in 2013 to say that Oakman and his girlfriend got in a fight, but Briles doesn't remember being told that "it was so bad the police were called." His assistant told him that he'd talk to Oakman about it, "so Coach figured it was being handled," he wrote.

According to a legal filing that would come out in February 2017 in a case involving Shillinglaw, the woman and her mother would tell her story to a Baylor employee in an academic department in January 2015, and the person would immediately contact Judicial Affairs, student life, the general counsel's office, and the Title IX office, where Patty Crawford had recently set up shop.

The regents also heard more about a volleyball player who in April 2013 told her coach—head volleyball coach Jim Barnes—that five football players had gang-raped her a year ago at a party off campus. Her story would end up being one of the most debated, contested, analyzed, and revealing narratives of the entire saga, as it became a flashpoint for what Coach Briles and others in the athletic department knew—or didn't know—and how such heinous allegations could be swept away without an investigation. It would be the subject of press releases, media columns, and, a full year later, a lawsuit filed by the former volleyball player herself that further heightened the outrage.

On February 11, 2012, Erica* went to an off-campus party at an apartment where Baylor football players lived. "She was just at the party, it got late. They were drinking," Barnes told us, recalling what she told him a year later. He said the volleyball player told him, "I was in a room with someone and then someone else came in and then it got out of hand." According to her lawsuit, Erica believed she'd been drugged. Her friend noticed one football player trying to repeatedly pull her into a bathroom, and she recalled another player—one whose advances she had deflected the day before—who kept grabbing at her throughout the night. Erica recalled her friends leaving, and another player picking her up, putting her in his vehicle, and driving her to another location. Before she knew it, there were at least four of them taking turns having sex with her; Barnes said she had told him five. She said once more football players tried to engage in sex or sexual acts with her, she told them, "no," and that she did not want this to happen, he said. "She just said, 'It just got out of control, and I couldn't stop it.'"

* Pseudonym

"And then I'm like, 'Oh no, [Erica].' And she goes, 'Yes.' And I go, 'Five?' And she goes, 'Yes,'" Barnes said. "She made the impression that five guys raped her. I clearly understood that. . . . I could tell how sensitive she was even thinking about it again."

Barnes said she didn't share many details, but her lawsuit states she remembers "lying on her back, unable to move and staring at glow-in-the-dark stars on the ceiling as the football players took turns raping her" and following that, she remembered hearing them yell, "Grab her phone. Delete my numbers and texts."

Barnes said Erica had been embarrassed, thinking perhaps she brought this on herself, and she didn't tell anyone at the time what happened. But word spread among the athletes, and she'd see football players pointing at her and whispering to each other when she walked by, her former coach said. She said in her lawsuit that the football players kept texting her, trying to "paint a completely different picture of what had happened that night" with one saying the sex was consensual, that she'd "wanted it," and that he had nude photos of her and other players from that night.

According to her lawsuit, Erica told her mom, who would end up arranging to meet an assistant coach on July 11, 2012, at McAlister's Deli in Waco, where she gave him the names of the players Erica said were involved in her alleged assault. "Not surprisingly, [Erica's] mother never heard from the assistant football coach again," the lawsuit states. That coach was former strength and conditioning coach Kaz Kazadi, according to several sources.

Kazadi called two of the accused players into his office and questioned them, according to a legal filing by three Baylor regents in a 2017 defamation lawsuit (although the filing only referred to him as the coach who had met Erica's mom in the deli). The players insisted the sex was consensual and that they were just "fooling around" and it was "just a little bit of playtime." According to Briles's attorney, Kazadi told Briles in passing that he had met with the mother of a volleyball player who was concerned about her daughter "partying" with football players. "Briles asked if there was anything else 'we needed to do' and

Kaz said no," attorney Mark Lanier wrote in an email, adding that the first Briles heard it was a rape allegation was from Barnes in April 2013. It's unknown who else Kazadi told at the time, and he did not respond to requests for an interview.

When Baylor's new head coach Matt Rhule took over after December 2016, he didn't retain any of Briles's hires. The university announced in March 2017 that Kazadi was reassigned a spot outside the athletic department and remained a university employee.

Erica's lawsuit states that football players harassed her and her relatives via text messages, and harassed her verbally on and off campus. She had to face them at the training facility the volleyball team shared with the football team, and in spring 2013 she had to attend a class with two of the men she said raped her. She had to "put her earphones in and listen to music just to make it through the class each week." One football player, who she would later accuse of burglarizing her apartment, began harassing her via text message, telling her that he never came on to her because she was "easy" and "like coach said, we [Baylor football players] don't want easy."

She noted in her lawsuit that she saw a counselor at Baylor, and relayed the details of her assault including names of the football players, but the counselor never told her about any rights or options to report the assault or whether she could get any academic or other accommodations to help her while still on campus.

In April 2013, she reported to Waco police that her apartment had been burglarized. Her lawsuit states that several football players broke in, stole money and a necklace, and threw her clothes and belongings all over her room. No charges were ever filed, and a week later she met with Briles to tell him about the burglary (but according to her attorney did not mention the alleged rape). "Briles was short with [her] and hurried the meeting along," the lawsuit states, and she did not believe that coaches or the school ever disciplined the players. They continued to harass her. Briles doesn't recall ever meeting or speaking with Erica, his attorney said. He wrote that when Briles heard from his assistant coaches about two players involved in the break in at her apartment, he kicked both of them off the team. He said that she later asked assistant coaches to reinstate one of them, whom she had been dating.

When Barnes spoke to us about what happened in April 2013, he said that a recent breakup involving a player Erica had been dating made her situation worse, and she decided she couldn't take it anymore. She was leaving Baylor. And leaving Texas altogether. He said her parents were coming the next day to bring her home. "I was like, 'Whoa. Let's go to the police. Let's take care of this. I need the information so I can go report it,'" he said.

Erica wrote five names down on a piece of paper, and Barnes said he told her that he was going to take the information to athletic director Ian McCaw and get back to her before her parents arrived. After speaking with McCaw, Barnes said he went to Briles's office. "His first reaction right away was, 'Oh my God, Coach, is she okay?'" Barnes said. "He was sickened by it."

Barnes recounted to Briles how Erica was at the party and ended up in the room with those five football players, and said Briles responded by saying, "Oh my gosh. Why would she be in a room at this time of night with some bad dudes?" Barnes said that was a reference to those five as "some of the roughest guys on the team." Barnes said Briles told him to have the woman report the incident to the police, and Barnes responded with, "I am trying to get her to do that." Briles asked him if he'd spoken with McCaw, and Barnes assured him that he had.

When Erica's parents arrived, Barnes said he met with them and said, "We've got to go report this," but they told him they just wanted to take her home. However, they agreed to meet with Barnes one more time before they left Waco. In the meantime, Barnes said he went back to McCaw and told him Erica and her parents weren't going to report the assault to police, to which McCaw responded, "They need to report it for something to be done."

Barnes said he asked what else he could do, and McCaw suggested Barnes call Judicial Affairs. He wanted to know what options he could give Erica's parents before meeting with them the next day, so he made the call and he said to the person answering the phone—whose name he never got—"If there's someone who needs to report something, how do they go about doing it?" He said the judicial affairs person told him that the victim needs to come by that office or call. "I said, 'Well, that's what I'm attempting to do.'"

Barnes did not share any specific details of Erica's case during that call, but relayed the information to the woman and her parents. "Please, let's call the number right now and do this," Barnes said, but her parents refused. They didn't want her name or what happened to her to be revealed publicly. They just wanted to take her home. But Barnes persisted. "We can't let them get away with it. We've got to make this right, that they don't do it to someone else." But they adamantly refused, he said. Years later, Barnes said Erica, who he said agreed with her parents' decision to remain quiet, told him that she wanted the athletics department to take some action to "address those issues." Barnes said he is still bothered by it. "I was extremely upset with them that they did not want to report it."

But Barnes's version of those conversations contradicts the details in Erica's lawsuit and her attorney, who said no one ever gave Erica or her parents a number to judicial affairs or anything along those lines. "Contrary to statements made by those with knowledge of [her] sexual assault, neither [Erica] nor her parents ever indicated that they did not want to report the assault to judicial affairs. Instead [they] were told that it was too late for criminal charges and they begged [Barnes] and the assistant volleyball coach to tell them what, if anything, Baylor could do about the sexual assault."

Erica's lawsuit states she made the decision to withdraw from Baylor after taking a mission trip to Africa with some of the football players, one of whom told her that he heard eight guys actually had sex with her that night in February 2012. That was her breaking point. She left Baylor and transferred to another Division I university where she played volleyball in 2013 and 2014. But according to her lawsuit, she made one more attempt to elicit someone's help in pursuing her allegations at Baylor; she, like other women before and after, confided in Baylor's football chaplain on a visit to Waco in fall 2013, and still nothing happened.

Barnes said that at the time he learned of the allegations, only one of the five accused football players was still on the team. Barnes said that player had already been suspended for an unrelated violation and that Briles, upon hearing about the gang rape allegations, cut him altogether. But Briles's attorney said that's actually not what happened, noting that all of the players were off the team by the time Briles heard of the allegations in spring 2013. At the time, Barnes said Erica appreciated Briles's handling of the incident and his discretion by refusing to speak about it or revealing her identity.

In a September 2016 interview with ESPN's Tom Rinaldi, Briles described the incident as "sketchy," saying that there were "different versions of what transpired" and "it was investigated within our staff." He also told Rinaldi that he didn't know about it until about a year after it had happened, and that he hadn't known the names of the players involved. The regents' legal filing would state that coaches' "apparent response was to engage in victim blaming," and that an assistant coach decided the accusations were in a "gray area" and there really was no evidence of a sexual assault.

One former assistant football coach who spoke to us on the condition of anonymity said that he and his colleagues were under the impression that it was a consensual "gang bang" and not a "gang rape," and referred to comments that a female witness made about the volleyball player making encouraging statements to the football players while they were having sex. That type of response from football players when issues like these would come up wasn't uncommon.

"You know, and you've got to understand, some of these guys, if I want to ask a question and say, 'Hey, did these guys do this?' I mean, those guys will immediately spin it to where, 'Coach, that girl's had sex with him ten times and with forty guys on this team,'" the former assistant football coach said. "Right, wrong, or indifferent, I know that's not politically correct to say. I know that's not the right thing to say. But that's reality. That's what those guys would say. Does that make it right if they were to do something wrong? Absolutely not. I

think you know good and damn well that none of us would ever con-
done that. But that's just the way a locker room is."

What struck the regents most about that incident—beyond the
actual act itself—was that no one actually shared the details of the
allegation to Judicial Affairs, which has an obligation to look into a
report of sexual violence even without the alleged victim's cooperation. The logic behind that policy is to protect other women from an
individual on campus who might pose a threat of sexual violence and
to detect any signs of a larger problem within a department, team, or
other group. A statement from McCaw's attorney said he was "was
faced with a situation in which he desired to honor the wishes of the
alleged victim" who did not want to report the incident to police, and
he directed the victim's coach to judicial affairs, also noting that no one
at the time had instructed him or anyone else on proper Title IX protocol. Barnes said he and Briles adhered to typical department policy
at the time, which was to report such incidents to the athletic director;
the school has no record that McCaw himself followed up with Judicial Affairs. Barnes said he pestered McCaw several times, but that the
athletic director repeatedly told him there was nothing they could do
if Erica didn't want to contact Judicial Affairs herself.

On December 2, 2014, Barnes said McCaw brought him into his
office, sat him down, and told him, "Jim, you've done a great job.
You've done everything we've asked. We decided to go in a different
direction," and McCaw stood up and walked out. "I said, 'Ian, you just
signed me to an extension. I just signed a top-ten recruiting class who I
told them I'd be here. Can you at least give me a reason?'" Barnes said
he never got one. The eleven-year head coach said he'd just finished his
second losing season; missing Erica had hurt the team in 2013, and then
2014 began with five starters suffering career-ending injuries, but it still
didn't add up. During his interview with Pepper Hamilton attorneys in
May 2016, they pointed out that he was fired just as Baylor's new Title
IX coordinator Patty Crawford was coming to campus. Barnes said, "I
don't believe they wanted me and the Title IX person to meet."

The February 2017 regents' legal filing noted that even though at the time Baylor wasn't training its faculty, staff, and coaches on proper Title IX reporting protocol, the onus was still on Briles and McCaw to have reported the incident to Judicial Affairs (Barnes was not named): "Coach Briles and McCaw knew that judicial affairs had jurisdiction for investigating sexual assaults. Indeed, on April 23, 2013, the very same day Coach Briles learned about the student-athlete's account of being gang raped, he was forwarded a letter stating that judicial affairs had investigated and cleared another one of his players of sexual assault allegations."

If Erica's incident and the 2013 Oakman domestic violence case were examples of allegations of sexual violence never making it out of the athletics department, an accusation against former player Myke Chatman involving a student athletic trainer with the football team was perhaps the reverse. The incident allegedly happened March 2, 2013, about a month before Chatman and Tre'Von Armstead were accused of raping Mary, and it was never reported to law enforcement. People who worked in the female student's academic program knew about it, but, according to multiple sources, at the time no one shared that information with the athletics department.

A former assistant football coach said he and many of his colleagues first heard about that incident in January 2017, in a lawsuit filed against Baylor by Mary, who said Chatman told her about the accusations involving the student athletic trainer. "We didn't know. Nobody told us. We had no idea," the former assistant football coach said. Although the lawsuit said the incident was reported to athletic department officials, and that "one staff member of the athletic training program warned the football team that they needed to get control over their players or else the football team would no longer have student trainers," sources with knowledge of the incident told us it was handled outside the athletic department. A Baylor employee in the woman's academic program—not in athletics and not in upper administration—responded to hearing about the student athletic trainer's assault by implying she "shouldn't be around male athletes" and should switch to working with another team, sources told us. Her case was reported to Judicial Affairs, but it never received a hearing and Chatman remained on campus until he was kicked off the team for a drug violation. "It's a huge deal," said the former assistant football coach, noting that Chatman transferred to Sam Houston State and played there for three more years. "If we would have known that, we would have told Sam Houston." Sources told us the employee who made that comment about her not being around male athletes was reprimanded, and the female student decided on her own to transfer to a different sport. Sources familiar with her case said she eventually went to the school's general counsel office and was provided tuition assistance, but she still suffered the emotional impact of the alleged assault and the school's initial inaction.

The regents would learn of even more alleged gang rapes. But there was more, much more, and it went beyond sexual assaults—and was equally as disturbing. The Pepper Hamilton attorneys pored through the emails, text messages, and other documents that the forensic analysis firm had extracted from servers and devices. And what those messages revealed was head-shaking, jaw-dropping, and eye-opening. Players brandishing guns, coaches working with Waco police to keep crimes quiet and circumvent any school punishment, and coaches arranging attorneys for football players.

When a freshman defensive tackle was ticketed for underage drinking in April 2011, Briles texted an assistant coach with the following: "Hopefully he's under the radar enough they won't recognize [his] name—did he get ticket from Baylor police or Waco? . . . Just trying to keep him away from our judicial affairs folks."

The regents heard about an exchange between Briles and an assistant coach in February 2013 regarding a female student-athlete who complained that a football player brandished a gun, and the incident was never reported to Judicial Affairs.

> BRILES: [W]hat a fool—she reporting to authorities.
> ASSISTANT COACH: She's acting traumatized. . . . Trying to talk her calm now . . . Doesn't seem to want to report though.

BRILES: U gonna talk to [the player].

ASSISTANT COACH: Yes sir, just did. Caught him on the way to class. . . . Squeezed him pretty good.

There were texts from Shillinglaw to Briles from September 2013 regarding a player who was accused of exposing himself and asking for "favors" from a masseuse, according to the texts the regents received. The woman had a lawyer but, Shillinglaw noted, "wants us to handle with discipline and counseling." Briles responded, "What kind of discipline . . . She a stripper?" When Shillinglaw said the incident happened at a salon and spa, Briles responded, "Not quite as bad."

They were presented with correspondence that showed Briles, Shillinglaw, and other coaches either trying to intervene or to circumvent school discipline. In one exchange from October 2013, regarding a player who had been suspended for multiple drug violations, Shillinglaw wrote that, "Bottom line, he has to meet with (Vice President for Student Life Kevin) Jackson tomorrow morning. If Jackson does not reinstate President (Starr) will."

Another exchange involved a player who had been caught selling drugs. Briles texted an assistant coach, "I'm hoping it will take care of itself—if not we can discuss best way to move on it." The crime was never reported to Judicial Affairs and Briles made arrangements for the player to transfer to another school. A text from the assistant coach read, "Him just hanging around Waco scares me," and said that another school (whose name was redacted in the texts released publicly) would take him. "Knows baggage," the assistant coach wrote.

And they heard examples of Briles and coaches actively trying to keep football player crimes under the radar, all the while trying to arrange legal representation for players—and this time, it involved even higher-ranking administrators. On September 20, 2013, Ian McCaw and Briles exchanged messages about a football player who had been arrested for assaulting and threatening to kill a male nonathlete. It was a player who multiple sources told us had ties to area gangs.

BRILES: Just talked to [the player]—he said Waco PD was there—
said they were going to keep it quiet—Wasn't a set up deal . . .
I'll get shill (Shillinglaw) to ck on Sibley.

McCAW: That would be great if they kept it quiet!

Sibley was in reference to Jonathan Sibley, a Waco attorney with
deep ties to Baylor sports; his grandfather had been athletic director and his father had played basketball there. He had also been Sam
Ukwuachu's initial attorney. And that exchange wouldn't be the only
one where regents saw coaches connecting players with Sibley.

In an exchange between Briles and an assistant coach on August
15, 2015, after a player was arrested for possession of marijuana:

BRILES: Shit—how about that—he's gonna b in the system now—
let me know what you think we should do. . . . I can get shill
(Shillinglaw) to call Sibley or we can. . . . Do we know who
complained?

The assistant coach responded that the complaint came from the
superintendent at the player's apartment complex.

BRILES: We need to know who supervisor is and get him to alert
us first.

While the attorneys did not make personnel decisions, they told
the regents about who was cooperative and who wasn't, who took
action and who didn't, and how the interview subjects responded to
the issues raised. They noted that the first time Briles was interviewed,
he recalled only "bits and pieces" of the gang rape allegation involving
the volleyball player, but in a later interview said he didn't remember
meeting with Barnes but "recalled hearing about the victim because
she had been in his office about another incident."

The attorneys also noted that when they spoke to Shillinglaw,
he said he did not remember meeting the woman who reported

Oakman's domestic violence incident and he did not recall getting the police report. But attorneys found her contact information in his phone along with emails indicating he had received the report and had asked an assistant coach to speak to Oakman's relatives.

On May 13, Baylor's media relations office issued a press release stating the board of regents had received a comprehensive briefing from Pepper Hamilton and were debating what to do next. It did not state whether the board would release the results of the investigation to the public, and any questions about that issue were deflected back to the press release.

CHAPTER THIRTY-TWO

TRUTH DON'T LIE

On May 18, 2016, while the Baylor board of regents was still deliberating about what to do after receiving a scathing presentation from Pepper Hamilton's lawyers, the public pressure on the university reached a tipping point. A whole plethora of allegations against football players surfaced, calling into question administrators, coaches, police, even Baptist clergy.

ESPN's *Outside the Lines* posted a story about several incidents discovered through police records, including one in which a woman told a reporter she informed football team chaplain Wes Yeary about being physically assaulted by her ex-boyfriend, who was a Bears football player. The woman said she was informed that President Ken Starr and football coach Art Briles knew about the incident, but she said no one reached out to her, nor did the university or Briles take action against her alleged perpetrator.

The alleged victim, Dolores Lozano, told police that on April 5, 2014, she was leaving Scruffy Murphy's—a Waco bar popular with students—and was trying to get into her friend's car when her boyfriend, football player Devin Chafin, started yelling and cursing at her. She reported that he grabbed her arm and slammed it against the window while her friend and his teammates—who she said had tried to hold him back—stood nearby. She told police it wasn't the first time he'd hurt her, and she detailed an alleged incident from March 6, 2014, during which she said Chafin "grabbed her around the throat cutting off her airway where she could not breathe momentarily and then slammed her against the wall hurting her arm and then throwing her on the floor of the apartment and kicking her." She told police at the time that she was not sure about pressing charges. No charges were ever filed against Chafin. On October 11, 2016, Lozano filed a Title IX lawsuit against Baylor, in which she stated Waco police never got back to her, despite her placing repeated calls to the department. The lawsuit also outlined her attempts to seek help from Baylor. She stated that she told Bears running backs coach Jeff Lebby about the first assault, when her bruises and cuts were still visible. She said Lebby told her he'd talk to Chafin about the incident, but Lozano said she was unaware of any action taken and no report was filed with Judicial Affairs.

Lozano, who was a student manager for the school's acrobatics and tumbling team, asked the team coach LaPrise Harris-Williams if she could take a leave of absence to deal with the emotional stress from the incidents. When Harris-Williams heard her story, she immediately reported it to her superior, associate athletic director Nancy Post, the lawsuit states. According to the suit, Post told Harris-Williams that "being involved with incidents like Lozano's were not [Harris-Williams's] responsibility," and Post—a senior athletic department official—took no further action, despite Harris-Williams's insistence that something be done. Harris-Williams claimed she was forced to resign a year later because she voiced her "discontent with the administrators."

Harris-Williams told us that she actually talked to other women with similar experiences at Baylor, and received a similar response from administrators.

"I did plead with the women that spoke with me to seek counseling, file police reports. In some cases I sat with them as they made phone calls to the police to determine what they should do next," she wrote in an email, adding that one woman told her about being turned away from the counseling center and "made to feel her attack was her own fault." "I brought the issue before my supervisor several times and was offered no help. There were coaches and staff members who were forced to take a fall so that Baylor could stay protected."

She recalled another student who shared "an unbelievably horrific experience with a Baylor football player." "She was scared and felt deserted by the university after her efforts to report were played down. I asked her what she was feeling at the time," Harris-Williams wrote. "She sat silent for a good while and then simply said, 'I feel like I'm wondering.'"

At the time, according to the lawsuit, Harris-Williams also reported Lozano's alleged assault to Yeary, who met personally with Lozano to discuss the incident. Lozano said she told the chaplain about concerns for Chafin and for her own well-being, and said Yeary only provided her with literature to assist her "spiritual self-worth and preservation." The second alleged assault would happen three weeks later.

The university, in asking the court to dismiss Lozano's lawsuit, didn't address any of the specific descriptions of her interactions with Post, Lebby, and Yeary; it stated that too much time had passed and that Title IX covers sexual violence and her claim wasn't valid because the abuse wasn't a sexual act. "Title IX is not a general student safety statute and does not impose upon universities the responsibility to manage the private interactions of its students. . . . Universities do not owe a legal duty to protect students from harm from fellow students." University officials also declined to discuss the case unless we could get Lozano to sign a waiver of her rights under student privacy laws, which her attorneys declined.

Former assistant coaches who spoke to us about her case had a different version, starting with Lozano telling a coach about going to Chafin's house intoxicated, causing a scene, and acting out of control to where the football player had to restrain her, but at no point did she say he hit her; Lozano's attorneys said that did not happen. The two students had a rather tumultuous relationship, and had recently dealt with some very difficult situations that had also involved their parents, the former assistant coaches said. Lozano has said, through her attorney, that she had been trying to help Chafin through some personal issues of his own—even reaching out to Baylor coaches and Chafin's own relatives for help—and that she also helped him with his academics. "Dolores' actions are commendable and her acts of maturity and heroism at such a young age show the strides she was willing to make for a man Baylor University simply turned their back on," her attorney Ricky Patel said in an email.

According to the coaches, the woman came to Lebby and told him that story because she was indeed concerned about Chafin's well-being and mental health. Nothing about the conversation led them to believe the woman was abused or wanted help, and they said she maintained a positive relationship with Lebby.

In June 2016, Waco CBS affiliate KWTX-TV quoted Chafin as saying he "grabbed Lozano to restrain her" following an argument, but he didn't believe he caused her bruising. The TV station also posted an excerpt of an email it claimed was sent from Lozano to Lebby a year after the assault allegations asking him for a job recommendation for the assistant director of athletic marketing at Baylor. It quoted the email as saying she admires "Baylor's convictions and mission to educate men and women for worldwide leadership and service by integrating academic excellence and Christian commitment within a caring community." She did not get the job, but now works as a sports media and public relations professional in Houston.

Another incident that became public as the regents were mulling the Pepper Hamilton findings involved cornerback Tyler Stephenson, whose girlfriend reported to police on April 3, 2012, that he was violent with her at his apartment and refused to let her leave or use her phone. "He then pushed me on the couch and wrestled me for my phone so that I couldn't call for help," she told police. The woman said she tried again to call 911 once outside, but "he charged me and picked me up and threw me against the [exterior] apartment wall. I hit my head and immediately felt dizzy," and she yelled for help. The report notes Stephenson ran away after three men approached him, and police confirmed the woman's account with a witness who saw the two fighting. Waco police prepared an arrest warrant for Stephenson but closed the case when the woman did not return several phone messages. According to the ESPN article in which the incident was first reported, Stephenson did not respond to questions. It's unknown whether he was disciplined.

Another case that came to light was a 2012 sexual assault allegation against All-American safety Ahmad Dixon, which turned out to be a false accusation: The woman even told a reporter she made the story up to get Dixon in trouble. Waco police noted in an incident report that officers had had several run-ins with the woman and her family over the years. Nevertheless, it was an interesting look into how quickly coaches found out when a player was accused of a crime and how they responded. The story quoted Dixon as saying an assistant coach called him within a day of the incident, but Dixon said he didn't know how the coaches found out. "They told me there wasn't much that they could do, other than to tell me to go to the police station and go from there," he said in a May 18, 2016, *Outside the Lines* story.

Dixon was also involved in another case—which was part of the aforementioned story—in which three football players were charged. A series of fights broke out at a fraternity party on campus in May 2011, and Dixon admitted he threw the first punch after a fraternity member tried to stop him from breaking into a line dance. Dixon and his teammates engaged in another scuffle with the fraternity member and his friends, which eventually spilled outside. According to the police report, three of the football players attacked a previously uninvolved Baylor student who was trying to walk to his car. They only stopped hitting him when a nearby group of women urged them to stop. The student identified the three players as defensive lineman Gary Mason, running back Isaac Williams, and Stephenson. According to the article, "while the athletes disagree on which of them hit him and when, statements to police and interviews conducted by *Outside the Lines* confirm that the student never threw a punch or made any physical advance on the other people involved. 'The young guy, I know that he had nothing to do with it. I didn't see [him] in the party or in the foyer fighting,' Dixon told *Outside the Lines*."

The police report noted the student had "major damage to the front of his face. His bottom lip was swollen twice the size of what it would normally be" and "about three to four teeth were knocked to the point that they were loose and leaning over." The officer also noted the student was reluctant to tell him what happened, writing, "he said that he has heard anecdotal stories of football players getting into altercations or disturbances and nothing ever being done." Mason, Williams, and Stephenson were arrested on charges of misdemeanor assault, but the McLennan County District Attorney's Office declined to prosecute. Mason and Williams declined to talk for the story, but Dixon said coaches did punish Williams: He was suspended from the football team until July and was required to do community service, extra running at practice, and cleanup duty in the weight room. The injured student died on August 8, 2012. His family and friends have refused to talk about the incident, and don't wish to disclose how he died.

The case was yet another look into how Waco police responded to incidents involving football players, and the department's desire to shield its information—a frustration already encountered by Baylor's fledgling Title IX department. The report noted a Baylor police officer provided contact information for some of the football players and that Baylor police lieutenant Kevin Helpert informed others at the university, adding that "there were supposed to be some administrative level meetings taking place concerning it, given that it was a university-approved function." Then, according to the Waco police officer's narrative, he asked that the police report be pulled from the computer system "so that only persons who had a reason to inquire about the report would be able to access it." A master copy of the report was placed in a locked office at police headquarters. The article quoted a Waco police spokesman as saying detectives can shield certain cases from public view if there are privacy concerns, which they've done for cases that don't involve Baylor. "Was this done specifically because this was a Baylor case and because it involved Baylor football players? I can't tell you that," he said.

In an interview on Sirius XM College Sports the next day, athletic director Ian McCaw responded to inferences from the story that there was collaboration between Baylor Athletics and Waco police. "Nothing to my knowledge. Student safety really is something that just has to be in place, and that's something that our administration, our board of regents are very committed to, and we're taking very strong steps to make sure that we have the best Title IX system possible. We built a very safe campus to protect the welfare of all of our students." (At that time, the text message correspondence between Briles and McCaw—in which Briles indicates that Waco police are going to keep quiet about a player arrested for assault and McCaw responds, "That would be great if they kept it quiet"—hadn't been made public.) Another case that wasn't reported at the time in the *Outside the Lines* story involved former running back Glasco Martin, whose ex-girlfriend alleged he forcefully barged his way into her apartment, went into her bedroom, and unbuttoned his pants and tried to pull her into bed with him. She ran into her bathroom, and when he went into her living room, she locked the bedroom door and waited for him to leave. Although Martin was a year removed from the team at the time of December 2014 incident, the woman told police that Martin had "been aggressive in the past and has even threatened her with physical harm if she did not do what he wanted." Police ended up issuing a misdemeanor arrest warrant and turned it into municipal court. "It was a misunderstanding," Martin said. "I got upset, and we worked it out afterward. I had a couple of hours of community service. It didn't happen exactly the way they said it happened."

The long list of other alleged criminal incidents naming Baylor football players on the heels of Oakman's arrest whipped social media and national sports columnists into a frenzy. Twitter filled with comments disparaging the school and its football program, accusing it of trying to win at all costs and covering up rapes. (Not coincidentally, many of those accounts were identified with rival Big 12 Conference schools such as Texas and Texas Christian University.) Defenders of the program discounted the reports as mere allegations and some blamed ESPN's coverage on an attempt for the network to bolster rival Texas and its ESPN joint-owned Longhorn Network. Then there was what many described as an odd and ill-timed tweet that Briles put out on May 19, 2016—and later deleted—which was a graphic listing Baylor football's academic statistics with the hashtags #TruthDontLie #BeCourageous #BaylorFootballBeAChampion.

It was the only public communication from Briles at the time, and he did not respond to media inquiries about the newly public allegations. The silence from Briles and Baylor had long been criticized, and now that criticism was reaching a fever pitch. Sports columnists pondered Briles's future as rumors started to swirl that the successful coach was now on the hot seat. Fox Sports senior college football columnist Bruce Feldman wrote that he received nine calls or texts from college football coaches about Briles in light of the new allegations. He quoted a coach as saying, "There are three big questions here: Who knew what happened? When did they know about it? And, what action was taken? This is a guy (Briles) who prides himself in being a players' coach and coaching his team like a high school team. It's really hard to believe that he didn't know about any of this stuff." *Fort Worth Star-Telegram* columnist Mac Engel wrote that Baylor and its board of regents could either "hunker down" with Briles and try to ride out the storm of bad publicity or fire the successful coach. "The board is expected to keep Briles, but two sources indicated firing him is being considered as the final solution to a scandal that continues to be a nightmare for the entire school for what is now approaching a full calendar year. . . . Consistent with the way it has completely bungled this story from the start last August, Baylor is not commenting other than to issue another vanilla press release."

In story after story, tweet after tweet, people were calling for more transparency. They knew the Pepper Hamilton investigation was finished, and there was one overriding demand: Produce the report.

CHAPTER THIRTY-THREE

UNPRECEDENTED ACTIONS

As public pressure mounted in May 2016, Baylor's board of regents already knew what its problems were and much of what it needed to do to fix them. Next would be to decide who would carry that plan forward. Prior to the meetings, the board's special committee—knowing where the evidence was leading—put together options on likely personnel options. Could they reduce salaries? Shorten contracts? Change titles? For Bears football coach Art Briles, could they suspend him six games and fine him $1 million, or would they have to fire him? The regents—a combination of corporate executive officers, pastors, businessmen and businesswomen, a political consultant, physician, and other leaders in their professions—weighed their options.

The regents deliberated, discussed, and prayed. And after a full-day session on Monday, May 23, 2016, with most of the board members meeting in Houston and the rest conferenced in on a call, they took a vote. They voted 24–6 to recommend suspending Briles with the intent to terminate for cause. They also voted 26–4 to seek athletics director Ian McCaw's resignation. The next day, they invited Briles and McCaw to come to a meeting—essentially giving them a chance to defend themselves—in a conference room in Clifton Robinson Tower, near campus.

When the regents invited McCaw in, he was prepared. He had a notepad and list of items he believed needed to be changed in athletics. When McCaw landed at Baylor in 2003, it was already the fifth stop in his athletic administration career, McCaw having originally hailed from Ontario, Canada. He served on a number of national boards and committees, and, outside of work, was a deacon at the Baptist church he and his family attended. McCaw admitted to the board there were problems, including the conflicting drug testing policy. He expressed frustration with close relationships important alumni and board members had with coaches that he said undermined his authority. Those issues were mostly money related, and we were told that Coach Briles would bypass McCaw and go to certain regents instead to renegotiate his contract. Along those lines, McCaw emphasized the need for the president to be *more* involved in athletics, and not only a "figurehead," because he—or any athletic director—needed support when trying to control a successful football coach and its program. McCaw laid out a series of steps he would take to improve the department's overall operations, including Title IX compliance. He was in there for about an hour, and once he finished, Briles was waiting outside.

When Briles came in, he seemed nervous. He apologized for what happened. He said he delegated down when it came to rules and punishment, and he knew he shouldn't have. He said he set up a system where he was the last to know about players' off-field problems, when he should have been the first to know. He said the football team's system for discipline was in house, not open house. At one point, he started to cry. He promised to do better. But there was something about Briles's response, unlike McCaw's, that didn't sit right with some regents. When Briles was asked what he would do to change things, he responded, "Tell me what you want me to do, and I'll do it." He admitted his failings but didn't provide a solution, other than promising to do better next time, the regents told us. One compared that comment to coaches saying after a bad game, "Next time we're going to pass the ball, we're going to run the ball, and score some points." "I didn't really get that he really got it," one regent said.

The regents had already spoken with Baylor president Ken Starr after the Pepper Hamilton presentations on May 11 and 12. Because the university and Starr ended up signing a nondisparagement agreement, few details have leaked about the nature of his discussion. Even though

Starr was getting regular raises and was supported by faculty, the internal strife with his executive council—the leaders of each division of the university—was getting worse and turnover was rampant. Speculation after his demotion led people to believe the board ousted Starr because of how he negotiated the settlement earlier that year with the Baylor Alumni Association, ending its decades-long strife with the board. But regents denied that, noting Starr wasn't a factor in key final discussions with the BAA and what involvement he had was not a concern to them. Several documents released during the course of Baylor's legal battles with the BAA would reveal, however, that there were tensions between Starr and certain regents whom he and other administrators—and even a fellow regent—had accused of trying to micromanage the university. In 2012, more than a year before the regents extended Starr's contract, he sensed they were concerned from an operational standpoint about how he was governing the university. In an excerpt from his book *Bear Country,* which was published in the *Waco Tribune-Herald* in October 2016, Starr wrote that he was summoned to outgoing regents chairman Neal T. "Buddy" Jones's office in April 2012 to meet with Jones and another regent for his end-of-the-year review. Jones, an influential state lobbyist, informed Starr that the regents wanted to implement a new organizational chart for the administration. Instead of having a clear number-two officer in the executive vice president and provost role, there would now be three senior officers reporting to him. The other vice presidents would no longer report directly to him, but to their respective senior officers. "It was simply presented to me, a fait accompli," Starr wrote. "The culture of the Baylor round table—all voices are equal, including my own—was to shift."

Over the next few months, Starr wrote, other regents suggested to him that his passion was law and he might be more satisfied working in an outside role such as chancellor, which would take advantage of his fundraising skills. In the summer of 2013, new regents chairman Richard Willis and regent Ron Murff informed Starr that an outside consultant was being hired to do a more comprehensive assessment of his performance. Susan Resneck Pierce, a former president at the University of Puget Sound in Tacoma, Washington, and a higher education consultant, met with Starr for several days on the Baylor campus in October 2013. Over breakfast, according to Starr, Pierce told him that his contract, which had two years remaining, would not be renewed. "A consummate professional, Susan made it clear that I was not what the board had in mind as CEO but that I could usefully play a different role in university-wide leadership," Starr wrote.

Starr told Pierce that he would resign so the board would have sufficient time to conduct a search for his replacement. Then, only a month later, the regents approached Starr about extending his contract as president for two years and giving him the additional duty of chancellor, which had been vacant for eight years. It was the first time a Baylor president had concurrently held the chancellor post, but Starr said he soon learned that it was only part of the regents' continued effort to nudge him out of control of the university.

"Quietly, I had been living on borrowed time," he wrote in his book. "For more than three years, the board's leadership had worked to ease me out of the CEO role and slot me instead into the non-executive position of chancellor, primarily a fundraiser. For various reasons, I was not satisfying the board's vision of a CEO. In their view, I was to be, instead, an outside person who built the university through raising money."

Through the turmoil between Starr and the board, members of the university's executive council said they did their best to keep up with the demands of Baylor's ever-growing student enrollment, and all of the regulatory mandates it was supposed to meet. But Starr was still the president. "If we had meetings and you got into some of the things that I think are important to operational decision making, Ken wanted to back-channel it, back-table it, 'we'll pick it up later,' task-force it, committee it, whatever. We didn't do it," said one senior administrator.

When interviewed by ESPN's Joe Schad on June 1, 2016, Starr would say he wasn't aware of the level of sexual assaults among Baylor students during his tenure at the university. When Schad asked him about the Pepper Hamilton findings, he said, "They, to be honest, are not findings. They are conclusions and recommendations," and he repeatedly cast his role as a leader who was simply ignorant to the problems below him, summing up his dismissal as "The captain goes down with the ship." He would say that every episode of which he was aware happened off campus, when, in fact, Baylor police alone reported ten cases of sexual assault in university housing or elsewhere on campus since 2010. His former chief of staff Karla Leeper told us she didn't recall a sexual assault case coming to him for an appeal ruling during her time. No one has come forward to say Starr knew about a sexual assault and covered it up. However, it was his lack of knowledge—and the many fingers pointing to his lack of involvement in the day-to-day business of the university—that led to the conclusion for some that while he didn't know, as president he should have. The board would decide to demote him from president, taking him out of any day-to-day operations of the university, but would allow him to keep the title and position of chancellor, which was a purely external role. He also would remain a professor in the law school. He would within weeks decide to step down as chancellor and later resign as law professor, leaving Baylor altogether.

In McCaw's case, they decided he could fix the problems in the athletics department with the right supervision and oversight. He was sanctioned and placed on probation, with the details of some sort of monetary penalty to be worked out. McCaw was told, specifically, that if the board ever learned of another instance in which he was pressured by alumni and/or coaches to "circumvent the rules" and he didn't come forward to the president, or if the president didn't help him and he didn't come to the board, then he would be fired. It was later told to us that issues with coaches—specifically Briles—going over McCaw's head and appealing to certain members of the board of regents had to do only with financial requests, such as contract negotiations, and not issues of student conduct. He abruptly resigned May 30, 2016.

Sources told us that in the days after he was sanctioned, McCaw talked to Baylor senior vice president Reagan Ramsower about the ongoing media attention and McCaw and Ramsower talked about whether McCaw should resign. McCaw decided it would be best for him and his family to move on, because as long as he remained, the story would be about him and the sexual assault crisis.

When it came to Briles, the board had his admission that he ran an internal disciplinary system, and they had the text messages and emails. They believed that Briles, like many other coaches, was being pressured by alumni and boosters, and, as can happen in that situation, "their judgment is going to be cloudy on who deserves a second chance, what has to be reported to the university." Regents were concerned about actions within the football program running afoul of several regulatory agencies—the U.S. Department of Education, the NCAA, and the Southern Association of Colleges and Schools Commission on Colleges, which provides Baylor's accreditation—not to mention university policy. "There was plenty of light being shined on this," one regent said. "If Art Briles is still our football coach, are any of those people going to think, *Well, he said he was sorry and he's changing. That's satisfactory for us*? I can't look straight in the face of those folks and say, 'Trust me. It's going to be okay.'"

Some regents were concerned about image and public scrutiny. Some were concerned about needing leaders who could right the ship. They needed someone who was more than only a football coach. They voted to fire Briles. "I always knew in my mind the question I had to answer for myself: 'Who is the right person in each of these positions to fix these problems?'" said regent J. Cary Gray.

Gray said he heard it said during the discussion that "[t]here are good people, even people who are good leaders, who are not the right leaders for the circumstances that they are dealing with." For Gray, the university was coming out of a crisis and had cultural issues that needed to be corrected. "Changes had to be made because these weren't the right leaders to lead us forward," he said.

For regent David Harper, the number of incidents—the sheer weight of that number—was a factor. "And then, ultimately on the football side it wasn't just the incidents, it was clear admission and other evidence there was a system in place, whether it was to avoid Title IX processes or our university process . . . to try to keep people out of the light of day," he said.

"There's been a lot said that the regents don't like football or we don't care about football and I think that's not true, you know, I love football," regent Kim Stevens said. "But when you look at the weight of the information, the number of cases against young women on campus, for me it kind of came down to, 'Where's our priority as the leadership of this school?' And our priority has to be taking care of our students and doing the right thing by them. And if that has to mean a crushing decision for the football program then that's what it is."

None of the decisions were easily made. There were dissenters, especially when it came to firing Briles. On the evening of May 24, 2016, after the regents had already voted once and after McCaw and Briles met with them to plead their case, the regents voted to place McCaw on probation with sanction. When it came to Briles, the board did consider a motion to reverse their decision to fire him, but the motion failed—by what's only been described as "an overwhelming margin." Baylor regents will not release the actual vote tally.

On May 25, regents Gray and Dan Hord, Associate General Counsel Doug Welch, and attorney Rick Evrard—whom Baylor had worked with before on NCAA-related matters—flew to NCAA headquarters in Indianapolis to report their findings and commit to helping the NCAA if it wanted to further investigate. That night, back in Waco, the regents and attorneys stayed up late crafting what they wanted to reveal to the public.

On Thursday, May 26, shortly before noon in Waco, Baylor's media relations department issued a press release announcing Briles's termination, Starr's demotion, and McCaw's sanctions and probation. They also posted two documents on Baylor's website, called "Findings of Fact" and "Recommendations." In the regents' opinion, the "Findings of Fact"—crafted by Baylor's attorneys—revealed as much about Pepper Hamilton's investigation as they could without violating federal privacy laws and jeopardizing the school's liability.

It was a summary of information. And although it didn't name names or say specifically who knew what and when, it was, in a word, damning. It was an admission of complete failure by an institution of higher education. As the regents would later put it, it was an "unprecedented institutional mea culpa." In fact, the word *failure*—or some derivation thereof—appears 41 times in the 13-page document. One of the first statements it makes is there was a "fundamental failure" by Baylor to implement Title IX and the federal Violence Against Women Reauthorization Act of 2013. It found that Baylor's efforts to implement Title IX were "slow, ad hoc, and hindered by a lack of institutional support and engagement by senior leadership." It continued:

> Baylor failed to consistently support complainants through the provision of interim measures, and that in some cases the University failed to take action to identify and eliminate a potential hostile environment, prevent its recurrence, or address its effects for individual complainants or the broader campus community. Pepper also found examples of actions by University administrators that directly discouraged complainants from reporting or participating in student conduct processes, or that contributed to or accommodated a hostile environment. In one instance, those actions constituted retaliation against a complainant for reporting sexual assault. In addition to broader University failings, Pepper found specific failings within both the football program and Athletics Department leadership, including a failure to identify and respond to a pattern of sexual violence by a football player, to take action in response to reports of a sexual assault by multiple football players, and to take action in response to a report of dating violence. Pepper's findings also reflect significant concerns about the tone and culture within Baylor's football program as it relates to accountability for all forms of athlete misconduct.

They faulted the school for not training its employees on how to handle complaints—including the practice of not pursuing cases where the victim wanted to remain anonymous despite a possible threat to campus safety. They faulted the school for not giving students enough information on how to report cases. The school wasn't adequately supporting people who complained of sexual violence, and it wasn't taking action to "prevent and address a potential hostile environment in

individual cases." It put the blame at "every level of Baylor's administration." According to the findings, Baylor had no one truly dedicated to carrying out Title IX compliance, and the people assigned to
bits and pieces of Title IX duties lacked the training or time to adequately perform them, and no one kept good records. Even when it did
appoint a full-time, trained Title IX coordinator in 2014, the university
failed to support the office with enough time or resources.

The findings also stated that of the cases that actually ended
up in the Judicial Affairs Office, the overwhelming majority didn't
move to a hearing and very few cases resulted in finding someone
at fault or handing out discipline. It dissected Baylor's approach to
investigating cases, stating that university personnel did not take into
account barriers to reporting, and in many cases would say things
that discouraged—rather than encouraged—people to participate in
the school's Title IX processes. In some cases, they didn't investigate
allegations of off-campus incidents, even though the school had the
jurisdiction—and obligation—to address those. And it tore apart
the methods and procedures the school used to adjudicate cases,
stating, "the investigations reviewed were wholly inadequate to
fairly and reliably evaluate whether sexual violence had occurred."
They weren't adequately trained, weren't making an effort to collect
evidence or interview witnesses, and weren't deciding cases based on a
preponderance of evidence, as federal law required. It stated:

In addition, the investigations were conducted in the context of
a broader culture and belief by many administrators that sexual
violence "doesn't happen here." Administrators engaged in conduct that could be perceived as victim-blaming, focusing on the
complainant's choices and actions, rather than robustly investigating the allegations, including the actions of the respondent.

It slammed the university's student code of conduct rules regarding alcohol or drug violations, with broad overarching condemnations:
"Once aware of a potential pattern of sexual violence, the university

failed to take prompt and effective action to protect campus safety and protect future victims from harm." And there were more targeted findings, such as stating that someone in the Baylor Police Department and an administrator in an academic program "accommodated or created a hostile environment, rather than taking action to eliminate a hostile environment."

On page 10, the focus turned to the football program, with an overall sentiment that administrators knew the program had problems and no one wanted to do anything about it. "Leadership challenges and communications issues hindered enforcement of rules and policies, and created a cultural perception that football was above the rules," it stated. The school and athletic department specifically failed to act in response to allegations of misconduct by football staff, even though other departments repeatedly raised concerns about how Baylor Athletics handled student or employee misconduct. It went so far as to say the choices made by football staff "posed a risk to campus safety and the integrity of the university." It referenced indirectly a gang rape and case of dating violence that football staff—even after meeting directly with the woman and/or a parent—did not report to anyone outside of athletics, and as a result no action was taken.

It kept getting worse: "Football staff conducted their own untrained internal inquiries, outside of policy, which improperly discredited complainants and denied them the right to a fair, impartial and informed investigation, interim measures or processes promised under University policy. In some cases, internal steps gave the illusion of responsiveness to complainants but failed to provide a meaningful institutional response under Title IX. Further, because reports were not shared outside of athletics, the university missed critical opportunities to impose appropriate disciplinary action that would have removed offenders from campus and possibly precluded future acts of sexual violence against Baylor students."

The findings brought up the concern about football coaches and staff having an internal system of discipline and at times "inappropriate involvement" in criminal matters or acting in a way that "reinforced an overall perception that football was above the rules and that there was no culture of accountability for misconduct." In some cases, instead of being forthcoming about the behavior of football players, the program dismissed them for "unspecified team violations" and assisted them in transferring to another school.

In addition, the university released a list of 105 recommendations by Pepper Hamilton on what it needed to do to fix its problems, and they spanned the entire university from the board of regents and administration to athletics, student conduct, counseling, health services, academics, and others. Included among those was a request for the school to reach out to victims—including those who had left Baylor— to see if they needed anything or if their case still needed a proper investigation.

The news of Starr, McCaw, and Briles being demoted, disciplined, and fired, respectively, and the extensive and exhaustive list of failures Baylor released was a shockwave. Never before in history had a student sexual assault scandal led to the firing of a Division I Power Five conference head football coach—and a prominent, winning one at that— along with the demotion of a university president. The irony was not lost on the fact that Starr—the man who had impeached a U.S. president over an act of extramarital, yet consensual sex—was now out himself after failing to address rape on his campus. From CNN to the *Corpus Christi Caller-Times* it made headlines in all the major newspapers and news and sports networks. Media in the United Kingdom, mainland Europe, and even New Zealand carried the story. It was global news, but back in Waco, it was personal.

Regent Gray tears up when he talks about it now. Within an hour of the announcement going out about the changes at Baylor, his son, a baseball player, texted him: "I love you, Dad." For many of the regents, thinking of their own children guided them through the process, including for Stevens, who had two college-age children at the time.

"It's not a very big leap to think about your daughter or your child being in a situation where they're either being assaulted or they're at a party where something like this is openly going on," Stevens said. "Not only does the victim go through the trauma of being assaulted, then they go to a place that is supposed to offer help that is essentially saying, 'It's your fault,' and turning them away and refusing them the help they need and deserve."

In those first few days, several regents indicated that initial feedback from friends was more of support and concern than criticism. "I really don't know what you all had to deal with, but it had to be horrible," one recalled a friend saying.

But those were regents who didn't live in Waco. For Stevens, the reaction was more mixed. People close to her were affirming and sympathetic and understanding of the difficult position she, as a board member, was in, knowing any decision was going to make some group of people angry. A few days after the announcement, she went to a festival in Waco and said she felt isolated. While most people said encouraging things, "there were a few people I ran into whom I've known for a while and they didn't agree with what we did and they were a little cool and standoffish."

In addition to the personnel decisions the board made regarding Starr, McCaw, and Briles, administrators decided to make at least two more personnel decisions. They terminated two athletic department employees: Colin Shillinglaw, assistant athletic director for football operations, and Tom Hill, assistant athletic director for community relations and special projects. There were plenty of people interviewed by Pepper Hamilton attorneys who failed in some way, and many, if not all, of those people lacked training. "We were not lacking in the courage to fire anybody if we needed to fire them," one regent told us. But the people whose conduct warranted termination were those who the attorneys believed were not forthcoming when asked about their knowledge of past incidents. According to the regents, Shillinglaw told the Pepper Hamilton attorneys he didn't remember meeting with defensive end Shawn Oakman's domestic violence victim or getting her police report, but they found her contact information in his phone and emails indicating he had received the report and had asked another coach to speak to Oakman's relatives about the incident. Shillinglaw has never responded to requests for an interview, and Baylor would soon change his status to being suspended with the intent to terminate and he would remain on the payroll. In April 2013, when Barnes heard about the incident with the volleyball player, he said he stepped into Hill's office and gave him a heads-up that the player was leaving. Barnes gave few details about what had happened but he made Hill aware that he had already informed McCaw and Briles. When Pepper Hamilton attorneys asked Hill about the incident, he said he truly didn't know what they were talking about, but Hill said they must have thought he was being deceptive. "Tom had nothing to do with this. He's not a part of this," Barnes said, adding that Hill was the guy who arranged courts and made sure the floors were clean, so an issue like this was far beyond his responsibility. "I felt like they really tried to make him one of the scapegoats."

Hill's firing would reveal how personally intertwined things could get in a town of 130,000 people; he and his wife jointly owned a houseboat with Stevens and her husband, besides having mutual friends and children the same ages. She and her husband ended up buying out the Hills' share of the boat.

Gray said that in talking with other regents, they have been able to face up to the doubters and naysayers, knowing they "did what we had to do to be true to our values."

"When I get accosted at the country club, I can just say, 'You know, I was burdened by the facts,'" Gray said.

Stevens injected faith into her perspective of the overall decisions the board had to make. "I think we have to look in the mirror and know we did the right thing and put our heads on our pillow at night and go to sleep. I think we all want people to like us and to feel good about what we do with our lives, but we all ultimately answer to an audience of one. And if we can't honestly stand really before God and say I did what was right, then it just trickles into the rest of our life."

CHAPTER THIRTY-FOUR

NOT ENOUGH

As a private school, Baylor had no legal obligation to release anything from the Pepper Hamilton investigation. It has historically been, as many private, religious schools are, a rather tight-lipped institution. Board meeting minutes weren't available to the public, nor was there even public notice of the meetings. Regents don't speak directly to media on controversial topics, even off the record, except in rare circumstances.

In fact, one of the key issues in a decades-long fight between the university and the Baylor Alumni Association was that some leaders were angry at the association for putting details about controversial topics in its magazine—airing the school's dirty laundry, so to speak—and in July 2013, the university bulldozed the alumni association's headquarters in what was seen by many as a retaliatory and unnecessary act.

Even within the athletics department, there were times when employees were instructed from above to not talk to media, even to counter what they believed were false allegations or incorrect information. The faulty theory was, "You can't report on silence," said one former assistant coach, assuming that media would eventually back off if the program didn't release information. The Baylor Police Department was allowed to operate in secret, too, until a Texas state law change in 2015 made campus police at private schools subject to state open records laws. Even then, the university chafed under the law by routinely refusing to release police records under the onus they were privacy-protected education records because they had been shared with the school's judicial affairs office, and once denying a reporter's request for a blank copy of a police incident report. The Texas Office of the Attorney General overruled Baylor in both cases.

So when the university released the thirteen-page summary of the Pepper Hamilton investigation, in which almost every sentence pointed out some way Baylor screwed up, there was a sense among leaders that such transparency would satisfy critics. In fact, many national sexual assault advocates praised the release and the school's actions, calling them unprecedented and forthcoming, but also noting that in the face of such public pressure, the school really had no choice. That's how it appeared to Shan Wu, a former prosecutor in the U.S. Department of Justice and current defense attorney representing college students in a variety of student conduct issues, including sexual assault.

"It's a big deal in big athletics to fire anyone like a coach. That's a statement," Wu said. "From a practical perspective, it also reflects the idea that the cat's out of the bag. If you go with your strategy of letting the report come out, then you really have to do something about what's in it. Given how egregious the problems were, it doesn't seem likely you could keep the same crew there and just do some reforms within it."

The problem was in Baylor's follow-up. Firing three top leaders was a start, said W. Scott Lewis, a partner with the National Center for Higher Education Risk Management who consults with universities on student conduct issues and Title IX compliance, but it couldn't end there if the school really wanted to change the culture.

"When you read the Pepper Hamilton report, you don't have to read too far between the lines: If this was the nice way to put it, how bad was it?" he said. "The Pepper Hamilton report talked about the problems but wasn't as specific to the problems as it could have been."

If there's one thing former chairman Ron Murff said he would change about how the board handled the sexual assault crisis in 2016, it would have been to provide more information in the "Findings of Fact" summary report.

"Although unsparing in its criticism, it lacked the kind of details people felt they needed to process the news and have confidence the board had no choice but to act. Then, by going silent, we created an information vacuum that others began to fill with conjecture, suspicions of cover-up, and self-serving leaks," he said.

One of the biggest doubters of the completeness of the Pepper Hamilton findings was Patty Crawford, who, despite being the Title IX coordinator, was not present for the presentation by the Pepper Hamilton attorneys, although she met with them to discuss implementation days later. By that point, Crawford hadn't even met football coach Art Briles. Yet she said the university asked her to handle media after the findings were released. "I said no. I know you're not telling me everything," she said.

On Thursday, May 26, 2016, when Baylor released the news of the Pepper Hamilton findings and personnel changes, the media relations office issued a lengthy press release with several prepared forward-looking statements. There was a real hope this was the zenith, the climax, the dénouement, or perhaps even the end of Baylor's scandal. Even though the board of regents had put out a lengthy tome full of damnation but short on actual details (not even a final tally of assaults or students involved), the hope was that the public would embrace its promise of change and the university could move forward. It would be respected, admired, and applauded for taking courageous, bold steps to address sexual assault.

"The depth to which these acts occurred shocked and outraged us," then-board chairman Richard Willis would say in a press release. "Our students and their families deserve more, and we have committed our full attention to improving our processes, establishing accountability, and ensuring appropriate actions are taken to support former, current, and future students."

It was followed up by a comment from Murff, who was then the incoming board chairman: "We, as the governing board of this university, offer our apologies to the many who sought help from the university. We are deeply sorry for the harm that survivors have endured."

The press release pointed out Pepper Hamilton attorneys reviewed "more than a million" pieces of information, but noted that details of individual cases would not be revealed. It announced the appointment of theology professor Dr. David E. Garland as interim president, a role he served in from 2008 through 2010, before Ken Starr was hired. It spoke of changes—mandatory training for all employees and students, $5 million already invested in expanded counseling services, new transfer procedures under way in athletics—and announced a special, high-level task force in charge of implementing Pepper Hamilton's more than one hundred recommendations.

Within weeks, Garland would promise that Baylor would be "the safest place on the planet" because of what happened. He deflected questions about the Pepper Hamilton findings and allegations of assault and specific actions by employees by saying it was his job to look toward the future, not the past. "My goal is that we become a model for the rest of the country, of how to address these issues," he said during an interview with Dallas ABC affiliate WFAA-TV in mid-June. "This is not an institution of football. It is an institution of higher education, and we happen to play football. Our major mission is to educate students. That's what we want the focus to be on."

But taking care of football *had* also been a priority: Athletic director Ian McCaw's last act before he resigned May 30, 2016, was to hire former Wake Forest University coach Jim Grobe as interim coach. Grobe was a man viewed nationally as a highly respected, steady hand, and a disciplinarian with a zero-tolerance policy for bad behavior. He agreed to take the job when legendary Baylor coach Grant Teaff called him asking for help.

Baylor had made bold, historic changes. And for a while, it seemed as if Baylor's chapter in the history of sexual assault scandals was over, or at least was on the rebound. Even Colorado attorney John Clune, who represented Ukwuachu's victim and would go on to represent three other female Baylor students, said he felt the release of the Pepper Hamilton summary and the resulting actions would turn a page.

"Schools rarely release that type of information and with such detail. After it was released, I expected Baylor would settle its lawsuits and begin to move on from the scandal. That didn't happen," he said.

In a testament to the power of football, politics, and public image, the story would indeed prove far from over. First there were the powerful alumni and donors who were convinced of two things: Baylor was making Briles a scapegoat for a much larger problem. Senior administrators and certain long-serving regents—specifically Vice President Reagan Ramsower, former chairman Richard Willis, and then-chairman Ron Murff—should be fired or removed from their positions as well because they were equally, if not more, to blame. In response to the federal Title IX lawsuit filed by Jasmin Hernandez (in which codefendants Baylor and its football coach were now at odds), Briles's then-attorney Ernest Cannon filed a copy of a letter he sent to Baylor's legal counsel stating that the university had used Briles as a "camouflage to disguise and distract from its own institutional failure to comply with Title IX and other federal civil rights laws," and that the regents did not provide Briles with any evidence to justify his firing. Soon after, Briles and the school would reach a financial settlement, which would prompt many supporters to ask, If he was truly fired for cause, why would the school feel compelled to pay him one cent?

Garland told Dallas ABC affiliate WFAA-TV in June, "I'm always interested in people saying 'we need more transparency,' when they ask me questions (about the findings). And I say, 'Well, if we hadn't been so transparent, you wouldn't have known to ask me that question.'"

Some of the school's most influential donors and alumni demanded evidence from the regents. Four of them met with Murff and four regents. There was a demand for Briles to be rehired or put on a one-year suspension. But the regents said that wouldn't happen, and they refused to disclose any more details about the investigation. They tried to reassure the donors that they had made the right decision and that keeping the people whom they found responsible for Title IX failures would not uphold the "mission of the university." One of the alumni responded, "If you mention Baylor's mission one more time, I'm going to throw up. . . . I was promised a national championship," according to legal documents filed in a case in February 2017. Although those documents and the regents and administrators who spoke to us didn't identify the donor, sources told us it was prominent Houston attorney John Eddie Williams, who would later become a founder of an alumni activist group demanding overhaul of the board of regents. Williams disputed that account, saying that every time he asked regents for details, he was repeatedly told, "If you just knew what we knew," to which he says he responded, "I'm going to throw up if you keep telling me that one more time. That's ridiculous. It's the argument of, 'Just trust me,' and frankly I didn't, and still don't." He said no one ever promised him a national championship.

"I see Penn State all over it, right? There are people that engage in hero worship," said regent David Harper, referring to the defenders of legendary Penn State football coach Joe Paterno, who was fired in 2011 in the wake of the child sex abuse scandal involving former assistant football coach Jerry Sandusky. "If you win a bunch of football games, then all other good virtues get ascribed to you. . . . They're not willing to accept that serious bad things could be happening, that mistakes could be made."

In fact, in the days before announcing Briles's firing, some of the regents called a Penn State trustee for advice, but were given more of a warning that they had to make the decision they thought was right and that there wasn't "any point in even trying to make anybody else happy." There were a lot of unhappy people at Baylor, especially about Briles's firing. In November, fans lined up outside McLane Stadium before a game against rival TCU and bought black T-shirts with the hashtag #CAB—for Coach Art Briles—or wore black at the game as a means of support for the fired leader, and many of those posting #CAB black T-shirt selfies to social media were women. As one regent pointed out, though, those black T-shirts were by far the minority in the crowd.

An activist group called Bears for Leadership Reform—founded in part by influential alumni donors such as Drayton McLane, for whom the stadium is named; aforementioned John Eddie Williams, whose name is on the field; and former Texas governor Mark White—demanded the board of regents release the evidence it claimed it had for all of the decisions it made. One of the group's founders was retired businessman, former regent chairman, and former Bears football player Gale Galloway, who was accustomed to saying that everyone in the athletics department was living at the "foot of the cross." He went so far as to offer a $10,000 reward for anyone who could find the "true reason" for the firing of Briles and the two other athletic department employees. They would accuse a core group of regents of manipulating the rest of the board. They specifically targeted Willis, the outgoing chairman and chief executive officer of Pharmaca Integrative Pharmacy in Boulder, Colorado, who stepped down June 1, 2016, after having served four years, breaking a twenty-year tradition of chairmen serving no more than two. And they questioned putting regent Murff in charge as chairman. Murff, who holds leadership positions among a few Dallas-based real estate management and holding entities, had been the chief financial officer of Guaranty Financial Group. The collapse of its Guaranty Bank in 2009, amid the crash of the home lending market, was touted as the tenth-largest bank failure in U.S. history and was tied to various lawsuits alleging impropriety, with one settled for $80 million and the other dismissed on appeal.

Murff said the criticism is "coming from a few people, who have been in authority at Baylor and are not in authority now, as well as die-hard supporters of the old Baylor Alumni Association, who continue to hold a grudge against Baylor and the board." He said calls for transparency have "become just another way to continue verbal sparring with the board over these old issues."

But the board's critics would imply that the regents had a long history of micromanaging the university—evidenced by emails uncovered in the university's lawsuit against its alumni association showing how regents were making day-to-day decisions on campus to undermine the association. Murff told us that the university was not aware of any evidence that sexual assault allegations were reported to current or former regents prior to the Pepper Hamilton investigation, nor that any regents knew that Baylor was failing to adhere to Title IX mandates. Williams, and other BLR supporters we interviewed, said they didn't have any documented proof, nor had heard any firsthand accounts, of regents or administrators conspiring to conceal sexual assaults or intentionally ignore Title IX rules.

"Our focus is not on athletics," Williams would say to a crowd of about 350 people at the Bears for Leadership Reform launch event in November 2016. "They may be a symptom of the problem, but we don't know. The buck stops with the board."

It also didn't help matters that through summer and into fall, athletics—if it was indeed just a symptom—appeared to have progressed into a chronic illness.

Baylor football players couldn't keep their names out of the news—and not good news. In the ensuing months, three more players would be accused of crimes. On August 1, 2016, wide receiver Ishmael Zamora was cited with a misdemeanor for animal abuse after he posted a Snapchat video of him whipping and kicking his dog, and Grobe suspended him for three games. On that very same day, offensive lineman Rami Hammad was arrested for felony stalking after his former girlfriend told police that from March to July, Hammad repeatedly harassed her and twice physically assaulted her, including once at Baylor's on-campus athletic facilities. Notable in the case was when the woman ran into a professor's office—and Hammad "began continually knocking on the door"—the professor first tried to call Hammad's coaches, and only when no one was available in the athletics department did she call the police. Even though by that point, all faculty were to have been trained to first ensure the student's safety and notify the Title IX office in such an incident. It was later revealed that in September 2015, Baylor Judicial Affairs had issued a no-contact order against Hammad, and he was the subject of a Title IX complaint in a separate case involving a female Baylor student, but in November 2015 that woman requested the case be dropped.

Hammad was suspended from the team after the felony stalking arrest. He has denied all of the allegations and has accused Baylor of being unfair in his punishment and the adjudication of his Title IX case, but he has not yet been willing to say anything more. He wrote a series of tweets in late October 2016, proclaiming his innocence and implying that he was being punished simply because the university needed to make an example of an athlete. "I remember sitting next to my ex when she said 'if you ever think about leaving me I'll ruin your life, and they will believe me over you,'" read one, and "Why can't I continue my education at least while you guys investigate. No rami but your an athlete. We have to show your punished at least," read another. And he wrote, "BTW..after talking to Fualk if anyone should be upset it should be him. He got kicked out without even having a trial..I guess I'm lucky?" which was in reference to yet another case that summer involving a Baylor football player—defensive tackle Jeremy Faulk.

While most of the crimes involving football players came from a reporter finding a police record, a woman coming forward, or a lawsuit being filed, there was an incident unlike any other. It involved defensive tackle Jeremy Faulk. Faulk was the one who said he wanted justice and wanted his story to be told. Faulk said that on May 31, 2016, coaches called him into the office to talk about an incident with him, another player, and a female student during the school's Diadeloso celebration in mid-April, and he told them he'd had consensual sex with the female student. (The other player, who was also a transfer, was already in the process of leaving Baylor, after expressing disappointment with Briles's departure.) Faulk didn't think much of it: If the woman was accusing one of them of nonconsensual sex, it surely wasn't him. He was so sure of it, he gave a reporter the woman's name and phone number to corroborate his story, according to a June 10, 2016, story on ESPN.com. But the story quoted the woman as saying Faulk and his teammate "forced me to do things that I didn't want to do against my own consent." The woman ended up telling Baylor police about her incident with Faulk and his teammates after police responded to a mental health call regarding the woman on May 5,

2016. In late May 2017, the woman was meeting with attorneys to consider a possible Title IX lawsuit against Baylor.

On the day after that first meeting with coaches, Faulk said he was brought back into the office and presented with a police report from an incident while he was a student at Florida Atlantic University, where he played in 2013 and 2014. The report was about an incident in which Faulk and a friend got in trouble after bursting into a teammate's room and teasing him and his girlfriend—who were both naked in bed—and threatening to pull off the sheets. Campus police came, but nothing came of it. According to the ESPN story, Faulk said that in a meeting with Grobe the next day, the head coach said that with all the Title IX controversy going on, the school—not Grobe but the school—was kicking him out, and Faulk should meet with compliance to get the paperwork to transfer to another school. Coaches actually first found out indirectly about Faulk's incident from a couple of regents, just as the Pepper Hamilton investigation was winding down in mid-May. Two former assistant football coaches told us that two regents went to Briles's office and told him there had been another sexual assault incident involving a football player, but couldn't give him the player's name. In that meeting, sources told us that the regents told Briles that the coach was going to be okay; his firing came about ten days later.

When Grobe spoke with Faulk, the decision had been made and Faulk was losing his scholarship, without which there was no way he could afford to stay.

There was one major problem: The Title IX office had never notified Faulk he was part of an investigation. Never. In fact, only after Faulk later emailed the Title IX office asking for a hearing and a chance to defend himself did he get a letter stating he had been accused of violating the school's sexual discrimination, violence, and harassment policy. But by then Baylor had already essentially gotten rid of him. Faulk's former coach from junior college, Jeff Sims, said in the ESPN.com story that he was particularly troubled by what was happening: Instead of perhaps suspending Faulk from the team while they investigated the allegations, Baylor was trying to shove him out the door without a chance to defend himself and to another school, no questions asked. (Grobe would say in an interview months later with Waco CBS affiliate KWTX-TV that while he and the athletic director did agree to suspend Faulk from the team while his case was investigated, Grobe did not make the decision to permanently remove him or strip him of his scholarship.)

"To me, that's the whole reason they got in trouble—either Jeremy's innocent, and they should go through the process, and he should get his scholarship back and play," Sims said. "Or he's guilty, and this girl should get some justice. . . . Now they won't give him his due process. Baylor is only worried about taking care of Baylor, and they're not worried about the men—or the women—in this process."

When the media carried the story in June about Faulk losing his scholarship and being kicked out possibly because of Title IX, no one was more surprised than Baylor's own Title IX coordinator. While Crawford had known about the incident for a while, she confirmed that the Title IX office hadn't even notified Faulk yet that he was being investigated, and the athletics department was still gathering records. In fact, Crawford would say later that she learned more about what happened with Faulk by reading the ESPN.com story than she did by talking to anyone at Baylor. That day, Crawford and her investigator Kristan Tucker—who would end up taking over for Crawford months later—went to Baylor's senior vice president for operations and chief financial officer, Reagan Ramsower, and complained.

"You have to trust me to do this job," Crawford told him. "You cannot go and interfere in these cases, because it's not only unfair to (Faulk) but it also hurts the victim because the victim is trying to heal, she's trying to navigate things. I'm working to make sure she can get to class and feel safe, and now this article is out there and she doesn't feel safe."

Faulk's case drew the ire of alumni and fans already upset with Briles's firing, who now blamed the school for overreacting to allegations against football players for fear of more bad publicity. When Faulk appealed the revocation of his scholarship and it came before the scholarship review committee, the chairwoman, Lyn Wheeler

Kinyon, then assistant vice president for student financial aid, believed there had been a miscarriage of justice. On July 6, 2016, the committee voted to reinstate Faulk's scholarship. But before they did, Kinyon would note that she sought and received assurance from Baylor's legal staff that the administration would not retaliate against her and the committee members for supporting Faulk's appeal. Kinyon believed that administrators like Ramsower would be embarrassed by the decision and would go after her and the committee members. Even so, within months of that decision, Kinyon's new supervisor complained about her performance, and Kinyon was fired in November. In mid-October, shortly after Crawford resigned, Baylor notified Faulk that the Title IX investigation would be suspended as long as he agreed to never seek readmission to Baylor and to never reenter its campus, according to a Title IX lawsuit Kinyon filed against Baylor in January 2017, alleging discrimination against Faulk and retaliation against her. In May 2017, Kinyon and Baylor reached an undisclosed agreement and her lawsuit was dismissed.

Crawford said the incident with Faulk—and others where she learned administrators took action on football players without her knowledge—also hurt her credibility with the coaches and made them less likely to want to report to her or involve her in any way. In fact, Crawford found out at a meeting on June 29, 2016, that Grobe was planning to have Brenda Tracy come to Baylor and address the team. It would end up being big news because Tracy, a nurse from Oregon, had recently gained a lot of attention for meeting with Nebraska football coach Mike Riley, who was the Oregon State coach when Tracy reported being gang raped by four football players. In a text message conversation between Crawford and the school's chief human resources officer, Cheryl Gochis, Gochis noted that the arrangement "reinforces that athletics takes care of themselves." In that same conversation, Crawford expressed her frustration about restrictions being put on her work and not being included in several actions the university was taking in light of the Pepper Hamilton recommendations, for example being left out of discussions with local law enforcement.

Ramsower, who, as one of the most senior members of the executive council, took over the university's response to the Pepper Hamilton recommendations, assigned someone else to oversee an action team leading the school's Title IX efforts.

Crawford thought the Pepper Hamilton investigation would pave the way for her and the Title IX office, but, instead, her initial concerns were stronger now than ever.

On July 12, 2016, she submitted a sixteen-page memo to Ramsower detailing her concerns, which basically boiled down to this: What Ramsower and the new team were doing was making it impossible for her to actually bring the university into compliance with Title IX. That was on paper. In her mind, and in her heart, she believed Ramsower and people like him in administration were still only concerned about the Baylor brand. She felt that was why they seemed to focus on high-profile, media-grabbing cases involving football players. "I was never given full facts from the university about why it was only about athletic culture . . . when I have seen even more cultural issues in Greek life, and other student clubs and organizations. Within the faculty, being harassing to students and other women in the workplace," she said.

She deduced that instead of making real change at Baylor, there was a rush to check off as many boxes on the 105 recommendations as possible by the end of summer so it would make for a nice, reassuring press release. And she had the sense that she was being excluded and marginalized because she had been doing her job "too well." Through her efforts and her advocacy, she had encouraged "too many" women to come forward, and such a high number of incidents was going to be a black eye for Baylor. She said that Ramsower, upon receiving the memo, told her in a meeting, "Some people might say that we would not be in the mess that we're in if you hadn't been doing your job so well."

Crawford ended up filing a complaint against Ramsower with the university's human resources office, after which, she said, things got worse: She wasn't getting the staff or resources she requested, and she was being told that she wasn't allowed to talk to board members.

"Institutional support means we're going to trust you to do the right thing. We're not going to come in and put our hands in every detail of your investigations. We're not going to go and expel people before they've had due process," she said. On September 26, 2016, Crawford filed a Title IX complaint against Baylor with the U.S. Department of Education Office for Civil Rights. It was the first known instance of a Title IX coordinator at a major university actually filing a complaint against his or her employer. The department had already received complaints against Baylor—including by Gabrielle Lyons, one of Crawford's former investigators, who had filed a complaint in April 2016—but it had not yet launched an investigation, noting in May that the department was aware Baylor was taking steps to satisfy Title IX. That position changed with Crawford's complaint, and Baylor joined the list of the more than two hundred colleges under investigation.

But Crawford wasn't done. She took her issues public, beginning a media crusade in early October by going on *CBS This Morning* to air her grievances and state that despite the high-profile firings and demotions and the failings publicized in May, senior leaders at the university were still standing in the way of true reform for addressing sexual violence. Baylor officials fired back, putting information on its website about all the financial and infrastructure resources it dedicated to Crawford and her office, including two salary increases, an increase in her staffing budget, a $50,000 discretionary fund, and, of particular note, a $12,000 weekend retreat for her and her staff at a spa resort in Texas Hill Country. The university also posted several emails and messages Crawford wrote to Ramsower and others at Baylor thanking them for their support—as recent as mid-September—and public comments she made to media in August commending Baylor for its dedication to Title IX. There was a July 30, 2016, handwritten card she gave Ramsower that read, "Thank you for your support of the Title IX team's growth and mental health. . . . We are all grateful for you and praying for you as you lead us into this new path." (It also noted, as an aside, that upon her departure Crawford's attorney asked Baylor to pay her a $1 million settlement along with retaining movie and book rights for her story, which her attorney and Crawford have denied and countered by saying during a mediation session, the mediator told Crawford and her attorney that Baylor would pay Crawford $1.5 million to keep her dispute and any information about Baylor confidential.)

Baylor blamed her departure on what it described as her lack of management skills and noted that three Baylor Title IX investigators left because they were frustrated with her specifically. When her management of the office didn't improve, "Crawford began seeking employment elsewhere and sought to blame Baylor for her own shortcomings," read a statement on Baylor's website. In response, Crawford provided the media with copies of performance evaluation reports, including one as recent as May 2016, stating Crawford "significantly exceeds expectations"—the highest rating. She released emails showing one of the investigators Baylor claimed quit because of her was actually fired for misconduct (although Baylor officials would later say she resigned). And months later, Lyons, the first investigator who Baylor claimed left because of Crawford, spoke publicly and said Baylor's claim was outright false. Lyons said she left because of the emotional stress of the job—she was having nightmares about rape and was worried for her safety while interviewing some of the alleged perpetrators—along with what she perceived as Ramsower's indifference to her and her Title IX colleagues, which prompted Lyons's complaint to the U.S. Department of Education, a month before the Pepper Hamilton report would ever come out.

Crawford had only started reporting directly to Ramsower that summer, and many who knew him told us it likely wasn't a perfect fit. They said Ramsower is, and always has been, a numbers guy, and perhaps not someone with the greatest of people skills, especially in dealing with such sensitive topics as sexual assault and domestic violence, but that shouldn't be taken as a lack of concern. At one point, Crawford accused him of yelling at her and asking that she not put any correspondence to him in writing, and Ramsower has flatly and repeatedly denied those allegations. In a later interview, Ramsower said he and Crawford had a clash of ideas about how much oversight Crawford should have over implementing the Pepper Hamilton recommendations, which Ramsower said touched on other broader student conduct concerns beyond Title IX. And he insisted that he wasn't trying to pay lip service to the demand for change, or assume it would be a quick fix. He pointed to what had been done already: doubling the counseling center staff, setting up a local after-hours crisis hotline, hiring more Title IX staff, mandatory trauma-informed training for Baylor police officers, to name a few.

"Changing the culture and the mindset of a community of tens of thousands of students and faculty and staff in central Texas as well as hundreds of thousands of alumni and others, that's a pretty tall order. It's going to take a lot of years to do that," he said.

To be sure, if Baylor officials were hoping to be on the path toward redemption, rebuilding, and rebranding after admitting such massive failures, they weren't on the right trajectory toward the end of 2016. And they were far from out of the woods. Baylor would end up facing two investigations by the U.S. Department of Education, one for Title IX compliance and one for its reporting of campus crime statistics under the Clery Act. The NCAA was checking into any potential violations of its rules, and the Southern Association of Colleges and Schools Commission on Colleges accrediting agency had also been investigating, and would end up sanctioning the school with a one-year warning. In February 2017, the Big 12 announced it would withhold 25 percent of future revenue distribution payments—an estimated $8.5 million in 2016–2017—until an outside review determined the university is complying with Title IX guidelines and other regulations. At the time, Big 12 commissioner Bob Bowlsby told ESPN that the Baylor scandal "just continues to ooze."

"I think everybody's pretty much in the barrel, but I don't know if anybody knows where the bottom of the barrel is," Bowlsby told ESPN. He said the review would also examine how the university was implementing Pepper Hamilton's 105 recommendations, as well as the role of the board of regents.

"There were contacts, back channels between individual staff members and board members that circumvented the leadership of the university and the athletics program," he said. "The university, I know, has taken steps to make the necessary changes there, but that's certainly one of the things we're going to verify."

He noted this was Baylor's third major scandal in recent history. In 1995, just a year before Baylor joined the Big 12, three former assistant basketball coaches were convicted on federal charges of mail and wire fraud in connection with an academic cheating scandal in which coaches were providing test answers to recruits to help them qualify for Division I eligibility. Former head basketball coach Darrel Johnson was implicated in the cheating scandal and fired from Baylor, but was acquitted of criminal charges. That was followed by the 2003 murder of basketball player Patrick Dennehy by a teammate, and the subsequent cover-up by head coach Dave Bliss, who wanted to portray the deceased player as a drug dealer to cover up illicit payments he had made to Dennehy, which were a violation of NCAA rules.

"They've shown over history that they backslide," Bowlsby said. "That's what we're really trying to avoid. We're trying to do something that's helpful."

By October 2016, there would be four Title IX lawsuits filed against Baylor, representing thirteen women, three of whom alleged being assaulted by a football player. By May 2017, there would be three more lawsuits: one filed by Mary, the woman who accused former football players Tre'Von Armstead and Myke Chatman of sexual assault; one filed by the former volleyball player who said she was gang raped by several football players in February 2012. The other one, the lawsuit filed by the former financial aid officer who claimed she was retaliated against for reinstating the scholarship of former Bears player Jeremy Faulk, was dismissed on May 23, 2017, after she reached an agreement with the school. Yet at the time, other media reports and sources who spoke to us indicated that at least four more women were considering filing lawsuits. Briles and the two athletics department employees who were dismissed or suspended in the wake of the Pepper Hamilton findings—Tom Hill and Colin Shillinglaw—had also filed lawsuits in Texas state courts accusing Baylor senior administrators, regents, and even Pepper Hamilton of defamation and libel, and Briles would also allege conspiracy to prevent him from getting another coaching job. (Briles's and Shillinglaw's suits would later be withdrawn. Hill's defamation and negligence lawsuit against Pepper Hamilton and a former regent, which would end up in federal court, was dismissed in May 2017.) The Bears for Leadership Reform activist group would continue its public campaign against Baylor and its board of regents, who turned down the group's demand for a third-party outside investigation and stood by the Pepper Hamilton findings.

With each new lawsuit would come not just another story of alleged rape or abuse, but accusations of continued cover-up. When Erica, the former volleyball player, filed her lawsuit in May 2017, it contradicted statements that current and former Baylor administrators had been issuing as recently as a few months earlier, such as the timeline of when athletic department employees first learned of her alleged gang rape, and the dispute over whether the woman and her mom were encouraged to, or discouraged from, pursuing an investigation into her alleged assault. It said Baylor officials "actively concealed" her options and that she was "manipulated into not pursuing her rights."

Her lawsuit also stated that as recently as fall 2015—around the same time the regents hired Pepper Hamilton in the wake of criticism over Sam Ukwuachu's case—Baylor officials had current and former members of the athletic department reach out to Erica to prevent her from speaking to reporters about her case and "clear Baylor officials of any wrongdoing in connection" with her sexual assault.

The university also took a beating in the Texas Legislature. In late March 2017, members of the Senate Higher Education Committee grilled interim president Garland on the university's transparency, accountability of its regents, and even specific personnel decisions—namely why Bethany McCraw, who headed up the Judicial Affairs Office during much of the time in question when women claimed their sexual assault reports were ignored, still had a job at the university amid all the other firings and resignations.

Senators were discussing a bill proposed by Senator Kel Seliger, a Republican from Amarillo, that would make the private university subject to state open records and open meetings laws—a move that would be unprecedented not just in Texas, but anywhere in the country. When Garland insisted that the school wasn't trying to cover anything up, Seliger fired back, repeating himself for emphasis, "I don't buy that for a minute. I don't buy that for a minute. Maybe you are today. But I think that is exactly what was going on." Garland tried to steer the emphasis to what Baylor has done—such as posting notices and minutes from regents meetings and allowing media to question board members after meetings, albeit not opening meetings to the public. But senators continued to press him about the Pepper Hamilton investigation and why the regents and employees—specifically McCraw—were not named. Garland responded by saying, "My inference would be they were trying to keep this confidential for the persons involved." Senator Royce West, a Democrat from Dallas, threw up his hands, guffawed, and said, "That's the whole point. That's the whole point of this." When senators pressed Garland for information on the Pepper Hamilton investigation, and he professed ignorance because he didn't come on board until after Starr was demoted, one senator questioned why Baylor chose someone to represent the school at the hearing who had no role in the investigation or resulting personnel decisions.

Senator West said he believed there was a "criminal conspiracy" among the athletics department and judicial affairs staff whereupon people turned the other way when they heard reports of sexual assaults. "That is just like committing sexual assault as the main perpetrator. To me, there is criminal liability. Whether or not the district attorney will indict that is altogether different."

The McLennan County District Attorney's Office was already looking into whether any of the previously unreported allegations of rape or abuse could be prosecuted. It was also trying to figure out whether any Baylor employees could be brought up on charges of witness tampering or obstruction of justice, based on a reference in the Pepper Hamilton findings that students were being discouraged from reporting assaults. After a group of Texas legislators called on the Texas Rangers, the state's top law enforcement agency, to investigate what happened at Baylor, the Rangers confirmed in March 2017 that they were conducting an internal review with the district attorney's office to determine whether administrators attempted to cover up misconduct and crimes committed by students, including football players.

Attorneys involved in the various lawsuits were pushing in court filings to get Baylor to release the materials provided to Pepper Hamilton attorneys, and were continually rebuffed by university lawyers who stated, among other arguments, that much of the information requested wasn't relevant to the individual victims' claims. The plaintiffs' attorneys in one lawsuit noted in May 2017 that Baylor's public statements of transparency and cooperation with outside investigators contradicted its reluctance and refusal to hand over materials in court cases pertaining to the victims. They wrote that they could, "recount numerous times Baylor has handpicked information from the Pepper Hamilton investigation and released it to the media to drive its desired football-focused narrative."

From all sides there was a drumbeat of dissent, of dissatisfaction, of doubt that the board of regents was telling the whole truth—that there was some deeper, darker secret about who was really at fault for Baylor's failings—and it would trail from the campus to the courtroom. And right or wrong, good or bad, it was really all about one thing: football.

CHAPTER THIRTY-FIVE

BEYOND BAYLOR

College football fans love to deflect attention somewhere else when bad things happen at their alma mater or favorite school. It has become as much of a tradition as tailgating and singing the alma mater. Baylor fans weren't any different when the sexual assault scandal broke during the spring of 2016. A few Baylor players, such as Tevin Elliott, might have been bad apples and did terrible things, but the Bears' problems weren't any worse than what was happening at other schools. At least that's what some of their fans wanted to believe.

In fairness, Baylor wasn't alone when it came to college football's sexual assault crisis. But the depth of its problems and sheer number of cases—and victims—set it apart from other schools. There were incidents of rape and interpersonal violence happening across the sport, and sadly, the ugly revelations in Waco didn't seem to stop some players from behaving badly. But the unprecedented fallout in Waco did at least cause a handful of university administrators to act swiftly and decisively, and women on college campuses—perhaps in part because of the courage of Jasmin Hernandez and other Baylor victims—seemed more willing to come forward with their stories of sexual assault.

W. Scott Lewis, cofounder of the Association for Title IX Administrators and partner at the National Center for Higher Education Risk Management, said what happened at Baylor had a profound impact on how other institutions responded to allegations of sexual assault and other violence. "The athletics departments I talked to and worked with, there was a tenor change," Lewis said. "They're saying, 'Hey, man, that's not going to be us, right?'"

College football coaches, athletics directors, and university presidents should learn one thing from Baylor, according to Lewis: "Pay attention—in a much bigger context. Things that happened twenty years ago as a matter of course—sort of 'boys will be boys' and we're going to turn a blind eye—those days are over. Those days are over. But that's a lot of tradition that isn't going to turn around overnight."

Unfortunately, even after the fallout at Baylor, incidents of violence against women were still occurring on college campuses, and schools didn't always choose to do the right thing:

• In March 2016, less than two months after ESPN's *Outside the Lines* initially reported on Jasmin and other Baylor victims, the parents of a former University of Kansas rower sued the school for false advertising and violating the Kansas Consumer Protection Act. The parents claimed Kansas falsely advertised that its campus was safe, because a Jayhawks football player sexually assaulted their daughter, rower Daisy Tackett, in the fall of 2014.

Another rower, Sarah McClure, who accused the same football player of sexually assaulting her in August 2015, joined Tackett's class-action lawsuit. The football player was never criminally charged. A judge dismissed the lawsuit in March 2017 stating the women, as former students, no longer had standing; both women later filed Title IX federal lawsuits against the school. The university's Office of Institutional Opportunity and Access conducted its own investigation and concluded that the football player had "non-consensual sex" with Tackett and violated the school's sexual harassment policy with McClure. He agreed to be expelled from Kansas in March 2016 and transferred to another school to play football. Both rowers made the rare move of publicly speaking out, with McClure revealing her identity on a YouTube video she posted in June discussing the alleged assault.

• In July 2016, the University of Tennessee agreed to pay eight women a total of $2.48 million to settle a lawsuit over how the school handled their allegations of sexual or physical assault by student-athletes. Five of the women alleged football players sexually or physically assaulted them and one said a basketball player raped her. Other claims were against students who were not athletes. Two former football players, A. J. Johnson and Michael Williams, were indicted on aggravated rape charges in February 2015 and were awaiting trial.

In a sworn statement in an amended lawsuit, former Volunteers defensive back Drae Bowles said he was punched in the mouth by one player and confronted by two others as retribution for helping the woman. Bowles also said Tennessee coach Butch Jones told him he "betrayed the team" and later apologized for calling him a "traitor." Jones denied making the statements.

• In October 2016, former Utah State linebacker Torrey Green was charged with raping or sexually assaulting five women in two years while he played football for the Aggies. A month later, he was charged with two additional counts of rape.

Four of the women told police in 2015 that Green raped them, but at that time he was never charged with a crime. After the women shared their stories with the *Salt Lake Tribune* in July 2016, the Cache County attorney's office reopened its investigation and police examined additional allegations against him.

According to the *Deseret News* in Salt Lake City, Green physically carried one woman into his bedroom, sexually assaulted her, and then asked her, "You aren't the kind of girl that would report rape? Because that would ruin my career." The NFL's Atlanta Falcons waived Green in August 2016 after the allegations resurfaced.

• The most scrutinized sexual assault scandal of the 2016 college football season occurred at the University of Minnesota. On September 2, the day after the Gophers' season opener, a female student named

Nancy* told Minneapolis police that she was gang raped by several football players at an off-campus party. She believed ten to twenty men had sex with her in defensive back Carlton Djam's bedroom; she couldn't recall an exact number because her recollection of the night wasn't clear and she wasn't sure if some of the men had multiple sexual encounters with her. She remembered some of the men holding her down by her shoulders while they had sex with her. She remembered more than one man having sex with her at once. She remembered seeing multiple men standing in the doorway, taking photos and videos with their phones as other men had sex with her. "The onlookers were chanting, laughing, cheering, and jostling for a position in line to have sex with [Nancy]," a report from Minnesota's Office of Equal Opportunity and Affirmative office noted, "[Nancy] remembers that men were arguing over whose 'turn' it was to have sex with her."

Based on time-stamped photos and text messages uncovered by investigators, they were able to determine Nancy was in the apartment from 3:15 a.m. to 4:20 a.m. on Friday, September 2. She remembered repeatedly wrapping herself in a blanket to try to shield her body from the men. "She became increasingly confused and repeatedly asked where all the people were coming from," the EOAA report said. "She repeatedly yelled at the crowd to stop sending people in the bedroom. She repeatedly yelled, 'I can't handle this many people,' and 'I don't want this to happen.' She yelled several times that she hated the onlookers, to which they laughed and someone responded, 'Ha ha, why?'" Nancy was eventually able to get dressed and leave.

While the Hennepin County District Attorney's Office declined to pursue criminal charges against them, the university's EOAA office charged ten players with three different violations of the student conduct code and suspended them from the team after a lengthy investigation. Five of the players were recommended for expulsion; four were recommended for one-year suspensions; and one was considered for probation (an appeals committee later expelled one student, suspended

---

* Pseudonym

another for one year, and placed one on probation; four were cleared, and three facing potential expulsion transferred to another school). Not all of the men were accused of having sex with the woman; some weren't even at the apartment where the assault allegedly occurred, but were accused of having video of the sexual encounters.

The EOAA report said an unidentified Minnesota player told investigators he and six other men "gathered around the bedroom doorway, 'saying things' and turning on and off the lights while [the woman] was having sex with one of the players." The report said the accused players provided investigators with different versions of what happened that night, and some of the players contradicted their own accounts of what occurred. "These discrepancies within and between the accused students' accounts led EOAA to discount their credibility," the report said. The EOAA accused the players of trying to conceal evidence and the identities of men who were at the apartment. One player even told investigators: "I wish she didn't remember my damn name."

Two days after the university released news of the suspensions, the Minnesota team announced it was boycotting all football-related activities—including its scheduled appearance in the Holiday Bowl in San Diego on December 27—until the suspensions were lifted. "All these kids' reputations are destroyed," quarterback Mitch Leidner said at the time. "Their names are destroyed, and it's extremely difficult to get back. It's very unfair for them, and that's why we're sticking together through this thing." Gophers coach Tracy Claeys tweeted a message of encouragement to his players that night: "Have never been more proud of our kids. I respect their rights & support their effort to make a better world."

On the morning of December 17, less than forty-eight hours after announcing the boycott, Minnesota's players agreed to return to practice and preparations for their bowl games. A day earlier, ABC affiliate KSTP-TV in Minneapolis published a copy of the EOAA report on its website. Public opinion about the Gophers' boycott changed dramatically once people read the horrific details of the alleged assault.

Even if the woman had consented to the sexual acts, which she adamantly denied, it was clear many of the players behaved badly. Hennepin County attorney Mike Freeman and other prosecutors and victim witness advocates from his office reviewed the EOAA report. In a statement, Freeman said that although the report "shined a light on what can only be described as deplorable behavior," the information was not significantly different from its own investigation and "our decision not to bring charges remains unchanged."

The Gophers defeated Washington State, 17–12, in the Holiday Bowl, and then Minnesota president Eric Kaler and Coyle fired Claeys and thirteen of his assistant coaches and support staff members on January 3, 2017. In an interview with the *St. Paul Pioneer Press,* Kaler said the university needed to do a better job of training its student-athletes about sexual assault and harassment because its message wasn't getting through. "I think clearly we need to do both more and different [training], because our student-athletes get an exceptional amount of training . . . and yet we don't seem to make the point," he said.

Lewis, the national campus safety consultant, said Baylor's decision to fire football coach Art Briles probably contributed to Claeys being terminated. The message was clear: College football coaches, even highly successful ones, were no longer untouchable in regard to their players' off-field issues. As CEOs of their programs, they were going to be held accountable for everyone's actions.

"I'm sure that aspect of it was definitely influenced by the Baylor situation," Lewis said. "There is some impact there."

CHAPTER THIRTY-SIX

SCOPE OF A SCANDAL

Four hundred.

That's how many reports of sexual harassment, violence, and assault Patty Crawford said she received during her almost two years as Baylor's Title IX coordinator. It was a figure she said her bosses would never let her release, because it was so high, although Baylor officials dispute that, stating that she counted incidents where the facts didn't justify categorizing them as Title IX cases. Baylor officials noted in a public statement the school's legal office was reviewing 125 reports of sexual assault or harassment from 2011 to 2015.

Crawford's former investigator Gabrielle Lyons—who was greeted her first day on the job by four women wanting to report a gang rape that allegedly happened over spring break—said in her six months there she handled at least 80 complaints, of which about 25 actually required a full-on investigation.

Whichever total you believe, it's a big number—especially after years of Baylor reporting single-digit sex offenses for the federal Clery Act. But seventeen would be the number that received the most attention. That's the number of women who reported allegations of sexual assault or domestic violence allegedly involving nineteen football players since 2011, and it includes four alleged gang rapes from 2012 alone, according to Baylor. Crawford said football player cases comprised about 10 percent of her work. That's a small percentage, but it's still an overrepresentation when you consider male student-athletes make up about 4 percent of the undergraduate male population at Baylor. Crawford found that even though football player cases were in the minority, they stood out—and not only because they received more attention from administrators and media.

"The cases that I've adjudicated have been terribly violent related to football players," she said. "From that 2012 time period, it was a real culture of gang rape. I never heard of such terribly explicit allegations."

One of the lawsuits filed against Baylor would state that football players would haze freshmen recruits by having them bring or invite women to house parties, where the girls would be drugged and gang raped. Football players would engage in a practice known as running "trains"—which is when several men take turns one after the other having sex with the same woman. "The gang rapes were considered a 'bonding' experience for the football players," the complaint stated.

That culture started long before 2012, according to one woman who was friends with a number of football players in 2009 and 2010. She described two scenarios where she was having consensual sex with one football player, and other men would slip into the room and try to start having sex with her. One time she successfully put a stop to it, but another time—when she'd been too intoxicated—she said a couple of guys coerced her into performing oral sex on them when she hadn't wanted to. The mentality among the football teammates was, "She slept with that player, and now she could sleep with all of us," or, to put it another way, she said, "You were one person's woman, so you were everybody's."

"They would just corner you and they knew how to do it. They knew when you were most vulnerable. It's just like they were predators," she said, adding that mentality was present among other male athletes at Baylor, even among the club rugby team, with whom she'd hung out as well. (In 2016, the club rugby team would end up being the focus of a Title IX lawsuit itself.) She said the younger guys saw what was happening, and that no one ever got in trouble for it, and the behavior continued. "It was just this weird mentality at Baylor that I haven't seen anywhere else," she said, noting that she's worked in athletic departments at three other Division I universities.

Crawford kept finding out about cases from several years ago, but there wasn't much she could do when the alleged perpetrators were no longer on campus. She noted her efforts were further complicated by women who complained of football players assaulting or abusing them but do not want to move forward with a formal investigation—which was an issue at other universities as well, where women refuse to pursue criminal charges because they fear retaliation or public shaming if they accuse a football player, or someone makes them feel guilty for potentially ruining a player's chance at a professional career.

Of the cases Crawford did adjudicate involving football players, she said every one of them was found to be responsible. If there were indeed seventeen incidents over five years, then Baylor's numbers are actually close to other college athletic programs recently studied. In 2015, ESPN's *Outside the Lines* published a report examining how often college football and basketball players at a sample of ten schools were accused of crimes, including sexual assault and domestic violence. (Although it included both sports, most cases came from the substantially larger pool of football players.) It found that from 2009 through 2014, Florida State had 18 cases of sexual assault, harassment, or violence against women. Missouri had the second most, at 12. A review of a database of sexual and physical assault cases handled by Waco police from 2008 through 2016—where the department noted in the database whether someone was a student—revealed that there were about 30 incidents involving male student nonathletes who were suspected of or arrested in connection with sexual assault, domestic violence, or physical assault. There were 16 incidents involving football players and 5 involving student-athletes in other sports—basketball, tennis, and track and field. Baylor police data were not included because the department withheld names of suspects who were not arrested.

However, in January 2017, attorneys for at least four women who reported being raped by Baylor football players filed a lawsuit on behalf of one of them and alleged there were actually 52 rapes by 31 football players from 2011 to 2014—a number much higher than any other reported. We learned that many reports came from accounts, or secondhand accounts, of women, and, when available, documentation from school officials or law enforcement and other sources.

Fans of any program will argue it's not fair to focus on football player crimes when the overall student body engages in far more criminal activity, but that argument doesn't take into account the disproportionate amount of weight and importance colleges give their student-athletes. Schools like Florida State, Missouri, and Baylor trade on the popularity of their athletic programs. There's a reason football and basketball programs are known as the "front porch" of a university. They get more publicity for the school's brand through television and online presence with the hope it will increase overall enrollment, which is where the real money is. Schools market their student-athletes as ambassadors to that brand, they become celebrities, and they are—for good or bad—different from regular students. And when they get in trouble with the law, it rightfully makes news.

Baylor was no different. Its climb in prominence as a university over the last several years was largely tied to the success of its football program and winning coach. On-field success won it sizable donations from its more senior and influential alumni and prominence in the community and beyond, with several coaches and other athletic department employees being featured on episodes of HGTV's *Fixer Upper,* the highly rated home remodeling show based in Waco. It was a positive symbiotic relationship, until the university's leaders decided to fire the beloved coach in the midst of a sexual assault scandal. After the announcement of Art Briles's firing, it didn't take long for football fan message boards and even some of those prominent alumni to start throwing around the word *scapegoat,* and then for speculation to swirl in late summer 2016 that the board of regents was going to vote on bringing him back—a rumor that regents whom we interviewed denied.

"Well, football's a big—obviously a big deal—a big deal in Texas. It's a big deal at Baylor. And we did have a lot of success," said regent Neal Jeffrey, an associate pastor at Prestonwood Baptist Church near

Dallas and a former Baylor quarterback and NFL player, in an interview with *60 Minutes Sports* on Showtime. "Art, in one sense, had us where we've never been before, and we were winning and things were awesome. And I think our main problem was it's hard to mess up awesome. And nobody wanted to mess it up."

The Pepper Hamilton summary came down hard on the football program, especially about cases it claimed football staff were aware of but did not report to Judicial Affairs. But Crawford, the Title IX coordinator who resigned in October 2016, said she saw the other side, with coaches who really cared about what happened but were never trained on what they should do. "They'd say, 'Patty, no one told me to report to you. When people come to me and they said they filed a Waco PD report, I trusted that Waco PD was going to do the right thing and that I thought these women would go forward with those reports,'" Crawford said, recalling one coach's comments.

But according to some of the women interviewed or documents reviewed, they did tell members of the football staff either about domestic violence or sexual assault with the expectation the coaches would do something—and nothing was done or the case wasn't handled properly.

When Pepper Hamilton attorneys started asking questions in the spring of 2016, an assistant coach who spoke to us on the condition of anonymity said he hadn't heard about 90 percent of the allegations they were bringing—including the alleged 2012 gang rape Jennifer reported—and said several cases, including some reported to police, never made it to the athletics department. He put the blame squarely on Judicial Affairs staff and their practice of being more interested in what a woman was drinking or wearing, and slapping her with a student conduct violation, than whether she'd been assaulted.

"Right, wrong, or indifferent, they're still allegations, but they never get followed up on, they never get talked about, they never reach our desk. Because of the Baylor code of conduct, they didn't want it reaching our desk," he said. "It was one hundred percent a systemic failure."

The assistant coach, who was with the program since 2008, also said he never heard about an incident in early 2010 between a female student and a player who had been on the team that previous fall that led to her leaving the university out of concern for her safety. In a letter the woman's father wrote to a Baylor administrator, he noted that he had spoken with an attorney from the Baylor Office of General Counsel, and that the attorney "concurred in our instinct to bring [his daughter] home as quickly as possible." The woman was taking classes and also working in the athletics department that semester. A verbal altercation over allegedly stolen property led the woman to believe that the former player, who she believed had gang ties, might come after her.

She left Baylor and transferred to another school. She and her parents tried for months, logging several phone calls, to have her unfinished sports ethics class graded as a withdrawal pass, instead of a withdrawal failure—which would reflect poorly on her academic record—and to get a tuition refund. She said she received a partial tuition refund but didn't get help with her grades. She provided to us a copy of a letter addressed to Brandon Miller, then assistant vice president of student success. Miller, who has since left Baylor for another university, said he recalled the incident, but didn't remember what action was taken or who else might have been informed, noting that standard procedure would have been to notify Baylor police, Judicial Affairs, and other administrators. But the woman said no one from Baylor reached out to her to discuss possible accommodations to address her safety, or discuss her allegations, which she said extended to other members of Baylor's football team at the time.

She had been seeing a therapist at Baylor's counseling center in distress after some encounters with football players in which she believed she was coerced into performing certain sex acts against her will. "I was so fearful of what would happen if I did say no, but I let things happen that I shouldn't have," she said. She said the culture of crime, of the rules not applying to athletes, and of Baylor officials turning a blind eye was nothing new, and she said it had been frustrating to see recent media coverage focus on just what happened in the past five years.

"This was a problem long before Tevin Elliot, and before Art Briles got to Baylor. This was a much bigger problem going on," she said. "What happened at Baylor, I don't think began nor ended with the football team, or the rugby team, or the basketball team. It was an epidemic. It was just being in denial about what was going on."

If her incident never made it to the coaching staff, it wouldn't be the only example. The March 2013 allegation that former Bears player Myke Chatman sexually assaulted a student athletic trainer was handled outside the football program. And Coach Briles stated in a legal filing that he was unaware in fall 2011 that Tevin Elliott had been convicted of misdemeanor assault, even though an email from Judicial Affairs had been sent to an athletic department administrator. Two former assistant football coaches also told us they were unaware of the conviction at the time. But there were other examples where incidents were reported to football staff but never made it to Judicial Affairs, such as the 2013 domestic violence report against Shawn Oakman and the 2012 volleyball player gang rape allegation. For many people outside the program—even other college coaches—it was hard to believe that Briles, the university's highest-paid employee, wouldn't know about his players getting in trouble with the law or being accused of an assault, especially in a small town like Waco. In early March 2017, Briles issued a statement in which he wrote, "Let me be clear: I did not cover-up any sexual violence. I had no contact with anyone that claimed to be a victim of sexual or domestic assault. Anyone well-versed in my work as a coach knows that I strove to promote excellence, but never at the sacrifice of safety for anyone. I did not obstruct justice on campus or off. When I was alerted that there might have been an assault, my response was clear: the alleged victim should go to the police. . . . I never knowingly played anyone with a sexual assault allegation."

Briles gave one formal media interview in the wake of his firing, and it was on ESPN's *College GameDay* with reporter Tom Rinaldi on September 10, 2016. In that interview, he took the stance that he wasn't aware of what was going on. "The way the chain usually works is the head coach is last to know. Head coaches are sometimes protected, in certain instances, from minor issues. Now, major issues I was always made aware of," Briles said. His comment didn't go over well with people who felt Briles was implying that sexual assaults weren't a major issue.

"There were some bad things that happened under my watch," Briles continued. "And for that, I'm sorry. . . . I was wrong. I'm sorry. I'm going to learn. I'm going to get better."

Rinaldi asked him what he would say to the victims if they were sitting in the room with them right then. He responded: "I'd tell them I'm extremely sorry. You know, my heart aches and we'd probably have a, hopefully a good cry session and then a talk session, and then hopefully a hug session. Because it just appalls me that somebody could victimize another human being. And there's no place in society for it. And I've never condoned it and never will." He would add later, "These players are part of our program and representatives of our program. And when they do wrong, then it reflects on me and the university. So I do feel responsibility."

The two former assistant football coaches told us that they and their colleagues handled reports of possible altercations involving their players the way they thought they were supposed to at the time, having not been trained on proper Title IX protocol until Patty Crawford arrived on campus. Her training was revelatory for them, and for the football players. A former football player, who started playing at Baylor in 2011 just as the Bears had emerged as a national power, said women "were going crazy" for football players, literally thrusting themselves on them at parties. "I came about at a time when everybody partied and partied hard," he said. Another claimed that women used alcohol as an excuse to engage in risky and promiscuous behavior, and when they woke up the next morning, and regretted what they had done, they would claim it wasn't consensual in an attempt to salvage their reputations. "Certain people can't live with those decisions that they've made," he said. When Crawford conducted a training session for the football team, one of the players said it was "eye-opening." *Don't take a woman home that you just met at a*

302   VIOLATED

*bar. Don't have sex with a woman who is intoxicated and hanging on you
at a party. If a woman is drunk, she cannot consent to sex.* "When she
said that right there, that spooked a lot of guys," he said. Even though
her lessons and legal terms were new to the student-athletes—and
coaches—the former player, and a former assistant coach, told us that
Briles and the other coaches had always tried to teach football players
to respect women, and, they believed, acted appropriately and fairly
when presented with accusations that football players had assaulted or
otherwise disrespected women.

Whether the number of football players accused of sexual assault
or violence ends up being 19 or 31 or something else, one of the assistant coaches we interviewed said he believes only one is guilty—Tevin
Elliott. "I think we had one horrible person. Awful guy," he said. "Did
we have some kids not acting right, not doing right? Absolutely. Did
we have a culture of rape and sexual assault? Absolutely not. In the
four hundred guys that we signed in nine years, were some of them
shitheads? Yes, just like the other hundred and twenty-five programs
in America. But serial rapists? Get out of here, absolutely not. A culture of sexual assault where it was just okay to force yourself on women
and to abuse women? Absolutely not."

Another former assistant coach had a different view. "Me, personally, I think there was a problem. I do. I don't think it's the only campus that has a problem," he said. "If I'm lucky enough to do this long
enough, I'm going to coach some bad guys. I'm going to coach some
guys who I'm going to have to kick off the team. . . . You get to know
a kid as good as you can. You feel like he's a good kid. Then the kid
makes a mistake. Or he turns out to be crazy or whatever, and you part
ways. To me that's not hard. It's unfortunate. You can't control kids."

One former Bears player actually offered less absolution of his
teammates than his former coaches, but still said the situation with
football was overblown.

"Half of that stuff was BS. Half of that stuff was real," one said.
"There are some guys who did what they did and they are guilty for it
and they [got] their punishment."

One of the student-athletes said he recalled one evening when the women who lived above him in a duplex had to rush their friend to the hospital after she had been drugged at a fraternity party. "She literally took one shot and a mixed drink and she was slap-hammered off her ass. She couldn't even hold her head up or her eyes open," he said, noting that fraternity guys drugging women to have sex with them was rampant, but hardly reported. And there were, indeed, many incidents of women reporting getting raped by male students who weren't football players.

In one lawsuit filed against Baylor, a female student said she was raped on February 28, 2015, after someone drugged and abducted her from a party at the off-campus "Rugby House," which housed at least seven players from the school's club rugby team (which was not under the oversight of the athletics department). According to the lawsuit, the woman had aspirations of working with special needs children. She was raised in a Christian home and abstained from drinking alcohol. During the party, she said she drank a can of Coca-Cola. About an hour into the party, she began to feel woozy and light on her feet. The last thing she remembers is being carried out of the house on the shoulder of a large male. The woman, who is five feet, four inches tall and weighs about 120 pounds, was too unconscious to resist, after someone placed an unknown drug in her drink, according to the lawsuit. The next morning, she woke up in a stranger's bed and found condom wrappers on the sheets. She told her mother, who immediately reported the incident to the Title IX office, whereupon she was advised that her daughter "made six at the Rugby House."

On March 20, the woman met with Crawford and Title IX investigator Ian McRary, when she said she was told that there had been five previously reported sexual assaults. Ten days after meeting with Crawford and McRary, she received an email from the Title IX office, which included a no-contact directive. The email included the name of an assailant and instructions regarding its enforcement. She wasn't sure why she received the email, since her assailant hadn't yet been identified. Immediately, McRary emailed her again and informed her that the no-contact directive was meant for another victim.

On March 31, McRary emailed her photos to possibly identify her assailant. The next day, she identified the man who raped her. McRary sent her another batch of photos, asking her if she recognized any of the other men in the photos as students who attended the party. He told her that he was investigating two other allegations of sexual assault that occurred at the same party. On April 9, McRary again emailed her a lineup of photos and asked if she recognized anyone. It was the last correspondence she received from the Title IX office about her case. Her alleged assailant was never arrested, and he didn't have a hearing to determine whether or not he was responsible for sexually assaulting her.

After reporting the assault, the woman said she was unable to get assistance in changing two of her grades to pass/fail so she could maintain the required GPA to keep her scholarship. The lawsuit said she reached out to the student life office and vice provost, but her appeal was denied, she lost her scholarship, and she had to drop out of school.

One thing Baylor regents and administrators are quick to point out is that Pepper Hamilton attorneys Leslie Gomez and Gina Maisto Smith were not tasked to investigate individual cases to find out whether the accused students were guilty; rather they were responsible for finding out if incidents had been properly reported and investigated. Regardless of what may be true about the incidents, and about who knew and whom was told and the exact person at fault, one fact is undisputed: Baylor, as an institution, didn't do the right thing.

"As disturbing as the acts of sexual violence were, I was also troubled by the lack of compassion some of our employees showed to the victims," said former regents chairman Ron Murff. "They might have followed policies as they were, might have done what was written down on the page. But they didn't take the problem to heart and actually follow through on Baylor's mission statement, which is to maintain a caring community based on Christian principles. This is our commitment to the world and the fact we failed to live it was quite disappointing."

One of the former assistant football coaches said, "There's not a doubt in my mind that the university failed women. That happened. That's real."

And football was a problem, but the problem was deeper than football. One former Baylor student who said she was raped by a classmate, not a student-athlete, described a somewhat love/hate relationship with the public's laser-focused attention to the football team when it comes to sexual assault.

"I know maybe one girl who was raped by someone on the football team," she said. "I know a crap ton of people who have been raped at Baylor. It's a teeny, tiny amount proportionally than the bigger problem. It gets all the attention."

But she also had a reverse argument. "Nobody would have paid attention to us if it wasn't happening on the football team, too. Because it happened on the football team, it helped give us some legitimacy and it helped us get our story out there."

CHAPTER THIRTY-SEVEN

NOT ANYMORE

A year after students protested the treatment of sexual assault victims in front of Ken Starr's house, and eight months after he lost his job, the university was still without a president. It was facing six federal Title IX lawsuits, with the definite possibility of more to come.

Former Bears football coach Art Briles spent much of his first season away from the sideline as a spectator at NFL practices and training camps, but he did attend one Baylor game, watching the first half of the Rice game from the stands on September 16, 2016. He hired superagent Jimmy Sexton to help him find a job, but no one seemed interested in hiring him. The University of Houston, his alma mater and former employer, sent out a news release in which athletics director Hunter Yurachek said Briles was not a candidate for the job, after media reports surfaced that he was. His son Kendal Briles landed a position as offensive coordinator at Florida Atlantic University, defensive coordinator Phil Bennett was hired at Arizona State, and former assistant director of football operations Casey Horny went down the road to the University of Texas. Defensive line coaches Chris Achuff and Jim Gush were hired by Navarro College, a junior college south of Dallas, and Briles's son-in-law Jeff Lebby and offensive line coach Randy Clements landed at Southeastern University, an NAIA school in Lakeland, Florida. The other former assistants would find their very association with Baylor to be toxic, with university presidents quashing any athletics director's attempt to hire them. When former athletics director Ian McCaw, who remained mostly silent since his resignation, was hired at Liberty University, school president Jerry Falwell Jr.—son of the late renowned Baptist televangelist—had to defend the hiring in the midst of student protest and media admonishment. Baylor officials hired Missouri's Mack Rhoades as the new athletics director and Temple University's Matt Rhule, the son of a Baptist minister, as its new football coach. Amid intense scrutiny of Baylor's past and present practices, other employees who worked in athletics would also depart, including one who sources told us was asked to leave after he was found to have flirted inappropriately with a female student athlete.

Baylor hired a public relations firm to help rebuild its image, but with every week or so bringing a new allegation, lawsuit, or dispute with a former employee or angry alumni, the university remained in the news defending some aspect of its sexual assault scandal. Moving on was moving slowly. Briles's lawsuit, filed by Stephenville, Texas, attorney Ernest Cannon, opened with a quote from the Ten Commandments, "Thou shalt not bear false witness against thy neighbor. (Exodus 20:16)," and accused the "renegade, self-dealing regents of a Christian university" of spreading lies about Briles, who the suit also tried to claim was not a public figure. Three of the regents named in Briles's libel lawsuit hired Houston attorney Rusty Hardin—known for high-profile clients including athletes such as Roger Clemens and Adrian Peterson—who said he made clear to Cannon that asking for the proof behind Briles's firing was "not going to be good for you." Briles withdrew the lawsuit. But when suspended athletics department employee Colin Shillinglaw filed a similar suit on January 31, 2017, naming even more people, including Pepper Hamilton, the regents fired back.

On February 2, 2017, they filed a fifty-four-page response to Shillinglaw's lawsuit that laid out multiple text messages, emails, and point-by-point narratives showing the type of exchanges Briles, McCaw, and the assistant coaches, including Shillinglaw, were having regarding student-athletes and allegations of criminal behavior and other misconduct. The response stated, "The football program was a black hole into which reports of misconduct such as drug use, physical assault, domestic violence, brandishing of guns, indecent exposure and academic fraud disappeared. In all, investigators compiled a lengthy list of such offenses, which had gone largely unknown to the rest of the university." The response—filed on Groundhog Day, nonetheless—was designed to put an end to the repetitious and ongoing criticism and legal filings accusing the regents of hiding the truth. It had its drawbacks, namely giving ammunition to all the women who had filed Title IX lawsuits and opening the school up to more possible NCAA sanctions, but the response, which was worded less like a legal document and more like a manifesto, seemed to be crafted for the court of public opinion.

"When a college football coach goes 6-7, 5-7, and 5-7 for three consecutive years, no one blinks an eye when the coach is fired," the response stated, an obvious nod to the recent firing of rival Texas coach Charlie Strong. "But when at least 17 women report sexual and physical assaults involving at least 19 football players, including allegations of four gang rapes, why is anyone shocked by his dismissal? Contrary to some people's belief, Briles was not a 'scapegoat' for the University's larger problems—he was part of the larger problem."

In March 2017, in a rare public statement, Briles issued something of a response, writing that "rumor, innuendo, and out of context messages, emails and comments have no place in a fact-finding mission. . . . I hope and pray that at some point, those feeding this disinformation will stop, and full disclosure rather than messaging misdirection will take place."

The regents, in their response to the lawsuit, stated that it would have been "irresponsible" for them to allow Briles and his supporters to "continue polluting the record." "The Board, including the named defendants, had a duty to respond in a measured, appropriate way and had a right to tell the truth, no matter how heart wrenching it may have been. And it owed that candor most of all to the victims of sexual assaults at Baylor who had been forced to suffer in silence for too long."

Indeed, mostly lost in the controversy of the last several months were the voices that started the uproar—the women themselves. When the regents listened to the volume of examples and details from Pepper Hamilton attorneys, it was possible to go numb to the fact that those names were people with lives and families and their own histories. When regent Kim Stevens and other executives met with a woman and her family who asked to address members of the administration, Stevens said hearing her firsthand account of her assault and how it reverberated through her family reignited Stevens's belief that she and her colleagues did the right thing.

"Because there are people, Baylor University students, who came to us, and their families trusted us to take care of them, and we failed," she said. "And we can't let that happen again. And so, let's always remember that there is always a human being, a young woman—many young women actually—who we failed as a university that we are committed to doing everything we can to make sure that that does not happen again on our watch."

Some of the women have reached financial settlements with the university. No fewer than fifteen have pending lawsuits. Some have married. At least one had a baby. Many are still in therapy. Some of them graduated from Baylor. Some transferred. Some still refuse to speak of what happened to them or want to speak of it no more. And yet others refuse to be silenced.

In the summer of 2016, Mary was discussing a settlement with Baylor. School officials did not investigate her allegation of sexual assault by former football player Tre'Von Armstead for two years, and when they finally did he was found responsible. She said the school offered her $29,000, mostly a reimbursement for the classes she took in the years following the assault, during which she said stress and anxiety caused her academic performance to suffer. She was ready to sign the form to get the money, when she saw the nondisclosure clause.

"If I took the money, I was not allowed by law to ever speak of this issue ever again," she said. She was stunned. "Baylor, although they're saying they're transparent, and they're trying to be forthcoming and they're sorry for everything that they've done, they're trying to very quickly silence the people that can talk about the wrongdoing that they actually did."

Mary never responded to the offer and within weeks contacted an attorney. She filed a Title IX lawsuit against Baylor in January 2017, which would include sweeping allegations against football players and coaches, including accusations they encouraged members of the Baylor Bruins to have sex with recruits, which coaches, Baylor officials, former football players, and several Bruins would vehemently deny. "I just feel like I need to be able to talk about it because they're not doing enough to make sure it doesn't happen again," Mary said.

Her lower grades derailed her plans for med school. Having been touched by the care and concern of the nurse who administered her rape exam, Mary was inspired to change her major to nursing, and upon graduating from Baylor in December 2014, she went to nursing school in her home state of Illinois. She now works as a nurse in Virginia.

When Amber wrote a blog post in February 2016 about her experience with Baylor after she said she was raped by a classmate, she became a very public face and name for the university's sexual assault crisis. She spoke a few times on national television and seemingly embraced her role as an outspoken advocate, encouraging women to come forward. But the blowback from her newfound fame and the messages of hate from Baylor supporters caused her to retreat. Her entire blog site has been taken down, along with her Twitter and Instagram accounts.

Just weeks before publication of this book, she demanded her name not be used if we were to share her story and details from a prior interview, and we honored her request. She said she wanted to regain her privacy so she can "continue to make progress in her recovery." In a blog post of February 4, 2016, she wrote about her struggles with post-traumatic stress disorder after describing her assault. "PTSD means that nearly every breath hurts and my bones feel swollen . . . A person touching me can send me into a fit of nausea, though I desperately want to be held. This is hell. Hell cannot be worse than this."

There are some positives in her life. She and her boyfriend got engaged, and after taking a year off after graduating from Baylor in 2015, she was accepted into and enrolled in a top-tier law school on the East Coast. Women still message her on social media with their stories of rape, and she said that's hard, but she's doing better and she wants to continue to help victims. Amber's experience at Baylor, even though it didn't end well for her, did effect change for future students who report assaults; in a letter from then-president Starr in February 2016, he wrote that because of what she shared with him about her experience, the Title IX office now makes reports available online to both parties in an investigation to minimize the burden of having to come to campus to view them. (Although we've heard conflicting accounts as to whether or not that's happening.) Her complaint also spurred Baylor's legal office to review the use of counseling records, and procedures for cases when the person making the complaint is both a Baylor student and an employee. Amber has said she's not entirely sure what she'll do with her law degree, although she'll most likely go into criminal law practice—maybe even prosecuting cases involving crimes against children or sexual assaults.

And then there's Jasmin Hernandez, for whom Baylor is still an adversary. She sued Baylor *and* Art Briles in her Title IX lawsuit in March 2016, but after the coach was fired two months later, his attorney moved to separate his defense from that of the university, because the two parties were now at odds. We were told that around the same time, Briles's attorney called one of Hernandez's attorneys and said the fired coach would come to a mediation to apologize to Jasmin and support her in her fight against the school. But Briles's current attorney, Mark Lanier, said that the coach's attorney at the time, Ernest Cannon, offered to meet with Jasmin but did not promise to apologize. Lanier wrote in an email that the closest the attorney came "was indicating that Coach Briles felt badly for what Jasmin had gone through."

He wrote that the mediator overseeing the dispute between Briles and Baylor advised against such a meeting.

The next morning, when Jasmin and her attorneys learned that Briles had reached a financial settlement with Baylor, and he didn't show up to the mediation, they said they believed they were used for leverage. Lanier wrote that Briles was actually willing to meet with Jasmin later in the day, but her attorney rejected that offer because Jasmin had a flight to catch. After not being able to resolve her claim in mediation, Jasmin's parents left convinced that Baylor was not taking her accusations seriously. Her father, Ostes, was so mad after meeting with Baylor attorneys that he was shaking. Suffice to say, the Hernandez family doesn't believe any sincerity coming out of Baylor's public statements, nor do they believe the school is fully rid of the bad actors—namely the administrators and regents—who caused the problem, or at least knew of it and did nothing.

"The lawsuit is a small price for Baylor to pay for what they've done to her, regardless of what the amount is, if anything," her father said. "She cannot get back those years that she lost. . . . I don't know how long it's going to take for her to turn her life around."

Everyone has been coming to terms with the fallout, including her parents' own struggle with Jasmin's admission of being, if not gay, then at least bisexual. "As a dad, I think she's going to come around," Ostes said. "I don't accept it, but what am I going to do to change it?"

Jasmin has been in and out of counseling. She has gone through trial and error with various medications. She's reconnected with some friends and lost others. It's changed her relationships with her brothers. "You don't realize how many areas it affects your life," her mother Candice said. "People think, 'Okay, you're sexually assaulted. Okay, the guy's in jail, just go on with your life.' There's so much healing. . . . She was in a really, really ugly deep, dark place."

Jasmin struggled for a long time with being disassociated with herself, stepping in and out of being present in her day-to-day life. Speaking out in public and putting her name on the lawsuit were steps she said empowered her and helped her become a new person. She believes now that she can be an advocate for other sexual assault victims. Part of her not wanting to settle the lawsuit with Baylor comes from her desire to push it to trial, to force Baylor to release documents and force regents and administrators to answer questions under oath, which she believes would achieve the transparency that so many other people seek—even if it's at a risk to her personally in the case.

"I don't think I need healing, because I'm already whole," she said. "Now is the time to take this new person, to express it outward, so that it has a benefit toward other people. I'll always be working on myself, but the important thing is I've done enough on myself so I can have an impact, and have an intent to benefit others."

But there are still personal goals, such as earning her academic degree. In the summer of 2013, Jasmin enrolled in a local community college, where it seemed as though she had to completely start over. Very few of her credits from Baylor would transfer to universities in California—which many women told us was a problem when they left, or tried to leave. Jasmin wound up in a History of Rock 'n' Roll night class to satisfy a core arts requirement, an experience she described as being the polar opposite of something she'd get in Baylor's Baptist curriculum. Only a few miles down the road was Cal State Fullerton, a highly regarded, 40,000-student university in the California state system. As a high school senior in the honors program, Jasmin was accepted to the college as a top student. But after leaving Baylor, she applied to Cal State Fullerton twice and was rejected. Her credits wouldn't transfer and her GPA was too low. She had essentially given up.

Jasmin's father worked in an office across the street from the Fullerton campus, and one day in the spring of 2016, he had a very strong urge to walk across the street. Ostes went into the admissions office and asked to speak to someone. They asked him what it was about, seemingly unaccustomed to a man in his fifties walking in without an appointment and wanting to talk to someone. He said it was a private matter. A man left for a bit and came back, telling him he couldn't just walk in off the street and talk to someone. He needed an appointment.

Ostes spotted a female employee standing nearby, pulled her aside, and asked to speak to her privately. "I said, 'I want to talk to someone in admissions because my daughter was raped at a university out of state and she can't enroll here because . . .'" He paused. "'I just want to talk to them.'"

"Hold on," the woman said, and walked back into an office.

She returned and ushered Ostes into a side door of another office, where he sat down in front of a woman at a desk. He briefly told her Jasmin's story, about Baylor and the rape. How Jasmin was admitted to Cal State Fullerton in high school, but couldn't transfer now because of her grades and nontransferable credits. After the woman listened, she excused herself for a minute and returned with a few forms. As she handed them to Ostes, she said, "Have her fill these out. Have her come and see me."

Ostes said he was so happy, he almost cried, and as he walked out, he saw the woman's name and title in her office. He realized he was talking to the director of admissions. When he returned with Jasmin, she met with the woman for a long time. And when Jasmin came out of the office, she was cleared to attend Cal State Fullerton that fall. Failed by Baylor, Jasmin now says she believes she's in a place where she can succeed. And with the new voice she's found, she's also changed her major: communications.

There was one more thing Jasmin had to do before she could register for classes. She had to complete an online training course, complete with videos and a quiz. It is mandatory for all incoming freshmen and transfer students. No one gets into Cal State Fullerton without completing it. It is the "Not Anymore" training program—on how to prevent and address sexual harassment and interpersonal violence.

"I was like, man, the school I originally rejected to go to Baylor is now where I'm finding this is the place for me, and it's better than I could have ever imagined," Jasmin said. "I stand for what they stand for. Of all the places I could have gone afterward, I think that this is such a perfect fit.

"I've come full circle."

POSTLOGUE: A NEW SEASON

On April 18, 2017, Baylor announced the hiring of Linda A. Livingstone as its new president. Beyond her credentials as dean and professor of management at the George Washington School of Business and former dean of Pepperdine University's Graziadio School of Business and Management, she made history by becoming Baylor's first female president in its 172-year history.

Livinstone isn't a Baylor alumna. She earned all three of her degrees from Oklahoma State University. But she did spend more than a decade on the Waco campus, first as a professor in the department of management and then as associate dean of graduate programs for the Hankamer School of Business from 1998 to 2002. Baylor's media release also pointed out her ties to athletics, noting that she was a member of the Faculty Athletics Council during her previous time at Baylor, and she was a four-year letter winner on the women's basketball team at Oklahoma State from 1978 to 1982, during which her now-husband, Brad Livingstone, played on the men's basketball team. And it noted their daughter, Shelby, plays volleyball at Rice University.

If you had to check off the boxes on someone who represented all interests in Baylor's recent turmoil, Dr. Livingstone would come close. She was the unanimous choice of the presidential search committee, which included one of the regent's current critics and major athletics donor, Drayton McLane. Livingstone's hire was described by some as part of the "glass cliff" phenomenon, when an organization makes a point of hiring a woman only in a time of crisis. And to be sure, Baylor was still in crisis with so many lawsuits and investigations pending. But Livingstone's hire was a sign of a tangible move forward. We were denied an interview with Livingstone for this book but she did answer questions submitted via email through university public relations officials.

She wrote that the recommendations from Pepper Hamilton were a "starting point." "It is incumbent upon me to make sure we, as an institution, continue on that path and ensure that the reforms and policies that have been put in place become an embedded part of the culture," she wrote. "Our Christian mission must inform everything we do—the organizational decisions we make, the people we hire, the way we do business. We understand that as a faith-based institution, we are held to a higher standard. We are called to not only meet that higher expectation but exceed it."

At the administrative level, Baylor was still tightly controlling its message and access to information and individuals through its public relations firm, but we found more openness within the athletic department in an interview with athletic director Mack Rhoades and head football coach Matt Rhule, who said they knew what they were getting into when they took their jobs at Baylor.

"If we did things wrong, we're going to handle it and we're going to face it head on, and we're going to take care of them as we need to," Rhoades said.

Rhoades and Rhule had some early experience with that involving two members of Rhule's new staff. In February 2017, Brandon Washington, the strength coach Rhule brought with him from Temple, was let go after he was arrested in connection with a prostitution sting. And in March, the school fired DeMarkco Butler, associate director for football operations, who was caught sending inappropriate text messages.

Rhule didn't shy away from talking about the incidents, and said he instead turned them into lessons for the team. "If it took letting a coach go to show the guys that we weren't going to be a team that enabled bad behavior, then I had to use that," he said.

Rhoades said the athletic department has already implemented new rules for vetting potential recruits and transfers, which are now required to answer five questions about their backgrounds that include incidents of violence. Transfers also will undergo a criminal background check and must sign a release giving Baylor access to any disciplinary or student conduct files at their current school.

Rhule said he has direct conversations with his players about affirmative consent and avoiding risky behaviors like group sex and sharing partners: "Did she say yes at every point along the way? Did she verbally say it to you? Did she lovingly say it to you?" And he talks about respecting women—all women—in every situation. "The hope is that instead of having a culture where if something bad starts to happen guys are cheering it on or videotaping it or whatever happens across the world, guys are intervening," Rhule said.

Rhule, Rhoades, and the rest of the athletics department staff also participated in the university's Green Dot training to teach bystander intervention. It's one of a number of new training programs implemented by Baylor, largely in response to the 105 recommendations from Pepper Hamilton issued in May 2016. A year later, the school announced that the "infrastructure and foundation are in place" for all 105 recommendations. Here are some of the accomplishments the university had listed on a Web page solely dedicated to its progress in lieu of the sexual assault crisis:

- The staff of Baylor's Title IX Office has been expanded, including the hiring of a full-time training and prevention coordinator, and the office is now one of the largest in the Big 12.
- A new Title IX policy, informed by leading experts in the field, has been approved, implemented and distributed to all faculty, staff and students.
- An amnesty provision has been incorporated into the Title IX policy to break down potential barriers to reporting, and an online, confidential reporting tool has been launched.
- Mandatory training for faculty, staff and first-year students has

been completed and additional training for upper-division students has been provided.

- A centralized database of student conduct information has been implemented across multiple departments.
- A mandatory drug-testing and education program has launched within the University's athletics programs ensuring compliance above Big 12 and NCAA standards.
- The staff of Baylor's Counseling Center has doubled in size to 21 professionals. Trauma-informed training and PTSD treatment training have been completed among the counseling center staff. Physical space for the counseling center has almost tripled and new specialists to assist with trauma recovery have been hired over the past year. Baylor's staff to student ratio of 1:750 is commensurate with top universities in the nation.
- A full-time Clery coordinator has been named and more than 600 employees designated as Campus Security Authorities have been identified and trained to reinforce Clery reporting obligations.
- The University President meets monthly with the Director of Athletics, Senior Associate Athletics Director for Compliance, and University Chief Compliance Officer to monitor compliance in all areas of the University.
- New student-athlete transfer policies and recruitment policies have been implemented.
- Baylor police officers have each completed an average of 100 hours of training—more than twice the number of hours required by the Texas Commission on Law Enforcement. Included in BUPD training is 32 hours of in-service training to cover Title IX and the Clery Act. Investigators have completed the Texas Sexual Assault Family Violence Investigators Certification Course and the Victim-Centered Interviewing and Forensic Interviewing Course.
- A Victim Advocate has been hired to assist complainants

throughout the investigative process, which includes helping the complainant navigate Title IX and criminal justice processes.

- Baylor police now video record all complainant, witness and suspect interviews to reduce the need for complainants to relay information more than once and aid investigators by allowing them to gather information firsthand.

- Baylor has strengthened its partnership with the Waco Advocacy Center and participates in McLennan County's Sexual Assault Response Team.

- A student-focused social climate survey is underway, the results of which will shape additional awareness and prevention training and communication strategies.

- Baylor's Board of Regents adopted more than 30 detailed best-practice recommendations for improvement to university governance that resulted from a comprehensive, independent task force review.

But all the lists and hires and press releases and outside analysis do not provide an objective measure of whether Baylor is truly succeeding. Baylor is a brand. Baylor sells a product. And like any entity, whether it sells airline tickets, cell phones, hamburgers, or college degrees, success is the bottom line of a balance sheet. For a college like Baylor, that means students—men and women—wanting to enroll. Of the $960 million in Baylor's total revenue from 2015 to 2016, about 68 percent came from tuition and fees; 5 percent came from athletics. Would this scandal deter potential students, especially women who made up 56 percent of Baylor's total 17,000-student enrollment in 2016, from coming to Waco? To that end, in March 2017, Baylor reported a record number of freshman applications, about 36,000. That news came as a surprise to many who had watched the scandal unfold amid intense social media admonition from moms and dads tweeting that they'd never send their daughters to Baylor.

But there were obviously people out there willing to give Baylor the benefit of the doubt, one perhaps exemplified by a tweet on April 18, 2017, from a Texas man reacting to the hiring of Dr. Livingstone that read: "Great news! My daughter and my dollars went to @Baylor so I'm thrilled! Now . . . let's keep cleaning up the mess!"

Former chairman Ron Murff also cited an April 20, 2017, guest column in the *Dallas Morning News* from a female freshman journalism major who wrote about her resolve to attend Baylor despite all the criticism and grief she got from friend and relatives.

"What she found was an openness around the topic of sexual violence—an openness on campus, in the classroom, among her peers," Murff said. "Her freshman orientation addressed it, her classmates were discussing it, and each one of her professors spoke about it on the first day of classes."

Murff said the topic of sexual assault is "being dealt with openly at every level at Baylor," which is a far cry from the environment Pepper Hamilton found where no one spoke of sexual assault and operated under the assumption of "It doesn't happen here." "As a Baptist university, where delicate subjects like sexual assault were never discussed, those changes are huge," he said. "It may take some time but I'm confident people will come to realize that how Baylor responded to this crisis has contributed significantly to the cultural sea change happening at not only religious institutions, but colleges and universities as a whole."

DRAMATIS PERSONAE

Alejandro, Juan: Baylor vice president for governance, compliance, and risk.

Amber: Baylor female student who alleged she was sexually assaulted by a classmate in March 2015.

Anderson, Jacob: Baylor fraternity president accused of raping a student on March 3, 2016.

Antwi, Celine: Baylor track-and-field runner who testified at Sam Ukwuachu's trial.

Armstead, Tre'Von: Former Baylor tight end who was accused of sexually assaulting Mary* at her apartment in April 2013. He was expelled from the university following a Title IX investigation and was indicted by a grand jury in March 2017.

Ashley: Nicole's friend.

Barnes, Jim: Former Baylor women's volleyball coach.

Barry, John: Baylor chief marketing officer.

Bennett, Phil: Former Baylor defensive coordinator.

Emily*: Mary's roommate.

Beth*: Sam Ukwuachu's girlfriend at Boise State University.

Bliss, Dave: Former Baylor basketball coach who was fired in 2003 for trying to cover up NCAA violations.

Bowles, Drae: Former Tennessee football player who was reportedly assaulted by teammates for helping a woman who said she was raped by football players.

Bowlsby, Bob: Big 12 Conference commissioner.

Bradshaw, Paul: Baylor senior associate athletics director for internal affairs.

Bratton, William, III: Former Baylor football player Tevin Elliott's defense attorney on his appeal.

Briles, Art: Baylor University football coach who guided the Bears to a 99-65 record and at least a share of back-to-back Big 12 Conference championships. He was suspended with intent to terminate after the Pepper Hamilton report criticized the culture of his program.

Briles, Jan: Art Briles's wife.

Briles, Kendal: Art Briles's son and former Baylor assistant coach.

Brittani: Nicole's friend.

Bryan, Antareis: Former Baylor cornerback who was accused of physically assaulting his girlfriend in 2010.

Cabler, Stephen: Polygraph examiner who administered Sam Ukwuachu a lie detector test.

Cannon, Ernest: Art Briles's former attorney.

Caroline*: Mary's roommate.

Chafin, Devin: Former Baylor football player who was accused of physically assaulting Dolores Lozano in two incidents.

Chatman, Myke: Former Baylor running back who was accused of sexually assaulting Mary in 2013 and a female athletic trainer for the football team. He was indicted by a grand jury in the case involving Mary in March 2017.

Chavez, Manuel: Waco police detective who investigated Phoebe's case, in which she alleged that Tevin Elliott inappropriately touched her and locked her in a bedroom, and Nicole's case, in which she alleged Sam Ukwuachu raped her at his apartment.

Childers, Mark: Baylor assistant vice president of campus safety and security.

Claeys, Tracy: Former Minnesota football coach.

Clements, Jerry: Baylor regent and Austin attorney.

Clinton, Bill: The forty-second U.S. president, from 1993 to 2001.

Clune, John: Title IX attorney from Boulder, Colorado, who represented the woman who accused Baylor player Sam Ukwuachu of sexually assaulting her, as well as three other women who claimed they were raped by Baylor players.

Coleman, Corey: Former Baylor wide receiver.

Coleman, Joe: Former Baylor board of regents vice chairman.

Counseller, Jeremy: Baylor law professor who conducted internal investigation into university's handling of Sam Ukwuachu case.

Coyle, Mark: Minnesota athletics director.

Crawford, Patty: Baylor's first full-time Title IX coordinator, who resigned in October 2016 and alleged the university's senior leadership wouldn't allow her to fulfill her responsibilities and that the school continued to violate Title IX.

Darling, Jason: Tevin Elliott's defense attorney.

Davis, Michele: McLennan County sexual assault nurse who examined Jasmin Hernandez and other female students who alleged they were sexually assaulted.

Dennehy, Patrick: Former Baylor basketball player murdered by his teammate in 2003.

Dixon, Ahmad: Former Baylor football player accused of instigating a brawl at an on-campus party in May 2011.

Djam, Carlton: Minnesota football player.

Doak, Jim: Former Baylor police chief.

Dotson, Carlton: Former Baylor basketball player who pleaded guilty to murdering Patrick Dennehy in 2003.

Elliott, Rodrick: Tevin Elliott's uncle.

Elliott, Tarnaine: Tevin Elliott's brother.

Elliott, Tevin: Former Baylor football player who was convicted of raping Jasmin Hernandez and accused of sexually assaulting three other women. He was sentenced to twenty years in prison.

Engel, Mac: *Fort Worth Star-Telegram* columnist.

Erica*: Former Baylor volleyball player who alleged five football players gang-raped her at an off-campus party in 2012 and would file a Title IX lawsuit against the school in May 2017.

Farmer, Tessa: Kansas State student who said she was raped at a fraternity house in March 2015.

Faulk, Jeremy: Former Baylor football player who was dismissed from the team in May 2016.

Garland, David: Baylor interim president and professor of Christian Scriptures.

Gibson, Stephanie: Baylor police sergeant who interviewed Nicole at the hospital following her alleged sexual assault.

Gochis, Cheryl: Baylor chief human resources officer.

Gomez, Leslie: Pepper Hamilton attorney hired by Baylor to investigate its handling of allegations of sexual assault.

Gonzalez, Catrina: Jasmin Hernandez's friend who was dating Baylor football player Tevin Elliott and invited her to the off-campus party where she was assaulted in April 2012.

Gordon, Josh: Former Baylor football player.

Gray, Cary: Baylor regent and Houston attorney.

Green, Torrey: Former Utah State football player accused of sexually assaulting seven women.

Griffin, Kiante: Former Baylor defensive back.

Griffin, Robert, III: Former Baylor quarterback who became school's first Heisman Trophy winner as college football's best player in 2011.

Griner, Brittney: Baylor women's basketball player who guided the Lady Bears to 2012 national championship.

Grobe, Jim: Baylor's interim football coach during the 2016 season.

Hall, Michael: *Texas Monthly* reporter who wrote about Baylor in 2003.

Hammad, Rami: Former Baylor offensive lineman accused of stalking his former girlfriend and sexually assaulting another woman.

Harding, Major: Retired Florida State Supreme Court justice who during a Title IX hearing found Jameis Winston not responsible for sexually assaulting Erica Kinsman.

Harper, David: Baylor regent and Dallas attorney.

Harris-Williams, LaPrise: Former Baylor acrobatics and tumbling team coach.

Helpert, Kevin: Baylor police lieutenant.

Henderson, Darnel: Former Arizona State running back who was accused of sexually assaulting a female student in 2004.

Henneberger, Melinda: *Washington Post* reporter who wrote about Lizzy Seeberg's death in *Catholic Reporter*.

Hernandez, Candice: Jasmin Hernandez's mother.

Hernandez, Elijah: Jasmin Hernandez's brother.

Hernandez, Jasmin: Baylor University student who accused Bears football player Tevin Elliott of raping her at an off-campus party in April 2012.

Hernandez, Matt: Jasmin Hernandez's brother.

Hernandez, Ostes: Jasmin Hernandez's father.

Hill, Tom: Former Baylor assistant athletics director for community relations.

Holmes, Christopher: Baylor University attorney.

Holmes, Sureka: Tevin Elliott's mother.

Hopper, James: Harvard Medical School instructor who wrote about rape victims' behavior in the *Washington Post*.

Hord, Dan: Baylor regent.

Howard, Chris: Former Baylor regent and president of Robert Morris University.

Howard, Xavien: Former Baylor cornerback.

Howell, Brent: Baylor police detective who received report about Tevin Elliott's behavior.

Hoyte, Elliot: Former Boise State football player and Sam Ukwuachu's roommate there.

India: Nicole's friend.

Jackson, Kevin: Baylor's vice president for student life.

Jayme*: Mary's friend and fellow Baylor Bruin.

Jeff*: The boyfriend of Mary's roommate, who confronted Myke Chatman and Tre'Von Armstead at her apartment.

Jennifer*: Baylor student who accused several football players of gang-raping her and another woman in 2012.

Johnson, A. J.: Former Tennessee football player accused of sexually assaulting a woman in February 2015.

Johnson, Matt: State district court judge who sentenced Tevin Elliott and Sam Ukwuachu.

Johnson, Myana: Waco police officer who responded to 911 call to Mary's apartment.

Jones, Butch: University of Tennessee football coach.

Jones, Neal: Former Baylor board of regents chairman and state lobbyist.

Kaler, Eric: University of Minnesota president.

Kinsman, Erica: Florida State University student who accused quarterback Jameis Winston of sexually assaulting her in December 2012.

Kinyon, Lyn Wheeler: Former Baylor assistant vice president for student financial aid, who filed a Title IX lawsuit against the university, which was later dismissed, claiming discrimination against Jeremy Faulk and retaliation against her.

Mathews, Charlotte: Waco police detective who was assigned Samantha's case and Mary's case.

McCaw, Ian: Baylor athletics director who was sanctioned and placed on probation when Pepper Hamilton findings were released. He resigned less than a month later.

McCraw, Bethany: Baylor chief judicial officer who found Sam Ukwuachu not responsible for sexually assaulting a female student.

McLane, Drayton: Baylor alumnus and billionaire business magnate who made largest financial donation for construction of McLane Stadium.

McRary, Ian: Former Baylor Title IX investigator.

Meggs, Willie: Former Florida state attorney who declined to pursue criminal charges against Florida State quarterback Jameis Winston.

Miller, Brandon: Former Baylor assistant vice president for student success.

Moody, Robert: McLennan County assistant district attorney who prosecuted Tevin Elliott and Sam Ukwuachu.

Munson, Lester: Former ESPN legal reporter who wrote about Darnel Henderson case.

Murff, Ron: Baylor board of regents chairman from 2016 to 2017.

Nancy*: Former University of Minnesota student who alleged she was gang raped by several football players in September 2016.

Nicole*: Former Baylor women's soccer player who accused football player Sam Ukwuachu of raping her at his apartment in October 2013.

Oakman, Shawn: Former Baylor player who was accused of physically assaulting his girlfriend in 2013 and sexually assaulting a female graduate student in April 2016.

Obama, Barack: The forty-fourth U.S. president, from 2009 to 2017.

Olivia*: Former Baylor student-athlete who alleged Tevin Elliott raped her while she was passed out drunk in her bed on Halloween night in 2009.

Orakpo, Mike: Former Colorado State player who briefly enrolled at Baylor before transferring to Texas State.

Paterno, Joe: Former Penn State University football coach who died in 2012.

Patton, Jim: Baylor professor of neuroscience, psychology, and

Schad, Joe: Former ESPN reporter who interviewed Kenneth Starr in June 2016.

Seeberg, Lizzy: Notre Dame student who committed suicide after she accused a football player of sexually assaulting her.

Seliger, Kel: Texas state senator.

Shembo, Prince: Former Notre Dame linebacker who was accused of improperly touching Lizzy Seeberg.

Shillinglaw, Colin: Former Baylor director of football operations.

Sibley, Jonathan: Sam Ukwuachu's defense attorney.

Simpson, Lisa: Former University of Colorado student who sued the university and alleged she was gang raped by several football players in 2001.

Sims, Jeff: Jeremy Faulk's junior college coach.

Skaggs, Bradley: Waco police sergeant who interviewed Jasmin Hernandez at hospital and investigated crime scene where alleged assault occurred.

Sloan, Robert: Baylor president from 1995 to 2005.

Starr, Kenneth: Former U.S. solicitor general and Whitewater special prosecutor who was hired as Baylor's president in February 2010. He was demoted to chancellor in May 2016 after the Pepper Hamilton findings of fact were released, and later resigned as chancellor and law professor.

Stephenson, Tyler: Former Baylor football player accused of physically assaulting his girlfriend in April 2012 and being involved in a brawl at an on-campus party in May 2011.

Stevens, Kim: Baylor regent and CEO of Blue Scout Media.

Strong, Charlie: Former University of Texas football coach, now employed by the University of South Florida.

Stroup, Crystal: Kansas State student who sued the university after she was raped.

Tackett, Daisy: University of Kansas rower who alleged she was raped by a football player.

Tagive, Peni: Former Baylor football player and Sam Ukwuachu's roommate.

Taylor, Phil: Former Baylor defensive tackle who was accused of physically assaulting a parking services officer in June 2009.

Teaff, Grant: Baylor's football coach from 1972 to 1992.

Ukwuachu, Sam: Former Baylor football player who was convicted of sexually assaulting a women's soccer player in October 2013. His conviction was overturned and a new trial was ordered in March 2017.

Weckhorst, Sara: Kansas State University student who said she was raped by two men at a fraternity party in April 2014.

Valverde, Shannon: Jasmin Hernandez's friend who drove her to the hospital after she alleged she'd been raped.

Vandenburg, Brandon: Former Vanderbilt player convicted of sexually assaulting an unconscious woman in June 2013.

Victoria: Nicole's friend.

Whelan, John: Former Baylor vice president for human resources.

Wigtil, Brad: Baylor police chief.

Williams, Isaac: Former Baylor running back involved in brawl at an on-campus party in May 2011.

Williams, John Eddie: Prominent Houston attorney and Baylor alumnus and booster.

Williams, Michael: Former University of Tennessee football player accused of sexually assaulting a woman in February 2015.

Willis, Richard: Former Baylor board of regents chairman.

Winston, Jameis: Former Florida State University quarterback who was accused of sexually assaulting Erica Kinsman. He was never charged by police and was found not responsible after a Title IX investigation.

Woodruff, Kristina: Waco police detective who investigated Lauren's case involving Tevin Elliott.

Wooten, Cheryl: Clinical psychologist at Baylor Counseling Center who treated Nicole following her alleged sexual assault.

Yeary, Wes: Former Baylor director of sports ministries.

Zalkin, Alexander: Jasmin Hernandez's attorney in her Title IX lawsuit.

Zamora, Ishmael: Former Baylor wide receiver who was suspended for three games in 2016 for repeatedly beating his dog with a belt.

TIMELINE OF BAYLOR SEXUAL ASSAULT SCANDAL

November 28, 2007: Former University of Houston coach Art Briles is hired as Baylor University's twenty-fifth football coach.

July 24, 2008: Baylor's board of regents fires university president John M. Lilley, saying he was unable to unite the school's students, faculty, and administrators. David E. Garland is named interim president.

February 4, 2009: Tevin Elliott, an outside linebacker from Mount Pleasant, Texas, signs a national letter of intent with Baylor as part of its 2009 recruiting class.

October 31, 2009: Olivia*, a Baylor female student-athlete, accuses Elliott of sexually assaulting her while she was passed out in her bed after a Halloween party. She never contacted police or university officials about the incident.

February 15, 2010: Pepperdine University law professor Kenneth Starr, a former U.S. solicitor general and federal circuit judge, is named Baylor University's fourteenth president. He will officially take office on June 1, 2010.

March 23, 2010: Bears cornerback Antareis Bryan is arrested for physically assaulting his girlfriend. Police officers observed she had a bloody lip and red marks on her arms. Bryan played in eight games in 2010, and the criminal case was dropped after he completed a pretrial diversion program.

March 19, 2011: Leslie*, a TCU student visiting Waco, Texas, during spring break, tells police and a sexual assault nurse that Baylor football player Tevin Elliott sexually assaulted her in the bathroom of a nightclub. Two days later, Leslie tells Waco police that she doesn't want to pursue criminal charges because the incident was a "he said, she said" situation and her actions might be considered "implied consent."

April 4, 2011: The U.S. Department of Education's Office for Civil Rights (OCR) issues the "Dear Colleague" letter to more than seven thousand colleges that receive federal money; it dictates the specific procedures that colleges must use to adjudicate allegations of sexual assault by students.

September 28, 2011: Phoebe*, a McLennan County Community College student, tells Waco police that Elliott inappropriately touched her and locked her in her bedroom. Waco police detective Fabian Klecka informs Baylor police detective Brent Howell about the incident.

November 4, 2011: Elliott is charged with misdemeanor assault for his actions in the incident involving Phoebe. He receives a Class C ticket and pays a $500 fine.

November 9, 2011: The tires on Phoebe's car are slashed, key marks cover the hood, and the word *bitch* is spray painted in gold paint on the driver's-side rear fender. She reports the incident to Waco police, and her mother notifies a Baylor police lieutenant.

November 18, 2011: Baylor Judicial Affairs sends an email to Elliott notifying him he is being charged with misconduct related to the allegations in Phoebe's report. The email is copied to an administrator in the athletic department.

December 10, 2011: Quarterback Robert Griffin III becomes the first Baylor player to win the Heisman Trophy as college football's best player.

December 29, 2011: The Bears defeat the University of Washington, 67–56, in the Alamo Bowl to win their first bowl game since 1992. Their eleven victories tie a school record for most wins in a single season.

March 27, 2012: Baylor football player Tevin Elliott is accused of raping Samantha*, another student-athlete, at her off-campus apartment in Waco, Texas. Four days later, she calls police after Elliott blocks her car in a parking lot.

March 29, 2012: Baylor officials sanction Elliott and place him on disciplinary probation for misconduct and improperly touching Phoebe during the November 2011 incident at her apartment.

April 3, 2012: The Baylor women's basketball team defeats Notre

Dame, 80–61, in the NCAA tournament championship game to finish the season with a perfect 40-0 record. Junior Brittney Griner is named national player of the year.

April 15, 2012: Tevin Elliott rapes Baylor student Jasmin Hernandez outside an off-campus party in Waco, Texas. Hernandez reports the incident to police and a sexual assault nurse later that morning. Jennifer*, another Baylor female student, alleges being gang raped by ten to fifteen other football players at what has been described as the same party.

April 27, 2012: Briles suspends Elliott from the Baylor football team for an "unspecified violation" of team rules. Waco police arrest Elliott three days later for sexually assaulting Hernandez.

June 6, 2012: Upon hearing news of Elliott's arrest, Olivia reports her alleged assault from 2009 to Waco police.

July 2, 2012: Former Penn State football player Shawn Oakman transfers to Baylor after Nittany Lions coach Bill O'Brien dismisses him from the team following an incident in which he allegedly grabbed a woman's wrist during an altercation at an on-campus eatery.

January 10, 2013: Baylor football player Shawn Oakman's girlfriend accuses him of physically assaulting her. A police report indicates the woman told police he shoved her face into brick walls and a cabinet and clutter on her bed, hurting her lip, which an officer said was swollen. The woman doesn't want to pursue the case and no criminal charges are filed.

March 2, 2013: Baylor football player Shamycheal Chatman allegedly sexually assaults a female student athletic trainer with the football team. No criminal charges are filed. Baylor officials outside the athletic department handle the incident internally and the female student switches to a different sport. Around the same time, Chatman is kicked off the team for an unrelated marijuana violation.

April 2013: Erica*, a Baylor volleyball player, tells then-volleyball coach Jim Barnes that five football players raped her at an off-campus party a year earlier. Barnes shares the players' names with McCaw and Briles. McCaw tells Barnes to tell Erica to call the university's legal affairs office.

April 18, 2013: Baylor football players Tre'Von Armstead and Myke Chatman allegedly sexually assault Mary*, a Baylor student and

member of the Baylor Bruins recruiting hostess program, at her
apartment following a party for the school's annual Diadeloso
celebration. After initially telling police that "nothing happened,"
Mary reports the incident and has a sexual assault exam two days later.

May 20, 2013: Sam Ukwuachu, a defensive end from Pearland,
Texas, makes an official visit to Baylor after he is kicked off Boise
State's football team. He enrolls at Baylor for summer school the
next month.

May 22, 2013: Mary declines to pursue the case against Armstead
and Chatman after police forensic officers are unable to retrieve
text messages from her cell phone. Baylor police detective
Charlotte Mathews suspends the case.

October 19, 2013: Nicole*, a Baylor women's soccer player, accuses
Ukwuachu of raping her at his apartment. She calls police and
has a sexual assault exam at a hospital the next day.

November 11, 2013: The Baylor board of regents votes to extend
Ken Starr's contract and assign him the new title of university
president and chancellor. He is the first Baylor president to hold
the titles of president and chancellor simultaneously.

January 21, 2014: Baylor chief judicial affairs officer Bethany
McCraw rules that Nicole's sexual assault allegations couldn't be
proved by a "preponderance of evidence" and declines to pursue
student conduct charges against Ukwuachu.

January 23, 2014: Elliott is convicted of two felony counts of sexually
assaulting Hernandez and is sentenced to the maximum twenty
years in prison and fined $10,000.

February 2014: Prompted by the off-campus mugging of a male
Baylor student, the Baylor board of regents hired consulting firm
Margolis Healy to examine its campus safety program. Margolis
Healy produces a report in the summer of 2014 that is critical of
the campus police department and Title IX procedures.

April 5, 2014: Baylor student Dolores Lozano tells police that football
player Devin Chafin physically assaulted her during an argument.
She tells police that he also choked her, slammed her against a
wall, and kicked her during an argument on March 6, 2014. No
charges are ever filed against him.

June 25, 2014: A McLennan County grand jury indicts Ukwuachu
on two felony counts of sexual assault for allegedly raping Nicole.

He is arrested and released on $30,000 bond.

August 31, 2014: Baylor's football team defeats Southern Methodist University, 45–0, in the first game played at McLane Stadium, the university's new $266 million venue on the banks of the Brazos River. The stadium is named in honor of alumnus and billionaire Drayton McLane Jr., who provided the largest financial gift toward construction.

November 18, 2014: Patty Crawford becomes Baylor's first full-time Title IX coordinator. She previously worked as chief of staff and manager of special projects at Indiana University East in Richmond, Indiana.

August 20, 2015: Ukwuachu is convicted of sexually assaulting Nicole and sentenced to ten years of probation and 180 days in jail, which is the maximum incarceration allowed under Texas law when a jury recommends probation.

August 21, 2015: Starr orders Baylor law professor Jeremy Counseller to conduct an internal inquiry into how the university handled the sexual assault allegations against Ukwuachu.

September 2, 2015: Baylor hires Philadelphia law firm Pepper Hamilton to conduct a "thorough and independent external investigation" into how the university handled allegations of sexual assault and violence by students. Attorneys Gina Maisto Smith and Leslie Gomez direct the outside inquiry.

September 18, 2015: Armstead was suspended from the Baylor football team for an unspecified violation of team rules.

December 31, 2015: Lawyers representing Nicole, the former women's soccer player who was allegedly raped by Ukwuachu, reached an undisclosed financial settlement with Baylor officials.

January 31, 2016: ESPN's *Outside the Lines* broadcasts a story in which Elliott's victims spoke out publicly for the first time, and accused the university of being indifferent to their allegations of sexual assault.

February 3, 2016: Baylor University Title IX adjudicator F. B. "Bob" McGregor Jr., a Texas district court judge, permanently expels Armstead from the university for sexually assaulting Mary. Armstead appeals the ruling, but is denied on April 5, 2016.

February 8, 2016: About two hundred protestors gather outside Starr's on-campus home to show their support for sexual assault survivors. The protest was sparked by a blog post written by a female Baylor student who accused a classmate of sexually assaulting her on March 12, 2015. The university's Title IX office found him not responsible for assaulting her and reinstated him as an employee.

March 3, 2016: Baylor student Jacob Anderson, president of Phi Delta Theta fraternity, is arrested and charged with raping a female student in a secluded area behind a tent on February 21, 2016. He is indicted by a grand jury on four counts of sexual assault on May 11, 2016.

March 30, 2016: Hernandez's attorneys file a federal Title IX lawsuit against the Baylor board of regents, Briles, and McCaw in U.S. District Court for the Western District of Texas, in Waco. For the first time, Hernandez is identified as the victim and is no longer referred to as "Jane Doe."

April 13, 2016: Waco police arrest Oakman for allegedly sexually assaulting a Baylor graduate student at his apartment on April 3, 2016. She tells police Oakman "forcibly removed" her clothes, forced her onto his bed, and sexually assaulted her. He is indicted by a grand jury on charges of second-degree felony sexual assault on July 20, 2016; he tells police the sex was consensual.

May 1, 2016: A group of Baylor regents and administrators fly to Philadelphia, where Pepper Hamilton attorneys present them with the findings of their investigation, which focus on six cases involving sexual assault or violence, all involving football players.

May 11, 2016: Gomez and Smith, the Pepper Hamilton attorneys, make a presentation of their findings to the full Baylor board of regents in Waco.

May 23, 2016: The Baylor regents vote 24–6 to recommend suspending Briles with intent to terminate for cause and 26–4 to seek McCaw's resignation. The next day, Briles and McCaw are invited to a meeting to defend themselves. The regents vote on May 25 to place McCaw on probation with sanction, and a motion to reverse the decision to fire Briles fails by an "overwhelming majority."

May 26, 2016: Baylor issues a press release in which it announces that Briles has been suspended with intent to terminate, Starr has been demoted from president to chancellor, and McCaw has been sanctioned and placed on probation. The university also releases two documents called Findings of Fact and Recommendations, which highlights Pepper Hamilton's damning findings and the 105 steps it will be taking to improve its Title IX process.

May 30, 2016: Baylor hires former Wake Forest coach Jim Grobe as interim football coach. McCaw also resigns as athletics director immediately after announcing Grobe's hiring.

June 1, 2016: Starr resigns as chancellor, but remains on staff as a professor at Baylor Law School.

June 7, 2016: Baylor's Title IX office sends football player Jeremy Faulk a notice that he is the subject of an investigation. He found out days earlier that he, and another player, have been accused of sexually assaulting a female student in mid-April. No criminal charges are filed. Baylor sends the notice of investigation only after he has been removed from the team and has withdrawn from school. Faulk maintains his innocence and contends Baylor denied him due process.

June 10, 2016: Baylor announced the formation of two task forces and twelve implementation teams to implement the 105 recommendations by Pepper Hamilton.

June 15, 2016: Three women file a Title IX lawsuit against Baylor, claiming the school did not properly respond and investigate their allegations of sexual assault. The lawsuit will eventually include ten women who claim they were sexually assaulted from 2004 to 2016, including one who alleges a football player raped her.

June 20, 2016: A woman files a Title IX lawsuit against Baylor, claiming the university created a "hunting ground" for sexual predators. The woman alleges she was drugged and then sexually assaulted at an off-campus party.

July 13, 2016: Baylor hired Missouri's Mack Rhoades as its new athletics director.

August 1, 2016: Baylor offensive lineman Rami Hammad is arrested for felony stalking after his former girlfriend tells police he repeatedly harassed her and twice physically assaulted her. It is later revealed that Baylor Judicial Affairs had issued a no-contact order against him and that he was the subject of a separate Title IX case involving a different female student.

August 19, 2016: Starr steps down as a professor at Baylor Law School, ending his working relationship with the university.

September 26, 2016: Crawford files a federal Title IX complaint against Baylor with the U.S. Department of Education's Office for Civil Rights. It is the first known instance of a Title IX coordinator filing a complaint against his or her employer.

October 4, 2016: Crawford resigns as Baylor's Title IX coordinator, alleging the university's senior leadership won't allow her to fulfill her responsibilities and that the school continues to violate Title IX.

October 11, 2016: Former Baylor student Dolores Lozano, who has alleged being beaten up by former football player Devin Chafin in 2014, files a Title IX lawsuit against Baylor in which she alleges that she did not receive help after she told people in Baylor's athletic department about her alleged assault, and that the one coach who tried to help her was retaliated against.

November 3, 2016: Baylor releases a statement indicating that it is currently reviewing 125 reports of sexual assault or harassment from 2011 to 2015. Days earlier, media reports quoted Baylor regents as saying there are 17 women who have reported a total of 19 cases of domestic violence or sexual assault, including four alledged gang rapes, involving football players since 2011.

November 4, 2016: Baylor assistant coaches tweet their support of Briles, and a few hundred fans wear black T-shirts with #CAB in support of the former coach during Baylor's 62–22 loss to Texas Christian University the next day.

November 10, 2016: Several prominent alumni and donors— including Drayton McLane—launch an activist group called Bears for Leadership Reform, which demands transparency from the university and accuses Baylor regents and administrators of covering up their own actions in neglecting sexual assaults.

November 22, 2016: Baylor reaches an undisclosed financial settlement with two women who alleged being gang raped by football players in 2012. The women did not file lawsuits against the school.

December 8, 2016: Temple University's Matt Rhule is hired as Baylor's new football coach. On the same day, former Coach Art Briles sues three Baylor regents and an administrator for libel and slander; he will withdraw the lawsuit about two months later.

December 13, 2016: Fired former Baylor athletic department administrator Tom Hill files a defamation lawsuit against Pepper Hamilton and its attorneys. It is dismissed in May 2017.

January 25, 2017: Former financial aid officer Lyn Wheeler Kinyon files a Title IX lawsuit against Baylor alleging she was retaliated against, and her employment terminated, because she reinstated the scholarship of former football player Jeremy Faulk, who she alleged was wrongly accused of sexual assault and improperly punished by Baylor. She later reaches an agreement with Baylor officials and dismisses her lawsuit.

January 27, 2017: Mary files a Title IX lawsuit against Baylor, alleging it fostered a culture of sexual violence that included fifty-two rapes in four years involving football players, which led to her being sexually assaulted by Armstead and Chatman.

January 31, 2017: Suspended director of football operations Colin Shillinglaw files a defamation lawsuit against Baylor and four regents. He will withdraw it about two months later.

February 8, 2017: The Big 12 board of directors votes unanimously to withhold 25 percent of Baylor's future revenue distribution payments, potentially $8 million, until a third party verifies the school is making appropriate changes.

February 25, 2017: Texas representative Roland Gutierrez files a resolution asking for the Texas Rangers to investigate whether Baylor administrators and coaches covered up allegations of sexual assault. On March 1, the Texas Rangers confirmed they opened a "preliminary investigation."

March 22, 2017: Armstead was arrested and charged with three counts of second-degree sexual assault after a McLennan County grand jury indicted him for raping Mary. U.S. marshals arrested Chatman on the same charges the next day.

March 27, 2017: A three-judge panel from a Texas court of appeals overturns Ukwuachu's conviction and grants him a new trial. McLennan County district attorney Abel Reyna appeals the ruling to the Texas Court of Criminal Appeals.

April 18, 2017: Linda A. Livingstone, dean at George Washington University's School of Business, is named Baylor's first female president in its 172-year history.

May 17, 2017: Erica, a former Baylor volleyball player, files a federal Title IX lawsuit against the school, alleging she was raped by as many as eight football players in 2012. Her complaint alleges gang rapes were considered a "bonding experience for the football players."

SELECTED BIBLIOGRAPHY

Amber*. "Dear Baylor, I No Longer Have Affection for You." *A Book I'll Never Write,* May 18, 2016.

———. "I Was Raped at Baylor and This Is My Story." *A Book I'll Never Write,* February 4, 2016.

Anderson, Nick. "Lawsuit Alleges Kansas State's 'Indifference' to One Rape Helped Lead to Another." *Washington Post,* November 30, 2016.

Barchenger, Stacey. "Brandon Vandenburg Guilty on All Counts in Vanderbilt Rape Retrial." *Tennessean,* June 18, 2016.

Barron, Robert. *2 Samuel (Brazos Theological Commentary on the Bible).* Grand Rapids: Brazos Press, 2015.

Baylor University. "Baylor's Distinctive Role." News release, May 2012.

———. "Baylor University Board of Regents Announces Leadership Changes and Extensive Corrective Actions Following Findings of External Investigation." News release, May 26, 2016.

———. "Baylor University Board of Regents Findings of Fact." News release, May 26, 2016.

———. "Baylor University Report of External and Independent Review Recommendations." News release, May 26, 2016.

———. "Extravaganza/Bonfire." News release, October 14, 2015.

———. "Identity Crisis." *Baylor Magazine,* February 2005.

———. "Keeping Baylor Nation Informed," News release, September 3, 2015.

———. "Op-Ed by Baylor President Ken Starr Regarding the Big 12." News release, June 7, 2010.

Briles, Art, Plaintiff, v. J. Cary Gray, Ronald Dean Murff, David Harper, and Reagan Ramsower, Defendants. Llano County, Texas, 424th Judicial Circuit. Civil cause No. 19980. Court filings, 2016–2017.

Chozick, Amy. "Starr, Who Tried to Bury Clinton, Now Praises Him." *New York Times,* May 25, 2016.

Culp, Cindy V. "Baylor Learns to Balance Research, Teaching Through Controversial 2012 Plan." *Waco Tribune-Herald,* May 9, 2012.

———. "Baylor Makes Strides, but Falls Short of Top-Tier Research Goal." *Waco Tribune-Herald,* May 9, 2012.

———. "Baylor Officials Denied Building Campaign That Critics Say Raised Tuition Too Much." *Waco Tribune-Herald,* May 8, 2012.

———. "Baylor's Next Strategic Plan Offers Aspirations, Not Goals." *Waco Tribune-Herald,* May 11, 2012.

Dallas Morning News editorial board. "Sexual Assault Cases Demand Federal Investigation at Baylor." *Dallas Morning News,* February 2, 2016.

Doe, Elizabeth, Plaintiff, v. Baylor University, Defendant. U.S. District Court, Western District of Texas. Civil Action Cause No. 6:17-CV-00027-RP. Court filings, 2017.

Doe 1 et al, Plaintiffs, v. Baylor University, Defendant. U.S. District Court, Western District of Texas. Civil Action Cause No. 6:16-CV-00173-RP. Court filings, 2016–2017.

Doe, Jane, Plaintiff, v. Baylor University et al, Defendants. U.S. District Court, Western District of Texas. Civil Action Cause No. 6:16-CV-00180-RP. Court filings, 2016–2017.

Engel, Mac. "Baylor Should Distance Itself from the Baptists." *Fort Worth Star-Telegram,* February 2, 2016.

———. "Firing Art Briles Must Be on the Table for Baylor." *Fort Worth Star-Telegram,* May 18, 2016.

Ericksen, Phillip. "Baylor Faces More Accusations of Botched Response to Sexual Assault Allegations. *Waco Tribune-Herald,* February 8, 2016.

———. "'Please Don't Ignore Any More Victims': Baylor Community Gathers to Protest Sexual Assault Responses." *Waco Tribune-Herald.* February 8, 2016.

———. "Starr's Forthcoming Book Covers Years of Disagreements with Baylor Regents." *Waco Tribune-Herald,* October 29, 2016.

Fagan, Kate. "Griner: No Talking Sexuality at Baylor." ESPN.com, May 27, 2013. http://www.espn.com/wnba/story/_/id/9289080/brittney-griner-says-baylor-coach-kim-mulkey-told-players-keep-quiet-sexuality.

Feldman, Bruce. "College Coaches Join the Call for Answers as Baylor Allegations Keep Growing." Fox Sports, May 19, 2016. http://www.foxsports.com/college-football/story/baylor-bears-football-scandal-art-briles-other-college-coaches-speak-out-051816.

Flaherty, Colleen. "Baylor Faculty Members, in Switch, Back Their President." *Inside Higher Ed,* January 31, 2014. https://www.insidehighered.com/news/2014/01/31/baylor-faculty-members-switch-back-their-president.

Florio, Gwen. "Former Griz Beau Donaldson Sentenced to Prison for Rape." *Missoulian,* January 11, 2013.

Florio, Gwen, and Keila Szpaller. "Jordan Johnson Found Not Guilty of Rape."
    Missoulian, November 6, 2011.

Hall, Michael. "God and Man at Baylor." *Texas Monthly*, October 2003.

Hays, Julie, and Mikel Lauber. "Decision to Kick JC Recruit Off Team Was Not
    His, Baylor Coach Says." KWTX-TV, October 13, 2016. http://www.kwtx.
    com/content/news/Decision-to-kick-JC-recruit-off-team-was-not-his-Bay-
    lor-coach-says--396574711.html.

Healy, Jack. "Accusation in Montana of Treating Rape Lightly Stirs Unlikely
    Public Fight." *New York Times*, April 12, 2014.

Henneberger, Melinda. "Reported Sexual Assault at Notre Dame Campus
    Leaves More Questions than Answers." *National Catholic Reporter*, March
    26, 2012.

———. "Why I Won't Be Cheering for Notre Dame." *Washington Post*, Decem-
    ber 4, 2012.

Henry, Diane. "Yale Faculty Members Charged with Sexual Harassment in
    Suit." *New York Times,* August 22, 1977.

*Hernandez, Jasmin, Plaintiff, v. Baylor University Board of Regents, et al, Defen-
    dants.* U.S. District Court, Western District of Texas. Civil Action Cause
    No. 6:16-CV-00069-RP. Court filings, 2016–2017.

Hewitt, Kimberly D., and Tina Marisam. "Re: Case number: 7360." University
    of Minnesota Office of Equal Opportunity and Affirmative Action spe-
    cial report to University of Minnesota Office of Student Conduct and Aca-
    demic Integrity Director Sharon Dzik, December 7, 2016.

Hoppa, Kristin. "Baylor Fraternity President Charged with Sexual Assault."
    Waco Tribune-Herald, March 3, 2016.

Hopper, James W. "Why Many Rape Victims Don't Fight or Yell." *Washington
    Post,* June 23, 2015.

Kingkade, Tyler. "Consultant's Report Blames Sexual Assault Activists for Occi-
    dental College Unrest." *Huffington Post,* October 29, 2014. http://www.
    huffingtonpost.com/2014/10/29/occidental-sexual-assault-report-gomez-
    smith_n_6065176.html.

Kinyon, Lyn Wheeler, Plaintiff, v. Baylor University, Defendant. U.S. Dis-
    trict Court, Western District of Texas. Civil Action Cause No. 6.17-CV-
    00023-RP. Court filings, 2017.

Krebs, Christopher P., and Christine H. Lindquist, Tara D. Warner, Bonnie S.
    Fisher, and Sandra L. Martin. "The Campus Sexual Assault Study." Spe-
    cial report for the National Institute of Justice, October 2007.

KWTX-TV staff. "BU Grad Alleging Assault Sought Athletic Department
    Job." KWTX-TV, June 9, 2016. http://www.kwtx.com/content/news/BU-
    grad-alleging-assault-sought-athletic-dept-job-382285741.html.

LaBorde, Hilary, and Robbie Moody. "Pushing Past Red Tape, Getting to the Truth." *Texas Prosecutor*, July–August 2016.

Lavigne, Paula. "Baylor Didn't Investigate Sex Assault Claim against Players for Two Years." ESPN.com, April 14, 2016. http://www.espn.com/espn/otl/story/_/id/15191102/baylor-investigate-sex-assault-claim-football-players-more-two-years-lines.

———. "Baylor Faces Accusations of Ignoring Sex Assault Victims." ESPN.com, January 29, 2016. http://www.espn.com/espn/otl/story/_/id/14675790/baylor-officials-accused-failing-investigate-sexual-assaults-fully-adequately-providing-support-alleged-victims.

———. "Baylor Player Arrested Monday Faced Prior Sexual Assault Claim." ESPN.com, August 4, 2016. http://www.espn.com/espn/otl/story/_/id/17216980/baylor-offensive-lineman-rami-hammad-accused-last-fall-sexually-assaulting-student-violating-university-issued-no-contact-order.

———. "Lawyers, Status, Public Backlash Aid College Athletes Accused of Crimes." ESPN.com, June 15, 2015. http://www.espn.com/espn/otl/story/_/id/13065247/college-athletes-major-programs-benefit-confluence-factors-somes-avoid-criminal-charges.

Lavigne, Paula, and Max Olson. "As Baylor Reviews Transfer Athletes, Ex-Football Player Cites Unfairness." ESPN.com, June 10, 2016. http://www.espn.com/espn/otl/story/_/id/16083428/ex-baylor-football-player-says-get-fair-chance-clear-name-stay-school.

Lavigne, Paula, and Mark Schlabach. "Art Briles Acknowledges Role in Baylor Scandal." ESPN.com, September 10, 2016. http://www.espn.com/college-football/story/_/id/17510465/art-briles-former-baylor-bears-coach-says-takes-responsibility-mishandled-sexual-assault-allegations.

———. "Police Records Detail Several More Allegations Against Baylor Football Players." ESPN.com, May 19, 2016. http://www.espn.com/espn/otl/story/_/id/15562625/waco-police-records-reveal-additional-violence-allegations-baylor-football-players.

Lavigne, Paula, and Mark Schlabach, Brett McMurphy, and Jake Trotter. "Kenneth Starr Stepping Down as Baylor Chancellor." ESPN.com, June 1, 2016. http://www.espn.com/college-sports/story/_/id/15875833/kenneth-starr-resign-chancellor-baylor-continue-teach.

Layman, Melissa J., Christine A. Gidycz, and Steven Jay Lynn. "Unacknowledged Versus Acknowledged Rape Victims: Situational Factors and Posttraumatic Stress." *Journal of Abnormal Psychology*, 1996.

Leslie, Mike. "Baylor President 'Caught Off Guard' by Briles Rumors; 'Can't' Release Redacted Report." WFAA-TV, June 13, 2016. http://www.wfaa.com/sports/baylor-president-garland-caught-off-guard-by-briles-reports/242742630.

Lozano, Dolores, Plaintiff, v. Baylor University et al, Defendants. U.S. District Court, Western District of Texas. Civil Action Cause No. 6.16-CV-00403. Court filings, 2016–2017.

Mai-Due, Christine. "The 'New' Nixon Library's Challenge: Fairly Depicting a 'Failed Presidency.'" *Los Angeles Times,* August 16, 2016.

McCraw, Bethany J. "Written Investigative Report Regarding Complaint of Sexual Harassment or Violence." Baylor University Student Conduct Administration special report to football player Sam Ukwuachu, January 21, 2014.

McGregor, F.B. "Written Investigative Report Regarding Complaint of Sexual Harassment or Violence." Baylor University Student Conduct Administration special report to football player Tre'Von Armstead, February 3, 2016.

Messick, Graham, and Ashley Velie. "The Case of Beckett Brennan." CBS News, May 4, 2011. http://www.cbsnews.com/news/the-case-of-beckett-brennan/.

Morton, Clay. "Baylor University Drops Homosexual Acts from Conduct Rules." *Dallas Morning News,* July 7, 2015.

Munson, Lester. "Landmark settlement in ASU rape case." ESPN.com, January 30, 2009. http://www.espn.com/espn/otl/news/story?id=3871666.

Myerson, Allen R. "After 151 Years, Baptist Baylor Kicks Up Its Heels, Just a Little." *New York Times,* January 30, 1996.

Neighbor, Fritz. "University of Montana Fires Football Coach, Athletic Director." *Missoulian,* March 29, 2012.

Ohlheiser, Abby. "Why Baylor University's Sexual Conduct Policy No Longer Calls Out 'Homosexual Acts.'" *Washington Post,* July 8, 2015.

Pérez-Peña, Richard. "1 in 4 Women Experience Sex Assault on Campus." *New York Times,* September 21, 2015.

Power, Stephen. "Ex-Baylor Coach Is Acquitted; Three Ex-Assistants Guilty in Player-Eligibility Scam." *Dallas Morning News,* April 6, 1995.

Pressley, Sue Anne. "The Roots of Ken Starr's Morality Plays." *Washington Post,* March 2, 1998.

Rimer, Sara. "Baylor Faculty Members Condemn SAT Retaking." *New York Times,* October 15, 2008.

———. "Baylor Rewards Freshmen Who Retake SAT." *New York Times,* October 14, 2008.

Schlabach, Mark. "Art Briles, Chris Petersen Continue Finger Pointing over Sam Ukwuachu." ESPN.com, August 21, 2015. http://abcnews.go.com/Sports/art-briles-chris-petersen-continue-finger-pointing-sam/story?id=33239296.

———. "Baylor's Art Briles Is Built to Last." ESPN.com, November 5, 2013. http://www.espn.com/blog/ncfnation/post/_/id/87410/baylors-art-briles-is-built-to-last.

————. "FSU's Jameis Winston Not Charged." ESPN.com, December 5, 2013. http://www.espn.com/college-football/story/_/id/10082441/jameis-winston-not-charged-sexual-assault-investigation.

————. "Jameis Winston Denies Allegations." ESPN.com, December 3, 2014. http://www.espn.com/college-football/story/_/id/11975588/florida-state-qb-jameis-winston-denies-sexual-assault-allegations-hearing-statement.

————. "Jameis Winston, Sexual Assault Accuser Settle Federal Lawsuit." ESPN.com, December 14, 2016. http://www.espn.com/college-football/story/_/id/18281435/jameis-winston-settles-lawsuit-2012-sexual-assault-accuser.

————. "Lawyer: Defense 'Too Little, Too Late.'" ESPN.com, November 22, 2013. http://www.espn.com/blog/acc/post/_/id/63747/lawyer-defense-too-little-too-late?utm_source=twitterfeed&utm_medium=twitter.

————. "Minnesota President Stands by Bans: 'Much Bigger than Football.'" ESPN.com, December 16, 2016. http://www.espn.com/college-football/story/_/id/18294618/minnesota-eric-kaler-says-player-suspensions-alleged-gang-rape-based-university-values.

————. "Univ. of Tennessee Settles Lawsuit Regarding Sexual Assault Cases." ESPN.com, July 5, 2016. http://www.espn.com/college-sports/story/_/id/16809872/university-tennessee-reaches-financial-settlement-lawsuit-regarding-school-handling-sexual-assault-cases.

Schlabach, Mark, and Max Olson. "Boise St. Says Ukwuachu's Dismissal Unrelated to Abuse Allegations." ESPN.com, August 25, 2015. http://abcnews.go.com/Sports/boise-st-ukwuachus-dismissal-unrelated-abuse-allegations/story?id=33321673.

Shapiro, Michael W. "A Long Way to Go on Baylor 2012 Endowment Goal." *Waco Tribune-Herald*, May 8, 2012.

Shillinglaw, Colin, Plaintiff, v. Baylor University, David E. Garland, Reagan Ramsower, James Cary Gray, Ronald D. Murff, David H. Harper, Dennis R. Wiles, and Pepper Hamilton LLP, Defendants. Dallas County, Texas, 116th District Court. Civil cause No. DC-17-01225. Court filings, 2016–2017.

Smith, J. B. "Baylor 2012 Still a Work in Progress 10 Years Later." *Waco Tribune-Herald,* May 7, 2012.

————. "Stadium Rising: The Story of McLane Stadium, from Start to Finish." *Waco Tribune-Herald*, August 29, 2014.

Solis, Paula Ann. "Tevin Elliott Denied Retrial." *Baylor Lariat,* April 8, 2014.

Solomon, Dan, and Jessica Luther. "Details About Sam Ukwuachu's Final Days at Boise State Based on Notes from the School's Assistant Athletics Director." *Texas Monthly,* August 22, 2015. http://www.texasmonthly.com/articles/details-about-sam-ukwuachus-final-days-at-boise-state-based-on-notes-from-the-schools-assistant-athletic-director/.

————. "Silence at Baylor." *Texas Monthly,* August 20, 2015. http://www.texas-monthly.com/article/silence-at-baylor/.

Solomon, Jon. "Open Letter to Ken Starr: Stop Stonewalling About Baylor Rapes." CBS Sports, February 4, 2016. http://www.cbssports.com/college-football/news/open-letter-to-ken-starr-stop-stonewalling-about-baylor-rapes/.

Starr, Ken. "Safeguarding Baylor's Students." Letter to Baylor students, alumni, and faculty, February 7, 2016.

————. "Years of Tension Preceded Presidential Departure from Baylor University." *Waco Tribune-Herald,* October 30, 2016.

State of Texas, Plaintiff, v. Samuel Ukwuachu, Defendant. District Court of McLennan County, Texas, 54th Judicial District. Cause No. 2014-1202-C2. Court filings and transcripts of proceedings, 2014–2015.

State of Texas, Plaintiff, v. Tevin Sherard Elliott, Defendant. District Court of McLennan County, Texas, 54th Judicial District. Cause No. 2012-1543-C2. Court filings and transcripts of proceedings, 2013–2014.

Stuckey, Alex. "After Four Women Accused a Utah State University Student of Sex Assaults, No Charges and No Apparent Discipline." *Salt Lake Tribune,* July 27, 2016.

Trower, David. "Sex, Violation, Power: 'If We Don't Know About It, We Can't Do Anything About It.'" *Baylor Lariat,* December 5, 2013.

U.S. Department of Education. "Dear Colleague Letter." News release, April 4, 2011.

————. "Title IX and Sex Discrimination." News release, April 2015.

U.S. Office of Civil Rights. "Sexual Harassment: It's Not Academic." Educational pamphlet, September 1988.

Williams, Mará Rose. "Former KU Rower Allegedly Raped in Dorm Joins Class Action Suit Against University." *Kansas City Star,* June 9, 2016.

————. "K-State Was Wrong to Not Investigate Rapes at Off-Campus Frat Houses, Federal Government Says." *Kansas City Star,* July 5, 2016.

Wilson, Amy. "The Status of Women in Intercollegiate Athletics as Title IX Turns 40." NCAA Publications. Special report, June 2012.

Wise, Mike. "Death and Deception." *Washington Post*, August 28, 2003.

Witherspoon, Tommy. "Baylor Football Player Charged with Sex Assault." *Waco Tribune-Herald,* May 1, 2012.

————. "Former Baylor Football Player Indicted on 3 Counts of Sexual Assault." *Waco Tribune-Herald,* August 28, 2012.

INDEX